Organic Resistance

FLOWS, MIGRATIONS, AND EXCHANGES

Mart A. Stewart and Harriet Ritvo, editors

The Flows, Migrations, and Exchanges series publishes new works of environmental history that explore the cross-border movements of organisms and materials that have shaped the modern world, as well as the varied human attempts to understand, regulate, and manage these movements.

Organic Resistance

The Struggle over Industrial Farming in Postwar France

Venus Bivar

The University of North Carolina Press CHAPEL HILL

This book was published with the assistance of the Wells Fargo Fund for Excellence of the University of North Carolina Press.

The University of North Carolina Press has been a member of the Green Press Initiative since 2003.

Library of Congress Cataloging-in-Publication Data
Names: Bivar, Venus, author.
Title: Organic resistance : the struggle over industrial farming in postwar France / Venus Bivar.
Other titles: Flows, migrations, and exchanges.
Description: Chapel Hill : University of North Carolina Press, [2018] | Series: Flows, migrations, and exchanges
Identifiers: LCCN 2017033923 | ISBN 9781469641171 (cloth : alk. paper) | ISBN 9781469641188 (pbk : alk. paper) | ISBN 9781469641195 (ebook)
Subjects: LCSH: Organic farming—France—History—20th century. | Agriculture—France—History—20th century.
Classification: LCC S605.5 .B566 2018 | DDC 631.5/840944—dc23
LC record available at https://lccn.loc.gov/2017033923

Cover illustrations: Top, *Manifestation paysanne*; bottom, *Hersage traditionnel*. Both photographs © DR/Min.Agri.Fr.

To Michael Geyer, for reminding me to be bold

Contents

Figures and Map

Acknowledgments

Organic Resistance has been a part of my life for more years than I care to count. Along the way, it has benefited from the watchful eyes of advisors, mentors, new colleagues, and old friends. First and foremost, I would like to thank James Vernon for invaluable insight on how to transform the manuscript into a book. Leora Auslander, Paul Cheney, and Michael Geyer were instrumental in training me as a historian and in teaching me how to tackle a book-length research and writing project. For their reading of drafts and professional support, I am grateful to Kris Cohen, Kenny Cupers, Sean Dunwoody, Sarah Farmer, Barry Haneberg, Elizabeth Heath, Sara Pritchard, Christa Robbins, Susan Carol Rogers, Heather Welland, and Alexia Yates.

In France, I have had the good fortune of being able to share my work with several generous and welcoming scholars. Steven Kaplan has been of great assistance in helping me to think through the early years of organic farming and the obsession with purity. He also provided invaluable feedback on a later draft of the full manuscript. Alain Chatriot helped me to understand the influence of agribusiness and state regulation over the market. Christophe Bonneuil encouraged me to think more seriously about the environmental and scientific implications of this story. And François Purseigle was an enormous help in the very beginning, welcoming me to join a lively circle of rural sociologists when I was just starting my research. Lastly, my biggest debt owed on the other side of the Atlantic lies with Angéline Escafré-Dublet, who read early chapters, kept me company in Fontainebleau at the old site for contemporary archives, and continues to serve as my Virgil for navigating all things French.

On the technical end of things, there are several people who deserve a big thanks. Brandon Proia at the University of North Carolina Press has been everything that a first-time author could hope for. My anonymous readers offered thoughtful and helpful suggestions (one of them even provided me with a better title!). I am also indebted to Jean-François Lemaire for allowing me access to the private archives of his father; Simon Bréhéret at the municipal archives of Angers for eleventh-hour assistance in securing images from the Lemaire collections; Tiphaine Rault at the Ministry of

Agriculture for generously hunting down historical photographs; and Aurélie Utzeri at the archives of the Musée du Vivant at Agro-Paris Tech for her help in accessing the unprocessed papers of André Louis.

At Washington University in St. Louis, I would like to thank Liz Borgwardt, Alex Dubé, Douglas Flowe, Maggie Garb, Corinna Treital, and Lori Watt for their professional support and generosity. I am likewise grateful to my colleagues farther afield, whose intellectual collaboration and friendship have sustained me through the process of research and writing: Fredrik Albritton-Jonsson, Celeste Day-Moore, Victoria Frede, Daniel Immerwahr, Eddie Kolla, Peter Russell Simons, Maggie Taft, Tore Olson, and Damon Young.

Last but not least, I would like to thank my family for supporting me through the ups and downs of graduate school, the job market, and the first years of life as a proper professor: Olga and Jace Lasek, Emily Keenlyside and Todd Stewart, Amanda Kelly, Malcolm Fraser and Stacey DeWolfe, Émilie Côté, dad and Candy, Carrie and Bob Weston, Maija Anderson, Mary Nisi, Eric Elshtain, Jon Trowbridge, Bonnie Lennox and the Callanan Clan, Kristy Storey, Sonja Bennett, Peter Rizun, Jarusha Brown, Robin Richardson, Will and Rachel BLA, Dorothée Imbert and Andrew Cruse, and David Connelly.

Abbreviations in the Text

ACAB	Association of Independent Organic Agricultural Advisors (Association des conseillers indépendants en agriculture biologique)
AFAB	French Association for Organic Agriculture (Association française d'agriculture biologique)
AFRAN	French Research Association for a Standard Diet (Association française de recherce pour une alimentation normale)
ANMR	National Association of Rural Migrations (Association nationale des migrations rurales)
AOC	Standardized origins labeling (Appellation d'origine contrôlée)
APCA	Permanent Assembly of the Chambers of Agriculture (Assemblée permanente des chambres d'agriculture)
CAP	Common Agricultural Policy
CDJA	Departmental Center for Young Farmers (Centre départemental des jeunes agriculteurs)
CGP	French Planning Office (Commissariat général du plan)
CNERNA	National Research and Recommendations Center for Nutrition and Diet (Centre national d'études et de recommandations sur la nutrition et l'alimentation)
CNJA	National Center for Young Farmers (Centre national des jeunes agriculteurs)
ECSC	European Coal and Steel Community
EEC	European Economic Community
EU	European Union
FDSEA	Departemental Federation of Farm Unions (Fédération départementale des syndicats d'exploitants agricoles)
FIA	Federation of Agricultural Industries (Fédération des industries alimentaires)
FNAB	National Federation for Organic Agriculture (Fédération nationale d'agriculture biologique)

FNSEA	National Federation of Farm Unions (Fédération nationale des syndicats d'exploitants agricoles)
GABO	Western Organic Farming Group (Groupement d'agriculture biologique de l'ouest)
INRA	National Institute for Agricultural Research (Institut national de la recherche agronomique)
JAC	Young Catholic Farmers (Jeunesse agricole catholique)
OEEC	Organization for European Economic Cooperation
SAFER	Society for Developing and Settling Rural Land (Société d'aménagement foncier et d'établissement rural)
UFAB	French Union of Organic Farming (Union française d'agriculture biologique)

Organic Resistance

Departmental map of metropolitan France

Introduction

The Human Cost of Creative Destruction

> Rising levels of human capital enabled an agrarian nation to
> evolve into places as rich and complex as Manhattan and Silicon
> Valley.... Technology displaces workers in the short run but does
> not lead to mass unemployment in the long run. Rather, we
> become richer, which creates demand for new jobs elsewhere
> in the economy.
>
> —CHARLES WHEELAN, *Naked Economics* (2010, 104)

The shift to an industrialized agricultural system, designed to support an ever-expanding number of food consumers with an ever-diminishing number of food producers, is without question one of the most important developments of the modern era. Nowhere was the transformation of the agricultural sector effected so quickly and so thoroughly as in France. At the close of the Second World War, the agricultural sector was for the most part a backward holdover of the nineteenth century, and yet by the mid-1970s, France had become the world's second largest exporter of agricultural goods—second only to the United States. After three decades of concerted efforts, farms were larger and rationally organized; chemical inputs such as fertilizers and pesticides were routine; tractors and combine threshers dotted the landscape; and farm products were shipped to national, European, and international markets. Between 1955 and 1975, when this transformation was at its most intense, the active agricultural population was cut in half, and 40,000 to 50,000 farms disappeared every single year.[1] As farmers left the land, freeing up holdings for those who remained, the average size of French farms almost tripled, from fifteen to forty-two hectares.[2] Productivity levels soared. By the end of the 1980s, just 6 percent of the active French population was still working in agriculture—compared with 33 percent at the end of the war.[3] Whereas one French farmer had fed seven people in 1960, a generation later he was feeding forty.[4] A process that had begun in the United States at the turn of the twentieth century was delayed a good fifty years in France, yet France still managed to close the gap and catch up, becoming one of the world's leading players in agricultural trade.

There is a tendency, both popular and academic, to view France as a beautiful museum, the specter of Walter Benjamin's capital of the nineteenth century. It is known the world over for its art collections, public gardens, and pastry. But the history of postwar farming tells an entirely different story—one of economic success, cutthroat capitalist competition, and global domination. Through its membership in the European Union (EU), France is one of a handful of countries that controls the worldwide food system. As such, it exercises an enormous amount of power. This might not be readily apparent from the vantage point of the United States, given that the global influence of American agriculture is equally impressive. But if you talk to a farmer in Africa, where markets are overdetermined by food aid and preferential trade agreements with former colonial masters, she is likely to be painfully aware of just how much power France wields on the global stage.

This rise to the top was all the more staggering when one considers the lack of agricultural development through the fin de siècle. When cheap North American grain hit global markets in the late nineteenth century, largely the result of reduced transportation costs, the French responded with high tariff walls, insulating the agricultural sector from competition. Because the electoral system under the Third Republic (1871–1944) favored rural voters, granting these protections was a politically expedient move.[5] Moreover, a pervasive agrarian ideology viewed the peasant proprietor as the linchpin of political and social stability. Léon Gambetta, one of the architects of the new government, famously proclaimed that if the peasants were "shod with the clogs of the Republic," then France would be invincible.[6] But ultimately, protectionism held French agriculture back. From 1880 to 1910, French farming grew at a rate just one-third of that of European farming as a whole.[7] While the Danes and the Dutch chose to adapt to the changing market, creating greater efficiencies in production and distribution methods, the French lagged behind.[8]

The vast majority of French farmers continued to work as their grandparents had. They labored on small and poorly organized plots; draft animals did the heavy lifting; and their products were sold on local, or perhaps regional, markets. Apart from a small minority of wealthy producers, concentrated in the fertile areas around Paris and in the northeast, at the end of the Second World War, the bulk of French farmers were still mired in the nineteenth century. In just one generation, this would all change.

In tandem with its rise to the top of the global food market, France earned a reputation as a small-scale producer of quality goods, a reputation that was at best only partially accurate. French farming and food culture have often been held up as an alternative, or even as an antidote, to their American counterparts. But France is not the bastion of a healthy food culture that American pundits, Francophiles, and yes, even the French food industry, claim it to be. The aisles of French supermarkets are stocked with pork produced in concentrated animal feeding operations in Brittany, rice grown in the Camargue on a contract basis for giant corporations, and dairy products produced on behalf of the French behemoth Lactalis, the world's largest dairy company.

So where does the French reputation for quality come from? In the first decades of the postwar period, the watchword was productivity. Policy was overwhelmingly focused on sheer output—to raise agricultural incomes and to take advantage of export markets. But industrialization and anti-industrialization went hand in hand, and a small handful of producers and consumers resisted the industrial tide from the get-go. Biodynamic farming arrived in France in the late 1930s, and organic farming appeared a decade later.[9] Tilting at the windmills of modernization, farmers and agronomists such as Raoul Lemaire and André Louis worked tirelessly to promote alternatives to industrial production. And although the movement grew through the 1950s and 1960s, it was not until the 1970s that a critical mass of producers and consumers began to question seriously the productivist model.

Moreover, "quality" is a slippery term. It has meant different things to different people at different times. For the pioneers of organic farming, a quality product was a product free of chemical inputs and endowed with superior nutritional content. On the other hand, for the Ministry of Agriculture, quality in the 1950s referred to safety more than anything else. There were concerns that lack of refrigeration in the dairy industry was contributing to infant mortality rates. When state officials spoke of quality in this context, they were referring to dairy products free from dangerous bacteria. By the 1960s, however, the Ministry of Agriculture began to experiment with a new version of quality—a quality that claimed to characterize superior goods. This version of quality was largely an invention of marketing and was applied to such things as chicken, cheese, and charcuterie. In the 1980s, quality took yet another turn as the AOC system was expanded (AOC stands for *appellation d'origine contrôlée*, or "standardized origins labeling"). According to this system, rules governing provenance and production methods guaranteed yet another form of quality, which in this instance was associated with transparency. To say, therefore, that French agriculture prized quality is a largely vacuous statement, constructed on the heels of multiple advertising campaigns that sought to win both domestic and foreign consumers by convincing them that various, if not all, French products were somehow superior to their American or British counterparts.[10]

Just as the actual scale of artisanal production runs counter to expectations, the ideological origins of small-scale quality production are similarly unexpected. Many of the earliest proponents of organic agriculture had ties to the fascist politics of Vichy and the eugenics movement. Quality for these men was about purity and the regeneration of the French race. They were white and staunchly Catholic, and they believed that the best way to save French men and women from the degeneration that had led to the German occupation was to rebuild their bodies through a superior organic diet. Well-maintained soil would produce higher quality food, which would in turn nourish body and soul.

Alternative methods were likewise pursued as a means of escaping the long arm of the state. With state-mandated modernization came new regulatory institutions that controlled everything from the wheat varieties that could be marketed to the immunization of livestock. Moreover, modernization required a steep increase in inputs, and while many farmers were ready to take on debt to make that happen, many more were either unable or unwilling to do so. For these producers, organic production presented itself as a viable alternative. They could retain their liberty in the face of technocratic dirigisme while simultaneously avoiding the added costs associated with industrial production.

After the rise of the back-to-the-land movement in the wake of the student rebellions of 1968, the ideological underpinnings of organic farming underwent a radical transformation. The fascist chauvinism and Catholic content disappeared, replaced with a decidedly leftist countercultural ethos. That said, important elements remained. The antistatism was still there. It had simply changed its political valence, moving from the libertarian Right to the radical Left. And while the movement no longer espoused a language of racial purity, its adherents tended to be white and to hail from privileged backgrounds. José Bové, the poster child for French organic farming at the end of the twentieth century, was after all born to academic parents and grew up in Berkeley and Bordeaux.

Several developments in the 1970s led to yet another shift in the status of organic production. Surpluses had become a big problem throughout the European Economic Community (EEC). Because subsidies were tied to output, there was an incentive for farmers to produce as much as possible, regardless of what the market might bear. From the perspective of both the French state and the EEC, this aspect of the productivist model had become very expensive. Moreover, agricultural incomes were not improving as promised. The large-scale producers who were able to take advantage of the common market had done well for themselves. But the small- and medium-scale producers were struggling to get by. Lastly, the oil crisis of 1973 caused the prices of many agricultural inputs to rise. As a result, many farmers and policymakers questioned the logic of an agricultural model that relied so heavily on oil.

The state sought to mitigate the negative effects of these crises by encouraging farmers to move into value-added niche production. But in no way did the French retreat from industrialization. They simply learned how to complement quantity with quality. By co-opting alternative practices, the state neutralized both the fascist and the anticapitalist politics of organic production. No longer necessarily part of the Right or the Left, organic production became one choice among many for French producers and consumers

For the pioneers and the disenchanted urban youth who became back-to-the-landers, organic production was a question of ethical and moral standards. For the state, however, claims to quality were simply one more tool to build its agricultural empire. Systems were put in place to foster the growth of niche markets for high-priced goods as a means of maintaining the value of the sector while cutting back on its volume. For example, in the 1980s the French state commissioned the creation of a national database of regional and traditional foods and expanded the scope of the AOC system to revive the concept of terroir, a term that had been largely dormant since the 1940s. At the same time, however, the state was flouting the importance of place by relocating the production of Emmental cheese from its native mountains of the Savoie to the large processing factories of Brittany, maintaining that the move would improve efficiency.[11] Sometimes regional origins mattered and sometimes they did not. Terroir and mass production, quality and quantity, went hand in hand. Niche markets were precisely that—*niche* markets. They were never intended to supplant the mainstream.

Sources

One of the sources of inspiration for this book is a classical explanation of how the process of creative destruction leaves a handful of individuals in the dust while the community as a whole flourishes. In his *Naked Economics: Undressing the Dismal Science*, economist Charles Wheelan provides a condensed history of the United States, starting with a farming community that was entirely self-sufficient, in which everyone had enough to survive by trading with each other, but no one was particularly comfortable. The community then grew by one inhabitant with the arrival of an outsider who held a doctoral degree in agronomy. She invented an efficient plough and traded it for a share in the harvest. Farmers then had more food to eat because of the increased efficiency and the agronomist was able to feed herself. Moreover, a new job had been created: that of plough salesperson. It was a win all around. Then a carpenter arrived and offered to do all of the odd jobs that limited the farmers' time in their fields. Yields rose again, and yet another job was created. With the surpluses created by the increased yields, the community hired a teacher. The kids got smarter and became better farmers. Yields went up again. Over time, "Rising levels of human capital enabled an agrarian nation to evolve into places as rich and complex as Manhattan and Silicon Valley."[12] As the community and others like it evolved, an out-of-date plough designer might have gone out of business or a few farmers might have been forced into other work when surpluses saturated available markets. In other words, in the short term there were growing pains, but in the long run, everyone was better off. New jobs arose to provide employment for out-of-work plough designers and farmers: "Technology displaces workers in the short run but does not lead to mass unemployment in the long run. Rather, we become richer, which creates demand for new jobs elsewhere in the economy."[13]

Wheelan's story, intended for a well-educated audience with no background in economics, is the stuff of standard classical economic theory. It deals in aggregates. But what about that short term in which people are forced, as individuals, to contend with powers beyond their control? What happens in the space that occupies the distance between the short and the long run?

The individual stories of French farmers, overrun by the forces of technological development and economic growth, tell the tale. Each chapter therefore begins with an individual snapshot that highlights the broader themes of the text. A young farmer borrowed so much money from the local bank to industrialize that he was forced to live with the constant stress of knowing that he was one bad harvest away from total ruin. Another, tired of living with the same stress, abandoned industrialization altogether to join Lemaire in his crusade for organic agriculture. A mayor protested the mandatory redistribution of land in his village, convinced that the state had operated arbitrarily and had violated the property rights of his constituents. A brave and idealistic arrival from Algeria relocated to the countryside in the hopes of learning how to farm, in spite of the fact that he had no training and few contacts. And finally, a factory worker desperately attempted to return to farming, after being passed over for his older brother in the inheritance of his father's holdings, only to be frustrated by inflexible state regulations. That their grandchildren might be better off would have been cold comfort to these men who were thwarted by state policies in their fight to remain on the land.

Just as Wheelan's story is simultaneously about the large-scale economic forces of creative destruction and the small-scale changes that this destruction effects at the local level, the story of postwar French agriculture similarly toggles back and forth between the global, regional, national, and local. It is a story that is rooted in the broader themes of postwar French history: economic modernization and state planning, urbanization, European integration, and a growing disenchantment with the modern conveniences of consumer capitalism. One could easily envision Georges Perec's young couple in his novel *Les Choses* (Things) finally breaking free of their materialist desires and leaving behind their soul-crushing marketing jobs in Paris to take up organic farming in the Cévennes. Embedded in these larger narrative arcs that capture the world-historical events of the twentieth century are a host of smaller intersecting and overlapping stories: from a producer in the southwest objecting to the arrival of American hybrid corn, to the furious indignation of local residents who were shocked and horrified to find out that German farmers could buy land in their communities under the laws of the new EEC. One of the aims of this book is to illuminate how a small-scale farmer in rural France was tied to Paris or Brussels, or even Washington, D.C. The story of agricultural industrialization in postwar France is both very big and very small.

The postwar French state was a bureaucratic paper-producing machine. The National Archives are overloaded with an endless stream of state-generated paperwork. But buried amidst the soulless studies and reports is a remarkable cache of letters written by farmers from across the country to local, regional, and national public administrators. These letters stemmed from the creation in 1960 of regional land banks designed to monitor the real estate market in agricultural lands to ensure access to this most basic of agricultural inputs for young and ambitious farmers. Typically the result of a sale-gone-wrong, the letters most often took the shape of complaints in which farmers pled their case to those in charge, from the village mayor to the president of the Republic himself. The letters in this collection reveal how farmers interpreted state-mandated modernization, how they variously used it to their own ends, translated it into local practice, and in some cases, were ruined by it. Expressing themselves as citizens of France, the men (and very occasionally the women) who wrote these letters revealed how they understood themselves as political agents. On a more intimate level, they also revealed how they understood themselves as workers, spouses, parents, caregivers, and inheritors of an ancestral legacy.

Personal archives likewise proved to be invaluable in demonstrating how local voices responded to state planning. The papers of André Louis, located in Grignon at AgroParisTech, and Raoul Lemaire, housed at the municipal archives of Angers, tell the stories of two men who opposed industrialization by coming up with agricultural models of their own. Only recently made available to the public, these two collections are rich in material related to the origins and early development of organic farming in France. Moreover, as personal archives, they offer insight into the thoughts and motivations of these two pioneers by way of personal correspondence, notes, marginalia, photographs, and sketches. Having access to these two influential voices has allowed me to flesh out in detail how the early efforts of a small handful of men led to the rise of organic agriculture in France.

By investigating how a collection of individuals, located across the political spectrum, navigated agricultural industrialization, I aim to demonstrate how French citizens challenged state power, both successfully and unsuccessfully, in the postwar period. On that note, I am not interested in recuperating farmer voices to give them agency. On the contrary, when faced with a powerful state and the interests of the agricultural elite, most farmers held very little agency at all. Their voices are important, however, because they demonstrate how national and international politics were carried out at the local level, and how world-historical events were filtered through the thoughts, desires, and actions of decidedly non–world-historical peoples and places. While the national scale celebrates the success of the agricultural sector as a global economic force, the local scale highlights how the national narrative was contingent on the actions of individuals. While some cooperated, others resisted, and this resistance often shaped the national policies that were designed to further the modernization agenda. Moreover, the local scale reveals that while the nation as a whole might have benefited from cheaper food and a powerful export sector, thousands upon thousands of individual farmers were ruined in the process.

Land Use

Land is an essential input in agricultural production. Without it, you cannot farm. Moreover, land is a limited resource. How it is distributed reveals a good deal about national and local priorities. Agricultural lands therefore serve as an analytically rich medium for thinking about how a national mandate for modernization was filtered through the local practices of agricultural players. The rules governing how land could be acquired changed enormously during the postwar period. Through the various amendments, regarding everything from land sales and agricultural leases to inheritance, land use policy was central to the tenets of each and every postwar farm organization. It was also central to state plans for modernization. In the name of economic growth, during the postwar period the French government overhauled a system of property rights that had been in effect since the introduction of Napoleon's Civil Code.

Buried deep in the storage rooms of the French national archives is a cache of letters written by farmers to various representatives of the state, detailing their experiences with the national land management bureau, the Society for Developing and Settling Rural Land (Société d'aménagement foncier et d'établissement rural, or SAFER). The folders in this collection include not only the letters of farmers, invaluable as a rare instance of access to a set of voices that were rarely committed to paper, but also a wide variety of responses from the Ministry of Agriculture, the major farm unions, the President's Office, and the Ministry of Finance. Together these letters offer a rare glimpse into how state policy was variously accepted, manipulated, and outright refused by the men and women it was intended to serve. These letters also reveal how citizens positioned themselves vis-à-vis the state; how they negotiated their rights and responsibilities as members of the larger polity; and how they understood their various entitlements as citizens, soldiers, farmers, and workers.

Ultimately, the general success of the farm sector required the creation of large-scale industrial farms. To borrow a phrase from the infamous American secretary of agriculture Earl Butz, French farmers were likewise exhorted to "Get big or get out." Measures were put in place to increase the size of individual farms, to speed up the ceding of lands from retiring farmers to a younger generation that was more open to modern techniques, and to redraw the property lines of entire counties to increase efficiency through better parcel distribution. Long-term low-interest loans were made available through the Crédit Agricole and the terms of agricultural leases were rewritten to encourage innovation and investment on the part of tenants. Eager to overhaul agricultural production to take advantage of foreign markets and to facilitate economic development through the transfer of labor from the farm to the industrial and tertiary sectors, the state sought to remap the borders of rural France.

Further complicating matters, farmers were not the only ones in need of rural land. The state expropriated farms to build highways and hydroelectric dams. Belgians and Germans were keen on taking advantage of the newly formed EEC, and hoped to take up farming in France, where lands were considerably less expensive. Environmentalists wanted set-asides for conservation purposes. And by the early 1970s, weary urban French men and women, many of whom were beginning to question the productivist logic of the postwar era, were seeking refuge by way of second homes, regional parks, and recreational areas. Agricultural history is all too often told in isolation from broader historical narratives. But farming in postwar France was intimately bound up with urbanization, European integration, and the emergence of environmentalism as a mass movement.

Agricultural industrialization transformed the French landscape, the very ground on which the French nation was founded. The rural exodus, which had begun in the late nineteenth century and swelled through the 1950s, was not only a key factor when making land use and agricultural policy decisions, but also had a profound effect on the ordering of French society. France grew increasingly urban (and suburban) during the latter half of the twentieth century, a development that contributed to a variety of new land use policies, such as the transfer of agricultural lands to recreational areas and environmentally protected spaces, as well as the growth of tourism in rural areas. A growing nostalgia for rural life and an appreciation for the ill effects of industrial agriculture on the natural world likewise led to a greater interest on the part of urban consumers in products that boasted organic or terroir designations.

The changing balance between rural and urban France, along with the industrialization of agriculture, likewise had a profound effect on how farming fit into French culture. As farmers left the countryside in droves, and as those who stayed behind transformed their farms into agricultural enterprises, many lamented the passing of an older and more authentic civilization that had been rooted in the land. These lamentations often found expression in both the popular and academic press.[14] As shown in figure 1, an illustration published in a 1971 issue of the widely read magazine *L'Express*, urban consumers associated farmers with the soil. Unhappily turned toward

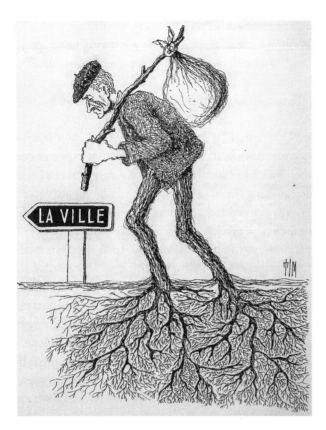

FIGURE 1
A peasant turns to leave for the city. *Source*: Pol Echevin, "Paysans. Au Secours!," *L'Express*, March 22, 1971; TIM (illustrator).

the city, a fate presumably imposed by his inability to keep up with the demands of agricultural industrialization, this farmer is literally rooted in the ground that he must leave behind. The diminutive size of the bundle slung across his shoulder, representative of his material possessions, stands in firm contrast to the elaborate root system that takes shape where his feet should be, suggesting that his life has been defined by production and not by the patterns of consumption that he will be forced to adopt in the city. Once he takes the first step in this ominous direction, he will have severed the tie between his body and the earth. And in destroying this root system, he will have unwillingly contributed to the social and cultural erosion of the countryside. Agricultural industrialization, and in particular its effect on the landscape, was ineluctably tied to profound social and cultural change.

As a centuries-old system of small holdings was converted into a combination of industrial agricultural enterprises, second homes, environmental preserves, and recreational areas, debates raged at the Ministry of Agriculture and the farm union offices about the proper use of rural lands. With these changes, the land came to embody different things for different people. For many farmers, it became a site of resistance; for a growing urban population, a means of escape and diversion; for a nascent environmentalist movement, a natural heritage to be protected; and for the burgeoning postwar economy, the symbol of an agricultural sector that had achieved unparalleled success.

THAT FRANCE IS THE WORLD'S SECOND largest agricultural exporter is a fact that is often met with shock and surprise—if not outright disbelief and indignation. The reputation that the French have built as being purveyors of all things gastronomically refined and artisanally produced makes it difficult to imagine that efficiency, productivity, and price might ever have trumped quality when it comes to food. The Michelin Guide, open-air markets, cheese wrapped in wax paper—these are the things that are called to mind when thinking about food and agriculture in France. Surely the French are too busy enjoying fine cheeses and perfectly prepared baguettes to see to the business of economic competition—or so the myth of the bon vivant would have us believe. The story of how agriculture was developed in the postwar period demands that these assumptions be questioned. It proves that the French are every bit as capable of global economic success as their neighbors. France is home to Danone, Unibel, and Lu, all of which focus their energies on the production of processed goods that line the shelves of such big-box stores as Auchan and Carrefour.

The stories of bucolic provincial France are well known. It is time to tell another story—a story that accounts for the multiple contexts in which the experience of postwar rural France played out: the domestic and international political economy, European integration, and the politics of transforming the French landscape. These larger frameworks produce an alternative history of both rural France and French economic development in the postwar period. In this narrative, rural France is a tumultuous place, engaged in a fierce back-and-forth with crucial national and global developments; farmers and their representatives are *simultaneously* keeping afloat a mystical belief in the sanctity of the *pays*, while shrewdly engaging in the bare-knuckle politics of international trade negotiations; economic development is brutally cutthroat; and France is a major player in the global death match of market competition.

CHAPTER ONE

The Industrial Ideal, 1944–1958

> After a long day of hard work, the American farmer returns home
> to join his family. Here he enjoys *a level of comfort too often unknown
> in France*: after taking his shower and changing his clothes, he
> relaxes in a rocking chair, a piece of furniture to be found
> everywhere in rural America. . . . The radio (often one of many in a
> single household), and increasingly the television, bring him the
> news. The radio, along with the telephone, the newspapers, and
> the automobile, shatter completely the difficult isolation that
> continues to weigh so heavily on so many of our own farmers.
>
> —ANDRÉ DOUZON, *Le fermier américain et sa famille* (1951, 17)

By the end of the 1950s, thirt y of the sixty farms in Bertignat (Puy-de-
Dôme) were either abandoned or barely maintained. Hit hard by rural
out-migration, the population had dipped precipitously, leaving its mark
on the landscape. H. P., however, a young farmer of twenty-eight, had decided to stay. With twenty hectares of pasture, potatoes, and cereals, H. P.
was one of the more successful farmers in the area. Many of his neighbors
had gone to work at the new pharmaceuticals factory that had been constructed after the war. Undeterred, H. P. fought to maintain his family farm
and, through modernization, to build a better life for himself. Joining forces
with over two thousand farmers in his county, H. P. put together a petition
demanding that (1) plots be redistributed to rationalize the structure of agricultural holdings, (2) that a land bank be created to monitor agricultural
land use in the area, and (3) that agricultural lands owned by absentee land-
lords be put in the hands of the farmers who farmed them.[1] These were
radical demands, especially when one considers that in the 1956 elections
60 percent of the very same county had voted for the extreme Right, a political orientation that typically refused alternative property-rights regimes.

In his efforts to modernize, H. P. carefully researched milk production,
which was where he wanted to concentrate his efforts. Over the course of
several years, he was able to change out his entire herd and replace his local
cows with Holsteins, known for their superior milk production. He also updated his outbuildings, purchased a tractor, and enhanced his pastures.
The improvements led him to double his milk production.

Nevertheless, the modernized production and the superior yields did not necessarily improve H. P.'s situation. By the end of the decade, he was making 800,000 francs per year. His expenses totaled 650,000 francs per year, leaving him with 150,000 francs in revenue. To put that number into context, H. P. had borrowed one million francs to buy the tractor, a debt that he was having trouble repaying in spite of his improved operations. If anything happened to his tractor or his fields, he would not be able to service his loan. Having to live constantly under the risk of failure was taking its toll. But at the same time, his improvements were not yet paying off, so H. P. decided to borrow yet another million and a half francs. Doubling down, H. P. hoped that this additional loan would eventually free him from his precarious situation.

According to Serge Mallet, the celebrated journalist and political activist, H. P. had worsened his condition. Comparing H. P.'s situation unfavorably to that of his father, Mallet wrote: "And so this innovative young farmer, this skilled agriculturalist, ultimately risks . . . living a life more difficult than that of his father, who had much lower operating costs. The slightest mishap, the smallest surplus crisis, constantly threaten to put him out of business."[2] H. P. had done exactly what the state had encouraged him to do. He had joined the ranks of the enterprising young farmers and had adopted the new modern methods. His yields had increased and his improved productivity was helping to build an agricultural export sector. But his own personal situation had not improved, and by Mallet's estimation, it had in fact deteriorated.

AT THE TIME of liberation in 1944, reconstruction was the top priority for the French administration. The war had cost France one-quarter of its total wealth. Agricultural and industrial outputs were a fraction of what they had been before the war—60 and 44 percent, respectively. Railroad tracks, bridges, and ports had all suffered substantial damages, and one million dwellings had been destroyed.[3] But "reconstruction" was an elastic term; it encompassed both the return to prewar standards *and* the drive to surpass them. Sights were set first and foremost on the immediate future, but they were also focused on the longer term. Areas that had been razed in the final days of the German retreat needed to be rebuilt and food production ramped up to end wartime rations. There were also plans for large-scale improvement projects, however, such as nationwide rural electrification and the expansion of industrial infrastructure, plans that would carry a badly bruised nation into a better tomorrow. This new France was going to be modern and powerful. It was going to move beyond the disgrace of the German occupation and the stink of Vichy, and it was going to reclaim its rightful place within the constellation of global powers.[4]

The agricultural sector was at the center of this drive to modernize. At liberation, France was still largely a rural country, and farming employed a full 36 percent of the active adult population (as compared with just 5.5 percent in Great Britain, 16 percent in the United States, and 20 percent in the Netherlands).[5] Because a modern economy was grounded in industry and services, many of those working in agriculture needed to be transferred from the countryside to urban areas.[6] Men and women who might have otherwise worked on farms instead took jobs in such places as factories, government offices, and retail establishments. This redistribution within the workforce in turn required a food supply system in which fewer producers were responsible for feeding an ever-increasing number of consumers.

Modernization was a transparent process for the French policymakers who oversaw reconstruction. This category has in recent decades become an object of critique for scholars investigating the history of development and modernization theory. But for midcentury French state officials, there was nothing questionable about modernization—no elements of instability in its meaning. These men and women who pushed the modernization agenda used the term without hesitation and easily agreed on its significance. Modernization meant the move away from an agricultural to an industrial and service-oriented economy. It required urbanization, increased purchasing power, and a cadre of well-trained citizens able to take up the white-collar work of both the public and private sectors. In short, a modern France would adopt the same trappings of the good life that had already been achieved in the more "modern" nations of the West: Great Britain, the Netherlands, and the United States.[7]

The methods by which this modernization was achieved were ruthless. At every turn, the state forced sacrifice on the countryside, maintaining that while a minority suffered in the short term, the nation as a whole was going to emerge triumphant.[8] Farmers lost their land, took on crushing amounts of debt, compromised their health with the application of chemical inputs, and left behind their communities—all in the name of modernization. Technocrats, neo-corporatist farm unions, the EEC, and the Crédit Agricole all worked to further the modernization agenda, and in doing so placed a series of demands and constraints on agricultural France, the most extreme being the near abrogation of property rights. While the full extent of these constraints and obligations was not reached until the 1960s, the state apparatus that ultimately drove French agriculture to modernize was established in the decade following the end of the war.

From national aspirations to improve standards of living by modernization, to dreams of global dominance, the ambition to rebuild was made manifest by a variety of actors at several different political levels. Domestically, the French Planning Office (Commissariat général du plan, or CGP), established in 1946, led the way on long-term reconstruction and modernization. Farm unions worked with the government to establish agricultural policy and accepted the demands made of their constituents in exchange for a seat at the negotiating table. Armies of public surveyors went into the countryside to rationalize the landscape and redraw property lines to improve productivity. Internationally, the agreements made at Bretton Woods and the push to foster freer global trade relations led the French state to introduce economic modernization schemes designed to improve the ability of French producers to compete in the global marketplace. Lastly, with the creation of the Organization for European Economic Cooperation (OEEC) in 1948 and the EEC in 1957, plans for the future of France were embedded in regional networks of commerce and power.

This is not to argue that the French case was not without its idiosyncrasies. While postwar modernization and agricultural industrialization were driven in large part by forces that operated beyond the borders of France, they were nevertheless unique to the postwar French experience. The rate at which France moved from the countryside to the city was unmatched. Only a centralized state authority, buttressed by a neo-corporatist labor model that enlisted union leaders to enforce state power, could achieve such a monumental transformation at breakneck speed while maintaining social and political stability. For example, while it took roughly two generations for the United States to overhaul its farm sector (from the 1880s to the 1940s), France completed the task in just one, prompting many to refer to this transformation as the "silent revolution."[9]

At the time of liberation, farming practices in France varied widely.[10] In the northeast, farms tended to be large and farmers engaged in high-input and high-yield production. They used the new chemical fertilizers and tractors, and concentrated on such crops as cereals and sugar beet. Relatively well-structured medium- to large-scale farms could be found in the areas circling Paris: the Beauce, Picardie, parts of the Loire, and Burgundy. In addition to cereals, these farms produced dairy, wine, and vegetables. The trees and hedgerows that broke up the lands of western France were largely absent in the northeast and in the areas surrounding Paris. Having so often been razed as battlegrounds, these parts of France were particularly amenable to well-organized farms and vast, open fields. Small-holders tended to be concentrated in the south and southwest, and produced table wines and dairy products. A subset of these farmers, found largely in Brittany and the mountainous regions of central and southeastern France, engaged in polyculture and remained isolated from markets and distribution networks. The small-holders of France, both those engaged in subsistence polyculture and those who were oriented toward small-scale market production, worked poorly structured farms and continued to rely on draft animals and plows rather than modern implements.

These variations notwithstanding, the vast majority of farms were small-scale. At the time of liberation, a little more than half of all French farms were less than ten hectares, a bar that would soon become the dividing line between what was considered to be a viable farm and a farm that needed to be sold off to expand neighboring operations (one hectare = 2.47 acres).[11] Farm products were by and large consumed locally; little, if any, paid labor was used; and the standard of living of farm families and farmworkers lagged considerably behind that of their urban counterparts. Much of rural France had yet to be provided with access to electricity, indoor plumbing, or serviceable roads. As the historian Gordon Wright once observed, and as Georges Rouquier captured in his 1946 documentary *Farrebique*, most farmers of this period had more in common with their ancestors of the early nineteenth century than with the new and improved versions of themselves that would develop through the 1950s and 1960s.[12]

The French agricultural sector had already come under fire for its sluggish output. Having relied on food imports during the First World War to cover shortages, by the 1920s many were calling for an industrialized farm sector that would be able to guarantee the nation's needs in times of both peace and war. Inspired by the ideas of Frederic Winslow Taylor and Henry Ford, French businessmen such as Louis Renault traveled to the United States to understand the new "scientific management." Principles that were first applied to industry quickly found their way to the agricultural sector. Like industry, agriculture would be run rationally. Industrial farms would be treated as businesses rather than as family homesteads. The bottom line would be prized above well-established customs and traditions. And to improve their efficiency, farmers would rely on new discoveries in technology, chemistry, and management.[13]

It was also the case that neighboring Denmark, Belgium, and the Netherlands were all more productive when it came to producing basic staples such as wheat. There was support to introduce measures that would help the French to catch up, but there was also support to maintain the status quo. The Third Republic championed the peasant proprietor and protected him with trade barriers and price controls. A century of revolt that stretched from the French Revolution to the Paris Commune had taught politicians that no government could survive without the support of the rural vote. French farmers of the Third Republic were catered to accordingly, and enterprising modernizers were forced to fight an uphill battle.

Peasantist dogma aside, the interwar period did witness some development in the agricultural sector. Rates of mechanization increased, which in turn improved yields. Farmers adopted horse-drawn rakes and harvesters, and improved their plowing systems. A small handful of wealthier farmers acquired more sophisticated machinery such as tractors and combine-harvesters. Improvements were also made in fertilization. As the Haber-Bosch process expanded beyond Germany and French companies discovered how to fix nitrogen on their own, these same large-scale farmers were purchasing synthetic fertilizers for their fields. These early efforts at industrialization were slowed not only by the politics of the Third Republic but also by the economic crisis of the 1930s, and then by the war and German occupation. It was not until after liberation, with the creation of a new republic and a new set of political and economic priorities, that earlier calls to industrialize the farm sector could be fully realized.[14]

The Politics of *Planification*

In the aftermath of the Second World War, plans for agriculture were both short- and long-term. Given that the French were still on rations well after liberation, ramping up food production was a top priority. Moreover, given the difficulties that the French state had encountered in feeding its population during the war, it had become a longer-term strategic priority to reduce imports and to achieve self-sufficiency in foodstuffs. In 1948, France enjoyed a bumper crop for the first time since the war and rationing was finally dropped in 1949.[15] Policymakers could finally begin to move away from the basic needs of reconstruction and to pursue agricultural expansion.

This is not to suggest that longer-term thinking about the French economy did not take place until prewar production levels had been reached.

Administrators in the Vichy administration had been planning for the post-war moment all along, and as the war began to come to a close, Charles de Gaulle's government in exile began to do the same.[16] The man at the center of these plans was Jean Monnet, the first director of the CGP. Monnet had been active in both business and politics his entire life, traveling the world as a representative of his family's cognac business, serving as an economic consultant both to his home government and to beleaguered nations abroad. For a brief time he also held a post with the League of Nations. He had spent the Second World War traveling between the United States and Britain, representing Allied interests in the acquisition of American war resources. At liberation, he was put in charge of the new French Planning Office.[17]

The CGP was established in 1946 and was tasked with coming up with five-year plans that would serve as road maps for the development of the French economy. Agronomist René Dumont, an ardent modernizer who would later experience a change of heart and run on the Green presidential ticket in the 1970s, was brought on as a consultant. The first five-year plan called for a widespread marketing campaign to get farmers on board: "With intelligent propaganda, we must prepare the psychological groundwork that will help farmers to understand that they have an interest in rationalizing their techniques. We must establish a receptive environment for the microbe of 'modernization' . . . by fostering an infectious outbreak."[18] As Dumont explained in his *Le problème agricole français* (France's agricultural problem), this rationalization of techniques would involve mechanization, land reform, chemical inputs, and careful seed selection. Modernization would transform French farms into industrial factories.[19]

It is not difficult to see why the standard dirigiste narrative of postwar development has held such explanatory power.[20] The five-year plans put forth by the CGP had a tremendous influence over French policy—so much so that the French word *planification* immediately calls to mind the statist policies of the postwar period. And while other areas of the government were plagued by leadership instability through the Fourth Republic, the CGP had just three directors between its inception and 1958 (by contrast, the Ministries of Finance and Justice each had fifteen, and the Ministry of Agriculture had nine). Moreover, the "plan" itself was everywhere: in the press, the National Assembly, and internal ministerial memos. Between the continuity and stability of the CGP and this broader culture of *planification* that took over during the immediate postwar period, there is much to corroborate the dirigiste interpretation of postwar French history.

From the Ministry of Agriculture to local farming associations, the silent revolution was very much a formal, legislated, and state-sponsored operation. It is entirely possible that agriculture would have modernized without the systematic intervention of the state—that enterprising farmers would have pioneered the way, pursuing both extensification and intensification in an effort to increase their own revenues. To be sure, many farmers in postwar France overhauled their operations on their own initiative. But without state intervention, widespread industrialization would not have happened with such astounding speed.

That said, French *planification* must be understood within the context of its constraints. The French state was not so powerful that it was able to realize its vision without having to answer to powers both below and above. French farmers, by way of both union and informal organization, pushed back when *planification* reached too far. Likewise, regional and global politics similarly shaped domestic policy. With the inauguration of the Marshall Plan in 1947 came the OEEC, and while full-scale European integration was still a decade away, it was clear from the outset that French plans would be devised within the context of European rapprochement. Monnet himself warned at the end of the war that if the nations of Europe foolishly rebuilt along economically isolationist lines, yet another violent conflict would be inevitable. Consequently, the dirigiste French state was shaped by both the American influence of the Marshall Plan and the promise of greater European integration.

One of the top priorities of the Marshall Plan in France was agricultural assistance. From tractors to animal feed, raw goods were shipped directly to French farmers, while teams of French bureaucrats, technocrats, farmers, and businessmen regularly toured the United States to study the (perceived) successes of the American model. The archives are replete with reports and photographs from the aptly named "productivity missions."[21] While production techniques were the focus of the tours, farmers and bureaucrats often marveled at the stately homes of the American farmer, complete with indoor plumbing, electricity, and often even kitchen appliances. In a 1951 report, an agronomist who had recently toured the United States with a productivity mission highlighted the creature comforts of the American farmer:

> After a long day of hard work, the American farmer returns home to join his family. Here he enjoys *a level of comfort too often unknown in France*: after taking his shower and changing his clothes, he relaxes in

a rocking chair, a piece of furniture to be found everywhere in rural America. . . . The radio (often one of many in a single household), and increasingly the television, bring him the news. The radio, along with the telephone, the newspapers, and the automobile, shatter completely the difficult isolation that continues to weigh so heavily on so many of our farmers.[22]

Mechanization, land reform, and chemical inputs would increase the yields required by the state to grow the agricultural export sector. But as we learned from H. P., increasing yields did not always translate to increased incomes. The promise of greater comforts at home served as an incentive to modernize and kept farmers motivated when their increased workloads and debt levels might have otherwise led them to return to their old methods.

These visits to the United States had a strong impact on French thinking about modernization. For example, agricultural trips to the American Midwest powerfully influenced the manner in which hybrid corn was adopted in France. Over the course of multiple visits from 1946 through 1949, French farmers and distributors forged relationships with seed sellers and facilitated the importation of American hybrid corn, which boasted higher yields than local French varieties.[23] The archives contain correspondence between the French Ministry of Agriculture and the Corn States Hybrid Service (founded in 1943 and acquired by Monsanto in 1997) discussing the donation of hybrid seeds to experimental stations in France and the possibility of long-term importation through the Marshall Plan.[24] By the 1950s, the grand patriarch of French rural sociology, Henri Mendras, was documenting how the adoption of this new hybrid corn had affected the social and economic relations of the southwest.[25]

The path toward a specifically American modernity, however, was pursued with trepidation. Americanization was both a promise and a threat. French policymakers and farmers traveled the countryside of the American Midwest on Marshall Plan–sponsored productivity missions, and all marveled at the efficiencies of mechanization and economies of scale, to say nothing of the household appliances and Formica tabletops of middle-class farm-family homes. But at the same time, many worried about the consequences of what came to be termed "Coca-colonization."

Americanization, as both a promise and a threat, is central to the history of agricultural development in postwar France, but it is not essential. One of the risks of framing French postwar economic growth entirely in terms of Americanization is that it makes it more difficult to see its domestic roots. The French were interested in Fordism and Taylorism long before the Marshall Plan was introduced—Renault visited the United States and met with both Ford and Taylor as early as 1911. The following decades witnessed a substantial expansion of state involvement in economic analysis and measurement. A cadre of technocrats began to emerge, and productivity was on the tip of these bureaucratic tongues, as new agencies such as the National Statistical Service created and monitored demographic and economic data. Many of the economic and political developments that followed the war certainly bore the stamp of American influence, but they were not defined by it. The "productivity" that was meant to be improved by these missions was the brainchild of both French and American technocrats.

These exchanges between the United States and France took place within the larger context of American farm and foreign policy. The reach of American influence into the realm of French agriculture was part of an already nascent program that extended well beyond the confines of the Marshall Plan. Supplying the French with agricultural aid was not just about buttressing a struggling postwar ally against the threat of communism. It was also about securing new markets for American goods. In the case of the French, deals were brokered to establish the regular importation of livestock feeds, while assistance in the form of tractors and combines stunted the development of the domestic farm machinery industry and created a captive market. The United States was engaged in similar practices all across the globe. It had already begun its export of hybrid corn as part of the Rockefeller Foundation's mission to Mexico and was beginning to make inroads in India. While the French were visiting the American Midwest, the green revolution was getting underway. By the early 1950s, the United States was using its agricultural policy as an instrument of foreign policy throughout the world, from Central America and western Europe to South and East Asia.[26]

If France had one eye on the American Midwest, the other was firmly focused on its European neighbors. Pierre Pflimlin, lifelong politician and minister of agriculture from 1947 to 1949 and 1950 to 1951, was especially interested in building a farm sector that was oriented toward European export markets. It was hoped that exports would kill two birds with one stone: lagging agricultural incomes and the uneven balance of payments.[27] Standards of living in the countryside tended to be well below those of urban France. With increased income through exports, farmers would be able to acquire both conveniences such as indoor plumbing and electric lighting and the widely reported comforts enjoyed by American farmers. The trade deficit was a similarly pressing problem. In 1937, it stood at 330 million dollars. By 1947, it had ballooned to 1.8 billion.[28] As reported in an analysis of the French economy, solicited by the European Recovery Program:

> The most striking feature of the French five-year program is the very marked increase planned in the production of basic agricultural commodities. The program intends to make France the largest western European exporter of basic foodstuffs. While, as noted above, the industrial output targets are, in general, in line with the prewar trends, the agricultural targets represent a radical alteration in French economic thinking, not only as compared with prewar but with 1946–1947. The economic strategists deemed it too difficult to achieve this equilibrium through industrial exports because of the difficulty of finding adequate markets.[29]

Consequently, industrial targets were attuned to interwar trends, while agricultural targets represented a "radical" shift away from the interwar economy. Agricultural transformation was at the core of state plans for post-war economic growth and development.

In particular, these efforts to increase agricultural production targeted net importers Germany and Britain. Data on the consumption preferences of the Germans and the British were collected and studied to maximize the profitability of expanding French exports. A member of the French embassy in Germany, for instance, reported on German food preferences by category: cauliflower was first for vegetables, grapes and apples for fruit, and so forth. He also added, with some chagrin, that Germans preferred white asparagus to green, which was unfortunate, as white asparagus was not produced in large quantities in France. Similarly, the German preference for beer over wine was viewed as a regrettable commercial loss.[30]

France was already moderately successful with the export of luxury food products, but to trade in the volumes necessary to repair the balance of trade and improve the incomes of farmers, the agricultural sector needed to export basic foodstuffs that were in higher demand. Pflimlin brought this message to his farmers when delivering a speech to mark the arrival of Marshall Plan tractors at the port of Le Havre. Rallying the troops, he proclaimed: "The task assigned to us is substantial. Specialists estimate that agriculture must account for one-fifth of the three million export dollars that we need to be earning by 1953. . . . This is a big number. So in addition to the high-quality products that have always distinguished French production, fine wines, liquor, foie gras, etc., a larger portion of our exports must be devoted to staple products. It is these products that the countries that might become our clients currently need the most. We must therefore export wheat, milk, dairy products, meat, fruits, and vegetables."[31] Aspirations to export to European consumers not only determined the quantity of agricultural yields; they also determined the content of those yields.

French economic motives aside, the decision to look to European markets was very much tied to the spirit of European cooperation that was promoted by both Marshall Plan bureaucrats and a small, though growing, group of French administrators. Indeed, various meetings held in the late 1940s and early 1950s to develop strategies for negotiating the end of Marshall Plan aid involved discussions regarding the expansion of European economic cooperation. French advocates for such cooperation hoped that agricultural surpluses, which were already a problem in the early 1950s, would be directed toward European markets, and that the revenue from these exports would increase farm-sector incomes and create a healthy balance of trade.

Rationalizing the Landscape

One of the chief obstacles to state plans for increasing productivity through industrialization was the structure of agricultural landholding. Most French farmland was heavily parceled. The census of 1946 revealed that there were 2.5 million farms in France, with an average surface area of 14.57 hectares. The average farmer held 42 discrete parcels and the average parcel was just 35 ares (one are = one hundred square meters).[32] It should be noted, however, that averages are difficult to read in this situation. Because areas in the northeast and the Paris Basin featured large well-structured farms, the averages are distorted. In most parts of France, average farm size and average distribution were much worse. To cite two examples, a farm of ten hectares in the Savoie was made up of 275 distinct parcels, whereas an 828-hectare village in Loir-et-Cher was composed of 5,075 parcels.[33] These numbers make for an average parcel size of 0.04 and 0.16 hectares, respectively. And while some of these plots would have been contiguous, the majority would have been dispersed throughout the county.

The reasons for this level of parceling were threefold. First, the Napoleonic Code dictated equitable inheritance, which meant that landholdings were supposed to be divided equally among all heirs. While there were ways around this legislation, it undoubtedly played an important part in the process of fragmentation.[34] The second factor that contributed to the parceling of French farms was the restricted availability of lands, which, when coupled with the relatively meager resources of farmers, forced buyers to take what they could get. A farmer might have saved for over a decade to expand his holdings, but when enough money was raised to make a purchase, his options were generally limited. Rather than sit on the savings until a nearby plot became available, more often than not, the money was reinvested in land as quickly as possible, even if the new property was located on the other side of the county. Lastly, when possible, farmers tended to prefer holding several different types of land. With counties made up of arable lands, forests, pasture, and vineyards, it was generally in the farmers' interest to hold strips in each of these areas in an effort to maximize self-sufficiency and to safeguard against natural catastrophe. Together, these three practices contributed to a heavily fragmented agricultural landholding system.[35]

This pattern of land tenure made it all but impossible to introduce mechanized production, which was fundamental to state plans for increased productivity. Indeed, mechanization was the top agricultural priority of the first five-year plan. In 1939, there had been just 25,000 tractors in use. The men at the CGP called for 250,000, a recommendation that Marshall Plan administrators seconded once they arrived on the scene.[36] They had their work cut out for them. In order for the acquisition of a tractor to be financially responsible, it was believed that farms needed to be at least thirty-five to forty hectares, much larger than the national average. Most existing farms were too small and too poorly organized to allow for the purchase of a tractor, or other agricultural machinery. More important, however, the lay of the land was such that the use of a tractor was inefficient at best and often technically impossible. Plots were often simply too narrow for a tractor to complete a turn. In an extreme example of how the technocratic approach to modernization often descended into absurdity, it was determined that in order for tractors to maneuver properly, plots must form a rectangle of at least fifty-nine meters wide by three hundred to four hundred meters long.[37] Moreover, it was common for plots to be several kilometers apart from each other, and oftentimes not accessible by roads. Fuel and time were lost in traveling by tractor from plot to plot, if it could be done at all. In short, advances in production techniques were being held back by the inefficiency of scattered holdings. As mechanization was key to the industrialization of agriculture, it was apparent to the engineers of postwar

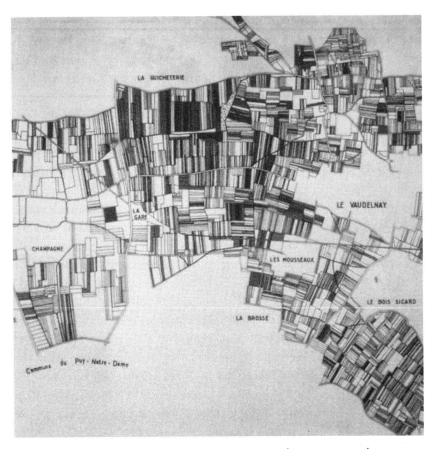

FIGURE 2 *Remembrement* before, Le Puy-Notre-Dame (Maine-et-Loire).
Source: © DR/Min.Agri.Fr.

economic development that the land tenure system needed to undergo a fundamental transformation.

The primary means by which this transformation was pursued through the 1950s was *remembrement*, a process by which the lands of a given county are exchanged and rearranged to consolidate holdings (see figures 2 and 3 for before and after results).[38] The CGP ambitiously called for a rate of land consolidation that was to reach one million hectares per year by 1950, a target that they failed to meet. Nevertheless, the numbers were impressive. Between 1945 and 1980, roughly 10.9 million hectares were consolidated (for reference, there are approximately 18 million hectares of arable land in France).[39] Indeed, *remembrement* played an influential part in the modernization scheme. It rationalized the landscape, both physically and conceptually. Fields were better organized and farmers were asked to think of their

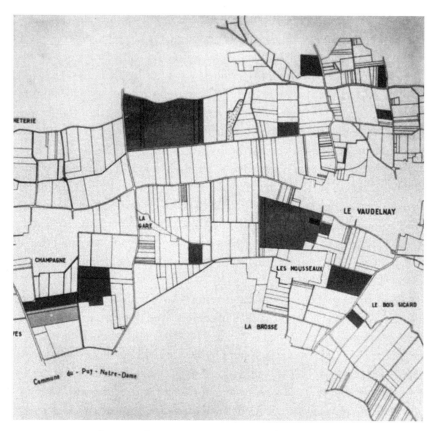

FIGURE 3 *Remembrement* after, Le Puy-Notre-Dame (Maine-et-Loire).
Source: © DR/Min.Agri.Fr.

holdings as rational businesses rather than as extensions of ancestral heritage.

Literally a re-membering of the constituent parts of the body, these redistributions metaphorically mirrored broader efforts to reconfigure a broken nation after the humiliation and defeat of the Second World War. Tied up with plans to modernize the economy and to develop exports for foreign markets, *remembrement* formed the (literal) groundwork of an agricultural policy that was part of a broader political agenda aimed at reasserting French power on the world stage. Asserting control over the French landscape through widespread *planification* symbolically marked the end of the occupation and the rebirth of the sovereign nation. Re-membering the constituent parts of the whole, the French state would be able to reassert the autonomy of its body politic.

Although *remembrement* had been practiced in France since the eighteenth century, it was not until the postwar period that it was pursued extensively and systematically. Prior to twentieth-century reforms, *remembrement* was a voluntary process that typically involved just a few landholders who agreed to pool and then redistribute their lands in order to end up with more rationally grouped holdings. And although efforts to redistribute lands were intensified in the late nineteenth century, largely on the open fields devoted to cereals production in the northeast, results were limited. Before the reforms were introduced, *remembrement* required complicated majority votes at several stages in the redistribution process (either two-thirds of the owners who accounted for one-half of the land, or one-half of the owners who accounted for two-thirds of the land). Consequently, even when a group of farmers was able to agree on exchanging lands, no small feat in and of itself, the process usually broke down before property actually changed hands.[40]

The turning point in redistribution efforts came with the close of the First World War. In those areas that had been destroyed during battle, *remembrement* was pursued with unprecedented drive. Given that property lines were no longer clear and that agricultural production had ceased for several years, there were far fewer obstacles to land redistribution: no crops were currently being grown and there was no system of trees or hedgerows with which to contend. As a project that was funded and carried out by the state, it also benefited from a top-down decision-making structure, eliminating the need for farmers to come together on their own initiative and reach agreement on how to redistribute holdings. From 1918 to 1941, *remembrement* took place in 685 counties, all of which had served as battlegrounds during the war.[41] While these numbers pale in comparison to those achieved during the 1950s, this early success provided an experimental arena in which the state was able to determine that new methods of land development and management could in fact be carried out with positive results.[42]

This early success prompted state officials to consider more seriously the possibility of widespread *remembrement*, but the economic depression of the 1930s prevented any real progress. It was not until the creation of the Vichy government, with its exaltation of the bucolic ideal, that restructuring in the agricultural sector once again became a top priority. The law of March 9, 1941, introduced two major changes to the *remembrement* process. First, the request for *remembrement* could now be made by those who did not own property, whereas previously all requests had been limited to landowners. This change was significant as it was often the younger, and as yet landless, generation that was most interested in modernizing landholding structures and production methods.[43]

Second, and most important, the complicated system of majority votes was abandoned. Instead, it was up to an individual in the county to submit a request for *remembrement* to the prefect, who would then decide, in consultation with the departmental Office of Rural Engineering, whether or not to proceed. If the decision was positive, the prefect would call for the creation of a commission that would then be in charge of making decisions for all of the property owners involved in the redistribution. Participants unhappy with any of these decisions would be allowed to file a formal complaint. Under the previous model, any disagreement among participants threatened to stop the entire process. The new legislation created a situation in which disputes would be addressed on a case-by-case basis, without interfering in the *remembrement* of the county as a whole.

That the near unanimous consent of all those involved was no longer required was an enormously significant change to French law governing landholding and marked the first step toward what would later be decried in the 1960s as a flagrant disavowal of property rights on the part of the French state. *Remembrement* became an extremely controversial practice, and as a result, future laws regarding agricultural property rights were decided with this controversy in mind. Although it is true that the right to the alienation of property, as inscribed in the Civil Code, was never in fact as absolute as some would suggest (the inheritance of property, for instance, was strictly regulated), the new law of *remembrement* considerably limited previously held freedoms.[44] With a central committee endowed with the power of having the final say, many residents in a given county were ultimately displeased with the end result. Owners could oppose the redistribution, file a formal complaint, and have their land reallotted all the same.

For many, *remembrement* was nothing short of political chaos—if not outright theft. Indeed, Mayor Nicolas Peneff, who oversaw *remembrement* in his southwestern county of Cadours, argued that this redistribution process was a radical overhaul that profoundly compromised property rights:

> Peasants have developed their lands, have built up a way of life and a way of work, sometimes over the course of several generations, have ordered their holdings through carefully negotiated purchases, sales, and exchanges. And in a few months, the administration topples this structure, and allots to [these peasants] the lands of their neighbors, takes away their lands, rebuilds roads, rips out hedgerows and fences.

Each and every day, you have to work these lands that are not your own and you have to see your own lands allocated to a neighbor—whom you may not like! Social revolution, radical political intervention—these are the terms of the new organization of land tenure.[45]

Although Peneff's words ought to be read with a grain of salt—his romantic musings on the peasantry are oftentimes peppered with dramatic flourish—it is nevertheless made clear in his memoir that *remembrement* had become a highly contested process.[46] Owners who had spent lifetimes building up their lands, which had equally been invested with the lives of their forefathers, suddenly found themselves at work on lands that they had never previously worked, lands on which they may have never even set foot prior to the redistribution. Such an enormous amount of change was often greeted with hostility and opposition.

In one case, a farmer in Peneff's county protested *remembrement* and formally requested that his lands not be included in the redistribution. Six years prior to the beginning of the *remembrement*, he had acquired fifty hectares of poorly organized and poorly tended farmland. Since then, he had invested a lot of money and labor into improving these lands. He had effected exchanges to improve the organization of the holdings, had worked hard to improve the soils, and had opened up the farm for larger-scale production by removing nine kilometers' worth of hedgerows.[47] This farmer had made great efforts to modernize his holdings and was then forced to give them up—at the expense of both his time and his money. While the portion of expenses that fell to residents was small (the majority of the expenses were covered by the state), any amount would have surely felt like an injustice to those farmers who had already done for themselves what they were then asked to do for the community.

Anger with the new procedures was likewise voiced in the halls of power. As the new laws governing *remembrement* were being introduced, a multipartisan group of representatives protested in Parliament that large-scale landowners would now be able to dominate the *remembrement* process at the expense of their less wealthy neighbors. Although they supported *remembrement* in general and recognized its economic benefits, they objected to the new process:

> As long as *remembrement* was a voluntary operation, the result of a free decision made by a majority of the landowners involved, there

were no general objections. That is no longer the case. Very often now *remembrement* produces a general opposition on the part of small- and medium-sized landowners.... Why is it like this now? Because the freedom of the property owners to decide on their own as a majority, and to come together as a *remembrement* association, has been replaced by an autocratic system that is imposed by a unilateral decision on the part of the prefect.[48]

Under the law of 1918, *remembrement* required widespread community support. Now that *remembrement* could be imposed at the request of one single property owner or public official, there was a risk that land reform would favor the larger landowners who held political sway in their counties.

Echoing the deputies' concerns that *remembrement* was becoming a tool of the powerful, Marg Charasse of Le Vernet (Allier), wrote to the Ministry of Agriculture in protest. Le Vernet had undergone *remembrement* in 1955 and she had been very unhappy with the results. She had started the procedure with two gardens, which were then replaced by a single garden, much further from her house, "doubtlessly in order to satisfy more important or more influential people." Given that another *remembrement* was slated to begin shortly, in 1961, she was demanding that the minister conduct a full investigation before the process began. In closing, she declared, "Like many small-holders, I am absolutely disgusted by what happened."[49]

In response to new property distributions, in counties across the country, angry farmers removed the new boundary markers that had been put in place by the surveyors, a practice of resistance that dated back to the enclosures of the early modern period.[50] In Antoigné (Maine-et-Loire), a member of the *remembrement* commission sought out advice from local authorities on how to deal with farmers who were refusing to comply with orders that they remove trees on lands slated for exchange. In some cases, farmers simply cut the trees at the base, leaving behind the stumps and the entire root system. In others, farmers removed the trees properly, but then failed to fill up the holes, leaving behind potential hazards. The commission worried that carelessly removed trees and large gaping pits in the landscape might damage the agricultural machinery that *remembrement* was to make room for in the first place. The commission likewise worried that farmers were leaving behind hazards on purpose, to protest the redistribution and to hassle the new owners of their land.[51] Clearly, the process was anything but straightforward.

The first step in the process that tended to elicit angry resistance was the determination of land values for the county. Once the request for *remembrement* was approved, a subcommission, in cooperation with landowners, was charged with the task of coming up with an abstract set of values by which the land could then be traded. The first task of those gathered at these discussions was to establish the best and worst plots of land in the county. From this determination, a series of classes, typically seven or eight, was decided on—the second best, the second worst, and so on, until the subcommission arrived at the middle. All of the plots in the county were then graded in relation to these classes, each of which was allotted a certain number of points. The value of each owner's holdings was then expressed as a function of this system. For instance, a farmer might own three plots in the ten-point category, two at seven points, and then nine at five points, for a total of ninety-nine. The only obligation of the commission, with respect to distribution, was to ensure that this farmer once again held ninety-nine points once the property lines were redrawn.

Because "best" and "worst" were defined in terms of *potential* productivity, rather than according to a concrete set of criteria, these discussions often lasted several days. Tempers flared as local politics and family feuds infiltrated the decision-making process. A farmer might be accused of not working his land to its full potential. Another might make excuses for why his land was not producing as much as it could. Some argued that potential productivity could not be measured adequately without first testing the soil, while others maintained that the use or absence of fertilizer would distort the results. Moreover, conflict was not simply attributable to the fact that it was in everyone's best interest to maximize their point designations. Age-old rivalries, family infighting, local politics, and a healthy dose of pride and indignation often worked their way into the discussions. Perhaps the most egregious act, however, was that those farmers who did attend the meetings tended to classify the lands of those who did not in the least valuable categories.[52]

While these preliminary discussions were intended to create a rational representation of a county's holdings, the process itself, rife with emotion, hardly encouraged rational behavior. In one case, a woman lost a piece of land that had been given to her by her godmother as a gift on her first communion. In the same county, a family lost its vines and the plum trees that had surrounded them. It had been a yearly tradition to gather the fruit to make eau-de-vie—a tradition that was lost once the lands had been given to a neighbor.[53] Elsewhere, an elderly woman who had previously held pasture was given arable lands that she was too old to plant.[54]

In an attempt to mitigate the conflict surrounding *remembrement*, the Ministry of Agriculture produced a number of promotional materials. A 1955 film, for example, took up the intergenerational conflict that often erupted between conservative fathers and modernizing sons.[55] In the film, it was the son who submitted the request to the prefect and who pushed for *remembrement*. And it was the father who responded, when faced with the prospect of exchanging his lands, "That which is mine, is mine—the land that comes from my parents—well—precisely because of that." His property was defined as his inheritance, as the legacy of his family line, and not as the simple dimensions of various plots of land, legally deeded in his name. At the same time, however, the father worried that if he did not modernize his holdings, his son would choose not to take over the farm. In this instance, it was the father's desire that the line of inheritance be maintained that forced him to compromise that very heritage, by agreeing to a process of land redistribution that could result in having to cede all of the lands that had been handed down to him. In the final scene of the film, after the new cadastral map has been posted, the wife of the modernizing son rode her bike out to the fields, bottle of wine in tow, to relay the good news and to celebrate with her husband and father-in-law. The voice-over explained that despite the difficulty with which the father had sacrificed his family holdings, he was nevertheless proud to have fixed things for a younger generation that had expressed a desire to stay loyal to the land. As a promotional piece for the Ministry of Agriculture, the emotional struggle between father and son was almost certainly overdramatized, and one should be careful not to draw general conclusions from one particular story. But it nicely demonstrated the general conflict that often lay at the center of debates regarding landholding, property rights, and agricultural modernization.

Ultimately, the vast majority of those who wished to continue farming as they always had lost out to the rationalizing demands of both the state and the market. The unique characteristics that distinguished one parcel of land, indeed one human experience, from the next, needed to be replaced by a uniform system of value—in this case, potential productivity. The development of a similar abstracting tendency in American agriculture has been well documented by historians William Cronon and Deborah Fitzgerald. In an analysis of how the midwestern wheat market was transformed by westward expansion, the railroads, and the emergence of futures trading, Cronon deftly explores the move from a qualitative understanding of the natural world and its productive resources to the market-driven designation of quantitative values in his discussion of the grain trade. Distributors, investors, and government regulators together "accomplished the trans-mutation of one of humanity's oldest foods, obscuring its physical iden-tity and displacing it into the symbolic world of capital."[56] Deborah Fitzgerald makes a similar argument in her analysis of how American farms were turned into factories in the early decades of the twentieth century. A vast complex of technocratic experts (agricultural engineers, bankers, ex-tension agents, etc.) and pioneering farmers adopted what she termed an "industrial logic," grounded in standardization, mechanization, specializa-tion, and efficiency.[57] The obsession with productivity that drove French planners to alter the agricultural landscape can be understood as a version of the abstraction or industrial logic that Cronon and Fitzgerald discuss in their own work.

Productivity was the centerpiece of French postwar planning. Beyond the productivity missions to the United States and the forcible redistribution of private property, there was the National Committee on Productivity, the French Association for the Growth of Productivity, and a host of other lower-level organizations and initiatives. Jean Fourastié, the French econo-mist who worked alongside Monnet at the CGP, was perhaps the most vocal proponent of this obsession with productivity.[58] He spearheaded govern-ment productivity initiatives and then popularized the ethos with such pub-lications as *La Productivité* (Productivity; 1952), published as part of the "Que sais-je?" series, devoted to providing a general audience with expert knowledge.[59]

Productivity was to be applied to all sectors. But because farm exports were the cornerstone of postwar plans for economic growth, agriculture was targeted with particular zeal. The men and women staffing the offices of the Ministry of Agriculture, the European Recovery Program, and the CGP measured yields, farm size, profits, and labor to come up with more effi-cient means of producing food. Outside the halls of government, experi-mental stations were established, agronomists were taught new tricks, the already modernized farmers continued to improve their operations, and the rest did their best to catch up. Productivity became the single most important metric by which agricultural production would be measured. And perhaps nowhere was this more true than in the realm of land redistribution. The rationalizing logic of productivity stripped the land of its ancestral ties and affective bonds, reducing it to a tool of production. With *remembrement*, farmland was assimilated into a rationalizing system that prized efficiency and productivity above all else.

While *remembrement* highlighted competing interests between farmer and farmer, broader state plans for economic development pitted farmers against an expanding array of nonagricultural interests. Modernizing the economy, in addition to increasing agricultural productivity, required widespread industrial expansion and urbanization, the execution of which often impinged on agricultural lands. Cities expanded into rural peripheries, urbanizing and suburbanizing the landscape. Railway and highway corridors bifurcated farms. And the recreational needs of a newly urbanized population required the construction of green leisure spaces.

To balance the needs of rural and urban France, no river, field, or public square would be left unmonitored, unconsidered. The already long-established French preoccupation with cultivating the landscape was given new meaning in the age of *planification*, and gained institutional authority in 1950 with a new branch of the Ministry of Reconstruction and Urbanism: *l'aménagement du territoire*. This is a notoriously difficult term to translate, as it covers several English-language concepts at once: organization, planning, layout, development, and improvement. Literally translated as territorial organization, this term is perhaps best understood by the English-language concept of regional planning (though in the French case, such planning was not limited to regions and often extended to the entire nation as a whole).

Above all, *aménagement du territoire* was about the rational use of space. In an effort to define its mission, Minister of Reconstruction and Urbanism Eugène Claudius-Petit presented to his fellow ministers what became the foundational text for this new branch of government: *l'aménagement du territoire* is "the search, within the geographical boundaries of France, for a better distribution of people, in relation to natural resources and economic activities. This pursuit is carried out with the constant preoccupation of providing people with better housing and working conditions and more ready access to recreation and culture. This pursuit is not, therefore, limited to strictly economic concerns, but is equally geared toward the wellbeing and development of the population."[60] As policy, *l'aménagement du territoire* concerned everything from public housing to environmental engineering. If managing France was a life-sized game of chess, the administrators of this new policy were responsible not only for the pieces but also for the board.[61]

One of the most pressing problems facing the new office was the balance between rural and urban populations. Although the transfer of labor from agriculture to industry and services was key to economic modernization, there were serious concerns about what might happen should that transfer happen too quickly and too haphazardly. The planners behind *l'aménagement du territoire* insisted that this demographic transfer be controlled, that it lead neither to an increase in the ranks of the potentially dangerous urban proletariat, nor to a shortage of young farmers able to take over operations once the older generation retired. The push and pull between country and city needed to be carefully managed to maintain a balance between social and political stability on the one hand and economic development on the other.

The emptying out of the countryside was a major cause for concern during the postwar period. The so-called rural exodus, which had begun in the late nineteenth century, quickened in the early 1950s and remained constant until the mid-1970s, with 40,000 to 50,000 farms disappearing every year.[62] Anxiety regarding the social desertification of the French countryside manifested itself in the popular press, in government policy, and in such academic works as Jean-François Gravier's *Paris et le désert français* (Paris and the French desert) and Roger Béteille's *La France du vide* (literally, "the France that is empty," but with a connotation that more closely approximates the English "void" or "absence," calling to mind the eerie image of an abandoned ghost town).[63] The depopulation of entire regions represented nothing less than the annihilation of civilization. For the French, civilization was something that had been built and cultivated on every square inch of the landscape. The conversion of any inch of this landscape into wasteland was tantamount to the diminution of French civilization itself.

One of the earliest efforts of the postwar period to manage rural populations was the National Union of Internal Migrations (syndicat national des migrations intérieures).[64] Established in 1948 by several key figures in the world of agricultural organizing, the union sought to mitigate the demographic upheaval of rural out-migration by relocating families from overcrowded areas, such as Brittany, to those that had lost much of their population, such as the Massif Central. The primary goal was to provide farmers with lands. The added benefit, however, was that these farmers would slow, if not stave off completely, the process of rural desertification.

In 1954, Minister of Agriculture Pflimlin expanded the organization by providing it with state funding and renaming it the National Association of Rural Migrations (Association nationale des migrations rurales, or ANMR). Upon the tenth anniversary of its founding, President Eugène Forget boasted that while 75,000 hectares had been left behind by migrating families, a full 283,000 hectares had been taken up in those regions that had suffered most from the exodus. He added that of these lands being taken up, 45 percent had previously been uncultivated. By installing farmers on previously fallow holdings, the ANMR was yet another means by which the state pursued its agenda of increasing productivity. But it also served another purpose. Moving farmers from overpopulated areas to those regions that had suffered most from the rural exodus, the ANMR ensured that villages that had previously run the risk of becoming ghost towns remained inhabited.

Forget was an important figure in the agricultural sector. He had served as the first president of the major postwar farm union, after having held positions in the Vichy-era Peasant Corporation. A Christian Socialist of the political center, Forget worked unremittingly to manage the factions of Left and Right that threatened to divide agricultural France. He believed in peasant unity and spent his career trying to improve the lives of French farmers, both as a political leader and as a model farmer himself, with a medium-sized holding that he operated according to the latest standards of efficiency and modernization. The ANMR was his first attempt at keeping farmers on the land, and in the 1960s it would serve as an institutional model for a much more radical approach to land reform.

The land use policy of this early postwar era was designed to maximize productivity and economic growth, whether in the agricultural or industrial sectors. Both rural and urban France were targeted by the five-year plans, and the challenge of *aménagement du territoire* was in determining how best to balance these respective spheres of both production and consumption. This equation was constantly changing, and as the postwar period progressed, rural productivity would become increasingly bound to the urban consumption of foodstuffs, natural parks, and second homes. At the end of the 1950s, while agricultural productivity still trumped the recreational and emotional needs of urban consumers, it was already clear that the chessboard was out of balance. As many of the nation's farmers failed to improve their standard of living while their urban cousins enjoyed unprecedented wealth and comfort, the unfulfilled promises of land reform and of *aménagement du territoire* led to discontent and defiance.

The Farm Problem

Although state efforts at agricultural modernization were proceeding steadily, change was not happening fast enough to remedy ailing incomes, and farmers took to the streets on multiple occasions throughout the 1950s to express their dissatisfaction. Unable to access the gains made by the French economy, many farmers were beginning to feel like sacrificial lambs. They were increasing yields, responding to the demands made by Monnet and Pflimlin, but they had yet to reap any rewards. The rocking chair and the radio of the American farmer remained elusive. Organizations such as the ANMR did their best to mitigate the consequences of the social and economic upheaval brought on by postwar growth, but on the whole those farmers who were left behind were beginning to question state plans that had resulted in an uneven improvement in standards of living. Although the agricultural sector as a whole was the centerpiece of the economic modernization agenda, individual farmers themselves were more often than not left to fend for themselves.

The disparity between agricultural and nonagricultural revenues was in fact growing rather than diminishing. Using one hundred as an income base for 1939, in 1950 urban French earnings had risen to 108, whereas rural earnings had risen to just 103. By 1957, the gap had widened considerably, with urban French at 142 and their rural counterparts at 125.[65] Farmers felt that the gap was all the more unjust given that productivity in their sector had in fact risen by 30 percent. But agricultural prices remained low, a must for the expansion of secondary and tertiary industries, as wages were tied to food prices. Between 1950 and 1988, the portion of income that French consumers devoted to food dropped from 42 to 19 percent. Conversely, farmers spent more and more on their inputs as industrial prices continued to rise.[66] As the gap between urban and rural standards of living continued to expand, farmers grew more and more disgruntled. Major waves of protest erupted in the countryside at regular intervals. State officials, syndical leaders, academics, and the national press all referred with increasing regularity to "the farm problem."[67]

When protests erupted in 1953, the national press widely reported on a beleaguered peasantry and the French Parliament once again revisited agricultural policy. The protests began in the south, where wine producers had been hard hit by a drop in prices. Tractors were used to block roads, a tactic that would persist through the decades to come, establishing the image of a tractor blockade as the new symbol of agricultural protest. For farmers, the tractor represented equally the investment they had made to modernize *and* the crushing debt that had resulted from the failure of the state to organize domestic markets and to secure foreign consumers. Productivity levels were rising, but incomes stagnated. Surpluses were starting to become a problem, especially for wheat, sugar, and wine. René

Dumont explained in the pages of *Le Monde*, "The violent actions of the peasants came as a surprise only to those who have ignored the gravity of their situation." Comparing the French and Danish agricultural sectors, Dumont concluded that without serious reforms, French farmers were doomed to suffer at the hands of their more efficient competitors.[68]

Similarly, sympathetic deputies in the National Assembly bemoaned the lack of support for the farm sector. Henri Bouret, a centrist MRP (Mouvement républicain populaire, or Popular Republican Movement) deputy from Côtes-du-Nord, bemoaned that the British were favoring Danish over French pork because it was less expensive. The high cost of agricultural inputs was making it impossible for Breton pork producers to match Danish prices. And the inability to find markets for their products translated into inferior incomes. As Bouret explained, the average annual income for French farmers was 219,000 francs, less than one-half the national average for incomes in other sectors (546,000 francs).[69] Meat producers in particular were more sensitive to market fluctuations as they did not receive the same kinds of government support that were on offer for the larger commodity crops such as wheat and sugar.

Along with lagging incomes, rising levels of debt put further financial pressure on French farmers. Keeping up with the standards of modernization was not cheap, and farmers increasingly began to rely on loans to mechanize, increase the size of their holdings, and install modern equipment (e.g., lights in outbuildings, refrigeration, irrigation). Agricultural credit was a double-edged sword for French farmers—necessary for the sort of expansion and updating that was required to remain viable according to increasingly strenuous requirements, and yet a burden of debt that demanded even greater efficiency and greater profits to make regular payments. The farm problem was as much about lagging incomes as it was about rising debt levels. In 1954, total agricultural debt was roughly 18 percent of the total value of agricultural production. A decade later, that number had risen to 50 percent (another decade after that, 70 percent, and by the early 1980s, a full 140 percent).[70] Debt levels forced farmers to intensify their methods in an effort to squeeze as much profit as possible from the land.

While the farm problem was often expressed through informal organization and protest, the two major farm unions of the postwar period offered a forum in which grievances could be aired to the minister of agriculture directly. The relationship between the state and the unions was one of neo-corporatism, "a system of interest intermediation in which a limited number of groups within a sector are formally incorporated into the public policy-making process (i.e., granted seats on public committees, commissions, or councils) and provided by the state with certain benefits in exchange for their cooperation and their restraint in the articulation of demands."[71] In other words, in exchange for maintaining order within their ranks, the major unions were given substantial power at the negotiating table.

The largest of these unions was (and still is) the National Federation of Farm Unions (Fédération nationale des syndicats d'exploitants agricoles, or FNSEA). Politically conservative, its leadership was largely composed of the older and wealthier farmers of the Paris Basin. Moreover, many of those in management roles, including the influential René Blondelle, who served as president from 1949 to 1954, had held positions in the Vichy administration.[72] Formed in 1946, on the model of the farm union that had been created under Vichy, its official mandate was to unify French farmers by pursuing a broad membership base. It did this chiefly by advocating for a wide variety of reforms: everything from price supports and rebates on farm machinery, to lower gas prices for farmers and better social security. Because leaders tended to command large-scale operations, however, the policy agenda of the FNSEA tended toward measures that were most beneficial to those farmers who were already deemed viable. For example, because these farmers had by and large already mechanized, and given that they were already in possession of well-ordered plots, land redistribution was not of immediate concern. Instead, price-support policies were the primary objective, the dividends of which disproportionately favored those already practicing high-yield and high-input farming. With their seat at the negotiating table, the leaders of the FNSEA consistently fought for policies that favored a minority of their constituents.

In spite of a policy agenda that skewed heavily in the direction of a small though powerful minority, the FNSEA retained a broad membership base through its ability to deliver essential services. With a network extending throughout all of France, the FNSEA was well positioned at the local level to offer farmers assistance with such things as credit and subsidy applications, tax forms, and the creation of cooperatives.[73] As a result, small-scale farmers who may not have agreed with all of the policy objectives of the FNSEA, and who in fact might have been indirectly harmed by them, nevertheless retained membership in order to benefit from these services.

Those farmers who advocated instead for more widespread reforms, such as land reform and better terms for tenant farmers, tended to support the National Center for Young Farmers (Centre national des jeunes agriculteurs, or CNJA).[74] Established following liberation to provide training for young farmers, the CNJA initially played a minor role in farm politics. But under the leadership of the dynamic Michel Debatisse and Hubert Buchou, the organization quickly emerged as an influential presence in the farm world. By the late 1950s, it had been invited to participate in the official policy-making structures of the state, a privilege that had previously been held exclusively by the FNSEA. Together, the two dominated agricultural policy for decades.

CNJA membership was limited to those under the age of thirty-five.[75] Because the farmers in leadership positions within the CNJA were of a younger generation than those within the FNSEA, they tended to be more liberal in their objectives. For instance, they argued that price supports benefited high-yield producers disproportionately and that overhauling the entire structure of the farm sector was the only way to improve the agricultural standard of living. Setting themselves apart from their more established counterparts at the FNSEA, they sought to represent those farmers who had the drive and the know-how to modernize, but lacked the resources to do so.

The most active members of the CNJA had been brought up by the Young Catholic Farmers (Jeunesse agricole catholique, or JAC), a reform-minded agricultural organization that had gained widespread popularity in the 1930s and 1940s. A mix of progressive Christian humanism and technical-economic rationalism, the JAC was founded in an effort to bring better standards of living to the countryside. Its Jesuit leaders promoted the professionalization of agriculture and encouraged rural youth to receive proper training in agronomy and to understand farming as a business. By the late 1940s, the JAC no longer required a religious commitment of its members, though a strong current of social Catholicism remained present in a rhetoric that privileged community over individuals, and celebrated the act of labor over the reward of profit.[76]

The success of JAC was formidable. In 1960, former members of the organization held forty-five of the eighty-five departmental presidencies of the CNJA and twenty-four of the thirty positions at the national level.[77] Raised on a platform of technical innovation, economic growth, and social progress, this younger generation of syndical leaders challenged the conservative agricultural bosses of the FNSEA who had been dictating the agenda for agricultural reform.

Determined to push further than price supports, CNJA leadership argued that a fundamental restructuring of agricultural production was the only means to increase farming revenues and to ensure the survival of farming in France. Unlike its old-guard counterpart, which (disingenuously) maintained that all farms could be saved, the CNJA was ready to accept strategic losses in exchange for the viability of the sector as a whole. This privileging of the whole over constituent parts was a direct result of JAC training. Building the service ethic of social Catholicism into the process of modernization, the CNJA argued that those who could not modernize ought to think of the good of the community. If they gave up their farms and ceded them to those who could modernize, the community as a whole might prosper.[78] Farmers were exhorted to sever their attachment to the land, to stop seeing it as an ancestral inheritance, and instead to view it as a tool of production like any other.[79]

Beyond the realm of organized labor, the interests of French farmers were also presented to the state through the Chambers of Agriculture.[80] As a semipublic body funded by the state, the Chambers of Agriculture was composed of delegates elected at the departmental level. Each department had a local office, and each administrative region had an office that was made up of departmental delegates. The national office, the Permanent Assembly of the Chambers of Agriculture (Assemblée permanente des chambres d'agriculture, or APCA), was staffed by the presidents of the departmental branches. At the departmental level, offices had substantial influence over how state funds were allocated. At the national level, APCA took part in negotiations with other branches of the state and was instrumental in determining the course of agricultural policy.[81]

The debates that engaged the FNSEA and CNJA largely ignored the truly marginal farmers, who were concentrated in the south and in mountainous regions. While the older and wealthier conservative leadership vied for political influence with their young challengers, a large cross section of the agricultural population was simply too isolated and too far behind to get involved. By the end of the 1950s, the Ministry of Agriculture estimated that 56 percent of French farms were smaller than ten hectares and were therefore classified as "marginal." As both the state and the syndicates chose to focus their energies on those whom they judged most capable of becoming economically viable producers, it became clear that these farmers would be left to fend for themselves.

Throughout the decade, the threat of domestic unrest, precipitated by recurring waves of agricultural protest, loomed large in a nation whose history was famed for its periodic outbursts of rebellion. The Fourth Republic, preoccupied by the war in Algeria, struggled to maintain stability on the home front without diverting precious resources from its military operations. As the colonial situation worsened, the French state grew increasingly incapable of addressing the mounting concerns of its farmers.[82] Accordingly, European integration, and specifically the integration of agricultural markets, grew more and more attractive as a means of assuaging rebellious farmers. What it could not afford to do alone—close (or even diminish) the gap between agricultural and nonagricultural incomes—its European neighbors would do as a community.

In the early aftermath of the Second World War, stability in Europe was of primary importance. Winston Churchill was calling for Franco–German reconciliation and the United States was hoping that a united western Europe would stand against the Soviet Union. Planning mastermind Monnet and Foreign Minister Robert Schuman were among the earliest French supporters of greater European integration. Monnet argued that fragmentation in Europe would make it harder to modernize the French economy. Without a larger consumer base, the mass production and mass consumption of American-style capitalism could not be fully realized. If Europe was going to take its rightful place alongside the United States in the pantheon of global powers, it needed an integrated market to promote growth and innovation.[83]

The economic benefits of greater cooperation were a relatively easy sell for a nation whose economy was struggling to regain its footing. But the political ramifications of integration were much more difficult to peddle. When Monnet and Schuman put forth a proposal for a European Coal and Steel Community (ECSC), many in the French legislature were nervous about how such a partnership might threaten national sovereignty. Moreover, not everyone was ready to leave the German occupation behind. The vote on the ECSC in the National Assembly was a narrow victory, with 337 votes for and 233 against.[84] Monnet, however, hoped that a softening of relations between the two traditionally oppositional nations might pave the way for greater European integration in the future.

Minister of Agriculture Pflimlin took another approach, suggesting that rather than form a supranational political entity, a customs union be established instead. To that end, Pflimlin kept his gaze firmly fixed on his European neighbors. Studies commissioned by the ministry regularly reported on how French agricultural productivity compared to that of its European counterparts. For instance, while the average French yield for grain was sixteen quintals per hectare, it was as high as thirty in Denmark and twenty-nine in Belgium (one quintal = one hundred kilograms). Statistics for other staple commodities such as sugar beet and potatoes were similar, with France lagging behind its more efficient neighbors: Denmark, Belgium, and the Netherlands (on the other end of the spectrum, Greece and Portugal consistently fell well behind France).[85] No question, French farmers would have to become more efficient if they were going to compete in a customs union with the Danes and the Dutch. But French production numbers were on the rise and surpluses loomed on the horizon. The acquisition of new European markets would provide outlets for this increased productivity.

The road to the common market was long and indirect. Between the formation of the ECSC and the ratification of the EEC in 1957, there were many points of disagreement and stress. The creation of the ECSC and dreams of an agricultural customs union did not render the common market a foregone conclusion. The French were incredibly hesitant to cede any national authority, and the British refused at every turn to allow for the inclusion of an agricultural policy. Ultimately, the vote to ratify the Treaty of Rome, the document that brought the EEC into being, was split in much the same way as the vote on the ECSC had been: in the National Assembly, it was 342 to 239, and in the Senate, it was 222 to 70.[86] With such conflicted results, tensions ran high during the negotiations process that followed ratification.

The French insisted that any and all versions of the common market include a Common Agricultural Policy (CAP). The two farm unions were quick to back this demand. In spite of their differences, both the CNJA and FNSEA supported European integration, albeit with serious reservations. With the signing of the Treaty of Rome, hopes were high within the unions that the common market would solve the problems of French agriculture, namely, insufficient revenues and the ever-widening gap between farming incomes and those of everyone else. The FNSEA publicly stated that French agricultural policy to date had been lacking and incoherent, and hoped that a common policy would succeed where it had failed. For both major farm syndicates, Europe, not France, would be the answer to the farm problem. That said, after a rather hopeless decade, it might have simply been the case that farmers were ready to believe that the EEC was going to be the panacea they had all been hoping for.[87]

To take advantage of the CAP, it was clear that France needed to realize extensive reforms. Without a modern and industrial farming sector, policymakers and syndical representatives alike worried that French producers would be unable to compete with the more efficient member-states.[88] Improvements had been made through the 1950s by way of *remembrement*, mechanization, the increased use of chemical inputs, and the planting of high-yield seed varieties. But these advances were haphazard and most farmers continued to lag behind. To survive the transition to the common market, the farm sector would have to submit to an even more aggressive modernization agenda and would likewise have to accept substantial losses as many farmers failed to meet the new competitive standards.

Ambivalence and anxiety over the transition to an integrated European market bore itself out in the press. By the late 1950s, French media were routinely publishing articles in which the EEC was presented as both a cure-all for the farm problem and a possible threat.[89] *Paysans* (Peasants), a pro-CNJA bimonthly review with a healthy national readership, began regularly featuring articles regarding the prospect of a common agricultural market by the late 1950s. While editorials retained a certain reserve with respect to how the market would be governed, the prospect of an expanded consumer base for French agricultural goods routinely elicited favorable responses. In a representative take on the possibilities of such a market, an article appearing in 1957 stated, "As we know, western Europe imports a lot of cereals, sugar, beef, and dairy products, and a significant portion of these imports are paid for in dollars. We will therefore work toward a preferential system between member-states. . . . It is clear that such a policy would be very profitable for our country, as it boasts a very large margin of expansion."[90] Although there was no doubt that a preferential trade agreement with importing countries could lead to significant profits for French agriculture, the degree to which France would be able to take advantage of the common market remained an open question.

It is perhaps not surprising, given how costly the CAP would become, that analysis has tended to focus on price policy and the subsidy system. But the CAP, and European integration more broadly, were instrumental in furthering deep structural reform within the French agricultural sector. The primary inspiration for agricultural policy in the 1950s, therefore, was not a French love of the land, or an attachment to terroir. The incentives that drove postwar farm policy were instead the promise of new markets and the threat of efficient competitors. In anticipation of the common market, agricultural improvement schemes, such as *remembrement*, were radicalized to speed up the process of modernization. If the 1950s had been a period of slow and uneven progress, the 1960s would mark a definitive turning point. By the end of the decade, with the common market in full operation, France was well on its way to joining the ranks of the United States as one of the most powerful agricultural nations in the world.

The Industrial Ideal

The average French farm of 1945 was akin to the average French kitchen of 1945. Both were self-consciously backward when compared with their more affluent Western counterparts. Refrigerators and Formica tabletops would bring modernity to the postwar home, while tractors and fertilizers would do the same for the postwar farm. Just as the domestic ideal presented a certain vision of the home, the agricultural ideal created a certain vision of the farm. It would be a certain size, it would employ mechanical and chemical inputs, and it would reach levels of productivity sufficient not only to feed the French but also to build a profitable export industry.

Building an ideal requires many actors across many different segments of the population. Indeed, it requires the creation of a new cultural category, a language with accepted definitions and standards. The industrial ideal was constructed by a wide variety of agricultural players. Men in government, such as Monnet and Pflimlin, were instrumental in devising and supporting the policies that promoted this ideal. Easier access to credit, for instance, would foster mechanization and expansion, while *remembrement* would increase productivity through consolidation. Working alongside the CGP and the Ministry of Agriculture were the farm unions, whose direct contact with farmers provided more informal methods for selling farmers on the new ideal. Local representatives modeled the new ideal, provided practical support for farmers seeking to benefit from state programs, and, as community leaders who held positions of authority, often dictated how policies such as *remembrement* were actually practiced. Although the FNSEA and CNJA were not always in agreement on how best to perform these roles, both certainly concurred that modernization was the best way for their constituents to improve their standard of living and narrow the gap between agricultural and nonagricultural incomes. And lastly, farmers themselves turned to the industrial ideal on their own, some because they had always been on the cutting edge, and others because they feared the consequences of falling behind.

The underlying assumptions about what did and did not constitute this industrial ideal were constantly laid bare in legislative texts, syndical initiatives, and the agricultural press. Fulfilling these criteria would guarantee viability, and remaining "viable" was everything in the cutthroat world of postwar French agriculture. Farms deemed "unviable" were marked for extinction, and those farmers who held such farms either raced to catch up or fell by the wayside. Making matters more difficult, as the years wore on, catching up required more and more. By the late 1950s, when the common market began to loom on the horizon, "viable" took on yet another meaning. It required keeping up with the more efficient Dutch. It required speeding up the process of modernization to ready French farmers for the onslaught of competition they would face from their fellow member-states. Moreover, while "viable" was applied in the immediate postwar years to any farm larger than ten hectares, by the end of the 1960s, the minimum size for a viable holding had risen to forty hectares. The bar simply kept rising. Catching up was a never-ending process.

At every turn, this amorphous concept of "viability" was used to bolster a ruthless process of attrition, in which those farms that failed to meet the industrial ideal were swallowed up by those that did. Farmers unable to meet these standards were a liability. Their lack of efficiency made it harder for the state both to keep food prices low and to build a booming export sector. An article in the newsweekly *L'Express* succinctly captured the stakes of the situation while covering recent agricultural protests: "The number of family farms must be reduced even further if we want them to be viable, if we want them to provide farmers with an acceptable standard of living, if we want them to stop adding to the high cost of living of French consumers, and if we don't want them to be a handicap on European and global markets."[91] This attrition was justified because it would improve standards of living for those farmers who survived, cut costs for consumers, and strengthen the French position in regional and global markets.

The industrial ideal that was established in the immediate postwar years would change very little until the 1970s, when a budding environmentalism and organic farm movement would bridge parallel discourses on quantity and quality. The core principle of the industrial ideal was productivity, and an entire bureaucratic edifice was mounted to promote it. In a report on agricultural productivity commissioned by the CGP, a simple equation designed to distill the objectives of the commission at once highlighted the tunnel vision of the technocrats behind *planification* and belied the absurdity of such a vision: Production = Surface x Yield.[92] Overhauling the entire agricultural sector was an enormous task of extraordinary complexity. It involved the desires of individual farmers, private property, a sometimes uncooperative landscape, and the dynamics of family relationships, to say nothing of the financing. This attempt to capture that process in a simple mathematical equation speaks to a blind adherence to an industrial ideal that did little to factor in the human cost of agricultural modernization.

CHAPTER TWO

Alternative Ideals, 1944–1958

> The impoverishment of our epoch stems, above all else, from the
> exacting commercial spirit and the mechanical industrial reasoning
> that have been applied to the development of agricultural
> production. Natural rhythms were forced to follow the artificial
> movements of the modern world, and the earth fell sick, and in
> turn so too did the plants and the animals.
>
> —ANDRÉ BIRRE, *Sol et Vitalité* (1950, 15)

Having adopted the industrial methods promoted by the state, many
farmers began to appreciate that while their yields might have improved,
their input requirements had intensified so much that their incomes had
barely increased. Moreover, their animals were getting sick because of the
change in their diets and the increased density of their living conditions.
For Joseph Racineux, the president of a local farm union in Chelun
(Ille-et-Vilaine), the new system ceased to be tenable. Racineux was the
owner-operator of a viable medium-sized farm of thirty-seven hectares.
With seven children, an elderly father, and a wife, Racineux benefited
from considerable household labor, but also employed a full-time farm
worker. He planted thirteen hectares in cereals (wheat, barley, oats), four
in vegetables (cabbage, beets, potatoes), and reserved twenty for pasture.
The majority of his income was derived from his sixteen cows and six
sows; he produced milk, beef, and pork for the market, and sold his pig-
lets to other farmers.

To maximize the yields on his cereal crops, Racineux applied chemical
fertilizers and herbicides. But after a few years of these intensive methods, he
noticed that his yields had ceased to increase. As he explained to a reporter
for *Agri-7*, the second most widely read agricultural paper in France: "I
noticed that I was not making any headway. I was spending more and more
while my revenues didn't increase. The parasites in my fields continued to
evolve. And as for my animals, it was a catastrophe: septicemia, sterility. . . .
In 1959, I spent 100,000 francs on veterinary services!"[1] Racineux was not
alone in experiencing higher incidences of livestock illness. Industrialization required that animals be subjected to a different diet to produce more
milk or to put on weight more quickly, and that they spend more time in

densely packed indoor environments. These conditions were less healthy and more stressful. The result was more sickness, in particular foot-and-mouth disease and bovine tuberculosis. Fed up with this new normal, to say nothing of the veterinary bills, Racineux wanted to abandon chemically intensive farming. But he didn't know how.

At around the same time that he was questioning the new industrial practices, Racineux came into contact with extension agents for Raoul Lemaire, a farmer in nearby Maine-et-Loire who was working relentlessly to promote organic agriculture. After doing some research into these new methods, Racineux stopped using fertilizers and other chemical inputs, and began using an organic soil treatment that had been developed by Lemaire. Eight years later, Racineux reported being entirely satisfied with the results. After an initial dip in productivity, his yields caught up, and most important, his animals were once again healthy. Inspired by his own success, he went on to work closely with other organic farmers in France to develop their ideas and grow their ranks.

Racineux's story was all too common. Many farmers discovered that the adoption of industrial practices had not really improved their bottom line. Yes, they were producing more, and meeting the demands of a state that was eager to build agricultural exports, but they were not necessarily earning more. This was the essence of the farm problem as discussed in chapter 1. Add to the disappointing revenue results the higher rates of livestock illness and the debt financing that was often required to purchase chemical inputs and to pay for veterinary services, and the modern farming techniques promoted by the technocrats at the Planning Office began to feel like a step backward rather than a step forward.

FRANCE IS OFTEN thought of as a bastion of gastronomic quality. From champagne to foie gras, and from Le Cordon Bleu to Julia Child, French food and cooking have served as standards for culinary excellence. But consumption and production are separate matters. While French food culture might have maintained its elite status, French agricultural production more often than not emphasized quantity over quality. Productivity was the standard by which agricultural production was developed. Pork was produced in closed concrete barns and vineyards were doused with chemicals, all in the interest of generating enough quantity to export to foreign markets. If quality entered the picture, it was typically defined in terms of safety rather than provenance. It was not until the 1980s, when terroir enjoyed a resurgence and urban consumers became more sensitive to the distance that separated them from their food, that this began to change. But even then, the state recognition of organic agriculture and the promotion of quality regional foods was really about appropriating alternative production and distribution networks to shore up value-added niche markets. The quality that was associated with terroir might have been given a more visible presence on the marketplace, but quantity continued to dictate both agricultural practices and agricultural policy.

While the French state, with support from the major agricultural unions, was pushing for an industrial agricultural ideal to modernize the economy, improve the balance of trade, and prepare for the common market, a handful of renegades were building ideals of their own. The productivity and efficiency of the modernizing technocrats were rejected for a new understanding of quality that formed the basis for early models of both biodynamic and organic farming. These outsiders refused the official version of modernization for a variety of reasons: health, nutrition, autonomy, and religion. Regardless of their reasons, however, these early pioneers were not antimodern or necessarily oriented toward the past. There was an important difference between these farmers who chose to farm organically in the twentieth century and those who had farmed organically by default in the past. These farmers were making a *choice* between the new industrial ideal and the alternative ideals that were being developed in response to what were viewed as the negative consequences of chemically intensive agriculture.

For many of the early advocates of organic farming, the alternative ideal was about maintaining independence, and opting out of the financial debts that came with chemical and mechanical investments. Pierre Page, a dairy farmer in the southwest, wrote to the extreme Right politician Pierre Poujade in 1956 to complain about the profits that accrued to the intermediaries between producers and consumers, and to question Poujade's support of those small businesses that functioned as go-betweens. While clearly a devoted supporter of Poujade in his defense of rural France and the small farmer, Page disagreed with the populist claim that small farmers and small businessmen needed to come together to defend a common interest. As far as Page was concerned, the growing network of food distribution in France did little more than displace money from his pocket to that of the shopkeeper who sold his food: "Shop keepers are nothing but distributors, parasites who produce nothing other than the smiles needed to sell their wares."[2] Page estimated that for every liter of milk he produced, middlemen skimmed 20 francs off the top. In a barbed description of how shopkeepers profit at the expense of farm labor, Page wrote: "Now I know that some common shopkeeper in Bordeaux wakes in the morning and opens the door to his milk shop to discover eight hundred liters of milk, and all he has to do to earn 3 francs per liter, or 2,400 francs per day, is sell it. This he earns without having to do anything more than ensure that his shop girls smile at his clients."[3] For farmers like Page, organic farming offered a means of foregoing the middlemen, of maintaining direct relationships with their buyers. This afforded them greater autonomy in their work and allowed them to reap the profits of their labor.

For his part, Pierre Poujade, a small-town shopkeeper who led a populist movement against the forces of big government, is a well-known figure in the political history of postwar France. He began his political career in 1953 when he rallied a group of merchants in his hometown of Saint-Céré, in the southwest, to resist a state crackdown on tax evasion. Their success led many merchants in nearby towns to approach him for advice on how to mount a resistance of their own. Almost overnight, Poujadisme was born. As a political philosophy, Poujadisme defended the small businessman and the craftsman against the technocratic elites of the rapidly expanding Fourth Republican state. It celebrated rural life and denounced urbanization and industrialization. In the 1956 elections, Poujadist candidates, including a young Jean-Marie Le Pen, won fifty-two seats in the French Parliament. And then, almost as quickly as they rose to power, they disappeared from view. With the advent of the Fifth Republic in 1958, the popularity of Poujadisme quickly waned.

While organic agriculture came to be identified with leftist politics after the rise of environmentalism in the 1970s, in its early years it was more often identified with right-wing extremism and conservative agrarianism. For a particular branch of early organic farming, Poujade was an inspiration. Most notably, Raoul Lemaire, one of organic farming's earliest pioneers, saw in Poujade a kindred spirit, a defender of rural France and the autonomy of the French farmer (see figures 6 and 7). Lemaire, in his capacity as a Poujadist candidate, would have had contact with Page and a number of other industrial farmers who came to Poujade for support. As a pivot point between the world of organic farming and the world of Poujadist politics, Lemaire had a strong hand in shaping the early ideology of alternative agriculture.

Just as the industrialization process was more ruthless than is commonly appreciated, the development of anti-industrial farming was both less progressive and less expansive than is widely understood. In its first decades, alternative agriculture was conservative, if not outright fascist, in its politics. Many of the postwar pioneers had supported the Vichy regime and continued to speak of purity and the threat of degeneration well after liberation. Maréchal Pétain, the head of the government under the German occupation, had lauded rural France as the true France, a message that dovetailed with early critiques of industrial farming: "The Land, she does not lie. She remains your respite. She is your fatherland [*patrie*]. A field that lies fallow is a piece of France that dies. An unplanted field that is seeded once again is a piece of France that is reborn."[4] Just as the proponents of industrialization sought to mitigate the effects of the rural exodus because they feared that demographic desertification was tantamount to the erosion of the French nation, so too did the Pétainists equate cultivation with civilization. But unlike their counterparts at the ANMR and in the offices responsible for *aménagement du territoire*, they rejected the industrial ideal as the very root of the problem.

Not all of the early proponents subscribed to these politics, however. While many located their conservatism on the extreme Right, others came to their anti-industrial stance by way of a Catholic belief in the relationship between God and the earth. Although the opposition was united in its refusal of the industrial model, it was by no means united in its politics or its vision for the future of French agriculture. As the movement progressed through the 1960s and 1970s, political differences became all the more apparent. For example, when the agitators of 1968 came face-to-face with Vichy-style conservatism, the language that had dominated the movement in the 1940s and 1950s was largely replaced by a new vocabulary that privileged such terms as environment and *territoire*.[5] What did remain of the founding fathers' dogma once the movement gained a leftist orientation was a respect for the land and twin demands for greater autonomy and the survival of small-scale farming.

In the early years of the postwar period, these advocates for biodynamic and organic methods were very much in the minority, and their influence on the national stage was minimal. The narrative of alternative agriculture ran in parallel to that of state-supported agriculture, and the two rarely intersected. By the 1970s, however, with the arrival of environmentalism and new state policies regarding conservation and pollution, these two strains started to converge. Shortly thereafter, the state co-opted alternative practices, created a discourse surrounding terroir and gastronomic heritage, and institutionalized organic production by way of official standards and labeling. Industrial producers co-opted what they could as well, leading to the development of "rational farming" (*agriculture raisonnée*), a model that allowed chemical inputs as long as farmers operated good judgment in their application. In other words, the alternative hard line was met with industrial compromise.

What happened during the intervening forty years? How did alternative ideals move from the conservative fringe, by way of the radical Left, into the mainstream? And what happened to these ideals as they were developed, contested, and transformed by a series of both state (e.g., the Ministry of Agriculture) and nonstate actors (e.g., farmers, consumers)? The pioneers of biodynamic and organic agriculture bequeathed to the twenty-first century a language, a set of priorities, and perhaps most important, a network of producers, distributors, processors, and consumers. If their ideologies fell by the wayside, much of their infrastructure survived. In chapter 1, we examined the beginnings of the precipitous rise of industrial French agriculture, setting the stage for its eventual triumph as a global trade powerhouse. In chapter 2, we will examine those who rejected the industrial ideal and laid the groundwork for future niche markets in "quality" goods, and an environmentally and health-conscious agriculture.

The Roots of Alternative Agriculture

The origins of alternative ideals in France were largely shaped by developments in Britain and Germany. In the early years of the twentieth century, an Irish physician and an English botanist went to India to conduct research, and in the 1920s, the Austrian founder of an esoteric spiritualist movement delivered a series of lectures on how farmers might apply spiritual philosophy to their agricultural practices. Together, these three men laid the groundwork for the emergence of an alternative agricultural ideal.

The English botanist Albert Howard spent the first decades of the twentieth century conducting agricultural and plant research in India. Starting with traditional Indian composting methods, he developed his own system, the Indore Method. To be sure, farmers had been using compost since the dawn of agriculture. What Howard contributed to this traditional practice, however, was the modern science of microbes. Starting from the premise that nitrogen was key to soil fertility, the premise that was driving the chemical fertilizer business, he sought to produce a compost that would naturally maximize nitrogen content without the use of outside inputs. After years of experimentation and refinement, Howard developed a system that allowed the farm to operate as a closed entity, free from outside inputs. Crop waste and manure were used to produce superior soil, which in turn would produce superior fodder for the livestock, which would then, again in turn, produce superior manure, and so the virtuous circle continued. In 1940, Howard published his findings in *An Agricultural Testament*, and established one of the fundamental principles of organic farming: soil, plants, animals, and humans were all interrelated and the health of each relied on the health of the others. In short, organic agriculture was first envisioned as a closed system.

While Howard was conducting his experiments in Madhya Pradesh, the Irish physician Robert McCarrison was also in India to pursue research of his own in the southern province of Tamil Nadu. Upon completion of his medical studies in 1900, McCarrison had joined the Indian Medical Service and likewise traveled to the subcontinent. While Howard was focused on the health of plants and soil, McCarrison devoted himself instead to the health of consumers, and spent the better part of three decades studying the effects of chemical inputs on food quality and human health. He determined that the increased nitrogen content of the soil, the result of chemical fertilizers, decreased the vitamin content of the food it produced, and that the traditional diet of the local tribesmen, composed of whole grains, vegetables, fruit, milk, and butter, afforded them superior health. This diet kept them free from the diseases, such as cancer, diabetes, and multiple sclerosis, that were common in those who consumed a diet of refined grains and processed foods. Upon his retirement, McCarrison returned to Britain and shared the results of his research when delivering the 1936 Cantor Lectures at the Royal Society of Arts. McCarrison ultimately failed in persuading the mainstream scientific community, but developed a devoted following with doctors, dentists, and farmers.[6]

Health was the primary category of concern for the earliest of the pioneers, from the health of soil and livestock to the health of consumers. By the late nineteenth century, decades before Howard and McCarrison had published their findings, French hygienists were already warning that long-term and repeated exposure to arsenic-based pesticides would lead to chronic toxicity.[7] In Germany, the Life Reform Movement was questioning an increasingly modern food system that relied on American imports and chemical inputs.[8] And all across Europe, farmers were reporting that their animals were falling ill after moving to a diet that relied on purchased supplements rather than on farm waste and pasture. It was not long before health professionals were cautioning that industrial agriculture was leading to greater incidences of disease—that consumers were compromised not only by the chemical inputs used to produce their food but also by the lower nutritional content of food that was grown in adulterated soil.

In 1924, a group of German farmers, who were concerned about a rise in sterility and foot-and-mouth disease in their cattle, organized a workshop in Koberwitz, Silesia, and invited Rudolf Steiner to deliver a series of lectures on how they might approach agriculture in a different way. Steiner, born and raised in Austria, had started his intellectual career as a Goethe scholar, and took an early interest in plants and chemistry. But he eschewed the mainstream science of the day, which he believed to be overly materialist. Instead, he subscribed to a vitalist understanding of the natural world, which held that living entities could not be entirely understood by the laws of chemistry and physics because they contained a "vital force" that governed their internal development. Building on this principle, Steiner founded a branch of esoteric spiritualism known as "anthroposophy," so named to emphasize the centrality of humanity to this new spiritual philosophy. With his teachings, Steiner sought to bridge the divisions between science, philosophy, and religion, and held that the material and spiritual worlds were bound together in an all-embracing, overarching unity. With an enhanced human consciousness, one could transcend the material and access the spiritual world. Working from this principle, Steiner pursued a number of intellectual pursuits, from agriculture to education.

The series of lectures that Steiner delivered at Koberwitz became the foundation for biodynamic agriculture and heavily influenced the organic movement that was soon to take shape in England. There were over one hundred people in attendance at the lectures, delivered at the estate of a local count.[9] Most were anthroposophist farmers, but there were also doctors, teachers, and scientists. Many of the attendees hailed from elite Prussian circles. In his eight lectures, Steiner provided broad outlines rather than a fully developed practice, something that his adherents would have to develop on their own. The most important tenet that Steiner put forth was that farms should be treated as living organisms, made up of different organs: crops, animals, soil, garden, fruit trees, and so forth. If everything was working properly, there was no need for outside inputs, and a farm could operate as a closed circuit.

This approach was not so different than the one that Howard was simultaneously developing in India. What *did* differ was the anthroposophist influence, and it was likely this influence that prevented biodynamic farmers from joining their organic brethren in their advance toward mainstream acceptance. Steiner drew from his vitalist understanding of the world to develop new methods for enriching the soil, and the results were nothing if not nonconformist. For instance, he encouraged his farmers "to put manure into cow horns and bury them for an entire winter so that the manure could capture the Earth's etherizing and astralizing rays and be transformed into a powerful fertilizing force."[10] Farmers were similarly exhorted to plant their seeds according to the phases of the moon and to build an intimate "personal relationship" to nature to harness the cosmic forces of the crops, animals, and soil. According to Steiner, only by introducing anthroposophist practices could farmers cultivate in the soil the vitality necessary to sustain healthy animals and crops. Needless to say, this mystical approach to agriculture differed dramatically from the more mainstream scientific approach employed by Howard.[11]

Steiner died shortly after delivering the lectures, in 1925. It was therefore up to the experimental circle that had been formed at the gathering to flesh out his ideas and come up with a defined agricultural practice. The first step was to coin the term "biodynamic," a combination of the biological character of fertilization, manures transformed into life through careful preparations, and the dynamic effects of the etheric and astral forces that were at work in the living organism of the farm. Steiner's followers then continued to work together, developing their methods through annual conferences held throughout the German- and English-speaking world. New preparations were advanced, in keeping with Steiner's ideas regarding the fertility of buried horns; pamphlets were circulated; and a journal was founded.

The most dedicated of Steiner's followers was Ehrenfried Pfeiffer. He also turned out to be the most influential; his works were routinely cited by French, British, and American farmers as their primary inspiration for adopting alternative practices. Pfeiffer first heard Steiner speak in 1920 and shortly thereafter went to work for him at the anthroposophist center in Dornach. It was there that he established an experimental agricultural station and worked on developing new compost preparations. Pfeiffer remained loyal to Steiner and his ideas, but his remove from the origins of anthroposophy allowed him to promote biodynamic farming in a more secular format that appealed to a wider audience of farmers who were not necessarily comfortable with Steiner's vitalist view of the world.[12] In addition to pursuing his research, Pfeiffer consulted on biodynamic practices throughout Europe and the United States, unstintingly traveling the globe to promote Steiner's methods. Even Howard, who had his reservations about the quasi-religious nature of it all, visited Pfeiffer to discuss alternative agricultural techniques. By the end of the 1920s, biodynamic farming had spread to England, Austria, Switzerland, and eastern France.[13]

The Sacred Mission

It was the French state itself that initially resisted industrialization, an unexpected twist given how enthusiastically the state would later embrace it. When American wheat began to flood European markets in the late nineteenth century, nations were left with a tough decision on their hands: try to compete or raise a tariff wall. Under the guidance of Jules Méline, France (in)famously opted for the latter. Under the Third Republic, agrarianism dominated farm policy. After the successive revolutions of the nineteenth century, the new republic turned to the countryside for social and political stability. Ultimately, however, agrarianism and protectionist trade policy were not enough to maintain a traditional agricultural sector. Industry was on the rise and cities were growing at a breakneck pace. More and more rural French men and women joined the rural exodus in search of better work and better lives. It was becoming clear that in spite of protectionist measures, agriculture would have to take a back seat to industry. This realization, and the productivist turn that followed suit, no doubt served as the foundation for the state's eventual about-face.

While protectionism and republican virtue might have formed the core of agrarian thinking in the early twentieth century, new ideas began to take hold through the interwar period. First, Henry Dorgères arrived on the scene with his rural right-wing extremism, calling all farmers to "raise the pitchforks!" in protest. Farmers were struggling to survive the economic depression of the 1930s, and the charismatic Dorgères appealed to their desire for justice. His rallies routinely attracted tens of thousands of supporters who wanted the small peasant-proprietor to remain the backbone of rural France. Although his movement failed to realize its mission, the direct political action that formed the core of its strategy lived on in successive agricultural organizations.[14] The widespread protests of the 1950s, for instance, were an inheritance of the Dorgèrist model.

These early proponents of a nonindustrial agricultural system began to develop a discourse of quality that subsequent generations would continue to develop. Bread in particular served as a lightning rod in the debates surrounding industrialization and agricultural policy. As historian of French bread Steve Kaplan has demonstrated, as early as the 1910s a handful of French doctors and nutritionists began warning consumers about the possible health risks of eating "mechanical bread," arguing that it could be responsible for a host of ills ranging from indigestion to cancer. In the 1930s, when the wheat market (and by extension, the bread market) came under strict regulation with the creation of a national wheat board, small-scale hands-on production served as a counterweight to the industrial bread machine. Farmers and nutritionists alike argued that new laws regulating the wheat market and the processing of flours favored large-scale industrial producers and their inferior grains, which in turn produced inferior flours and inferior bread. By the 1950s, largely as a result of several bread-related food-poisoning outbreaks, such warnings had migrated to the mainstream press. Faced with a public relations problem of epic proportions, the National Research and Recommendations Center for Nutrition and Diet (Centre national d'études et de recommandations sur la nutrition et l'alimentation, or CNERNA) embarked on a six-year investigation into the quality of French bread, the results of which were predictably bureaucratic. Consumers who were worried about their health, to say nothing of their safety, were urged to reject the white breads of the modern production process and instead to favor the brown breads of small-scale operations.[15]

Niche producers and small-scale processors emerged to satisfy this growing (albeit small) demand. One of the most active and ardent defenders of quality goods was the farmer and businessman Raoul Lemaire. In 1930, Lemaire founded the Société de vente de blé Lemaire, and in 1931 opened a shop in Paris where one could buy his natural Lemaire bread. For Lemaire, wheat was the bedrock of the French diet: "One could argue that the history of hard wheat is the history of France, and even the history of civilization. Is not wheat the noble grain? It is the divine plant, the sacred plant.... The scholars who have studied the composition of a wheat seed know its wealth, and it is this wealth that is being prostituted to the scandalous profit of private interest."[16] Lemaire regularly positioned the sacred mission of small-scale quality producers against their corrupt and profit-driven competitors. Just as Jean Monnet was fighting to return France to its former position amidst the constellation of global powers by way of industrial prowess, Lemaire and his compatriots were fighting to protect a power that they deemed to be much more important: the authority of France as the cradle of civilization.

The end goal for Lemaire was nothing less than the restoration of what he believed to be the true France, the France that served as an example of all that was good and holy in the world. But it would be wrong to see him as nothing more than a right-wing extremist vying for libertarian freedoms and the racial purity of the true France. Lemaire devoted his life to building an alternative agricultural model that was antistatist, antitechnocratic, and anti-industrial, and along the way he remained open to a variety of collaborators who did not necessarily share his understanding of the world. In the end, he subscribed to his own idiosyncratic brand of libertarian politics: an odd mixture of Vichy-era conservatism, Poujadism, and Catholic mysticism on the one hand, and on the other, a voracious intellectualism that embraced the work of Mohandas Gandhi and Rachel Carson.

Lemaire was born in 1884 in Villers-Bretonneux (Somme). His family ran a distribution business for, among other things, wheat and bread, and it was on the Saturday rounds with his brother, visiting area bakeries, that he began to think about how he might improve French wheat. French wheat, while abundant, was of insufficient quality for high-end purposes. Its gluten content was weak, and without enough gluten, dough was difficult to handle. To remedy this problem, imported wheats with higher gluten content supplemented the domestic supply. When Lemaire assumed the helm of the family business, at the age of twenty-five, he stepped up his efforts to develop a superior French wheat that would eliminate the need for imports from abroad. Before long, Lemaire was producing and milling his own high-quality varieties and was distributing his flour to bakeries in Roye, Versailles, and Paris.

Trying to gain a foothold, however, in a market that was heavily regulated proved to be next to impossible. For starters, by the 1930s there was an abundant surplus of millers in France. The miller unions were working hard to deal with their surplus problem, and the arrival of outsiders on the scene was hardly welcome. Moreover, there were rules governing which wheat varieties could and could not be brought to market and an official registry that listed the approved varieties.[17] Lemaire had difficulty in getting his own wheats accepted, and accused his competitors of using their influence to keep these varieties from being marketed. In 1934, he had his first of many run-ins with the Fraud Bureau, a government agency that was responsible for monitoring the markets and protecting consumers. Samples were taken from Lemaire's fields and determined to be other than what he claimed them to be. Lemaire then went before a judge and demanded a second test, the results of which were clean. According to Lemaire, the second test proved that larger interests were purposefully targeting him and keeping his superior wheat varieties from coming to market. He tried to gain political traction with policymakers in power who might support his plight for superior wheat, and even wrote to Eugène Forget, who was at the time the agricultural attaché at the Economic Council. In his response, Forget agreed with Lemaire that France ought to produce its own quality wheat but offered no more assistance than to join him in getting the word out to farmers and agronomists.[18]

These commercial and legal difficulties led Lemaire to embrace a more conservative politics. By his own account, he was a member of the French Socialist Party until 1933, when the organization ceased being "the party of liberty" and became instead "the party of dirigisme."[19] He became an ardent follower of Maréchal Pétain during the German occupation and remained decidedly right of center for the rest of his life, even running for office in the early 1950s on the extreme-Right ticket of Pierre Poujade. That said, he was a voracious reader and energetic supporter of organic farming, both of which often led him in unlikely directions. While he quoted Ayn Rand at length in his correspondence and writings, he was likewise interested in the agrarian thought of Mohandas Gandhi, and when he read Rachel Carson's *Silent Spring* he wrote to Poujade himself to declare: "I am no longer asleep. I am at the boiling point!"[20] For Lemaire, personal and professional freedom from an increasingly technocratic and bureaucratic state was the primary agenda. Anything and everything that supported him in this cause was fair game.

During the war, Lemaire made his way westward before finally settling near Angers, in the Loire Valley, where he would remain until his death in 1972. Here he continued to pursue his experimental wheat development and to grow his business, while also teaching genetics at the agricultural college. Needless to say, the massive scale of state planning that was introduced in the aftermath of the Second World War only fueled Lemaire's fire. Gone were the days of a state-sanctioned agrarianism that celebrated the smallholder and his independence. The postwar state pushed for quantities of scale and exercised its power to the fullest in an effort to achieve these new goals. No longer was it simply a question of fighting back against a strictly regulated wheat market. The agricultural sector as a whole was being subjected to increasingly expansive regulation. The Monnet and Marshall Plans now governed the broad outlines of agricultural development and newly created institutions such as the National Institute for Agricultural Research (Institut national de la recherche agronomique, or INRA) carried out the details. For Lemaire, *planification* was nothing more than an extension of the greedy reach of the technocratic state. In a letter to the president of the French millers' association, Lemaire bemoaned the new intensity of state intervention: "The Dirigisme to which we are subjected in FRANCE, especially with respect to Wheat, is ruthless, for the good reason that our Public Men who believe themselves to be everything are nothing, for they do nothing but move up the ranks, while the civil servants remain and maneuver as they wish. If only they continued to maneuver in the general interest of the Country all would be good, but if it is in other domains as it is for Wheat, we are headed for ruin and catastrophe."[21] Lemaire deeply distrusted government authority and viewed civil servants (*fonctionnaires*) as mindless and obedient pawns who subjugated the good of the citizenry to their own self-interest. In his view, the state worked primarily to perpetuate itself, and its bureaucrats worked to advance their careers. The good of the nation and its citizens was at best an afterthought.

While Lemaire was pushing for greater flexibility in the market in order to expand the production and distribution of his products, farmers were slowly but surely learning about the developments taking place in Britain and Germany. Farmers along the Swiss border in Alsace began to practice biodynamic methods as early as 1925, and by the eve of the Second World War, Steiner's ideas had spread all the way to the southwest, an area that later became a hotbed of biodynamic and organic activity.[22] Experimental farms were established, intended to serve as educational centers for those farmers who wanted to learn more about biodynamic methods, and it became even easier to learn about these new methods in 1938, when Pfeiffer published a French-language edition of Steiner's teachings, *Fécondité de la terre* (Fertility of the earth). Interrupted by the chaos of the war and occupation, these early efforts at building a biodynamic base in France were put on hold. Once the war was over, however, enterprising farmers and agronomists were ready to double down on their efforts to spread the word.

Given the scope of French plans for postwar agricultural modernization, the early French adherents of organic and biodynamic farming had much to worry about. Lemaire referred to government regulators as his "executioners," while one of the farmers who wrote to him cynically wondered if the "dirigiste state" might not crush the organic movement before it even had a chance to grow.[23] These early adopters looked upon state-mandated agricultural industrialization with suspicion, if not outright disdain.

André Birre, a civil engineer by trade and an advocate of natural foods by vocation, published a series of like-minded articles in the weekly agricultural newspaper *L'Epoque agricole*. In these writings, Birre addressed Monnet's plans for modernizing the French economy on the basis of an industrialized farm sector. While applauding the government for finally addressing the plight of French farmers in a methodical fashion, Birre maintained that these efforts privileged an urban desire for cheap abundance over the rural need for parity: "Agriculture and the peasant condition were subordinated to urban needs, desires, and ideas, without fully compensating them for the contributions they've made."[24] The plan for the future of France was overly one-sided. Agriculture was going to be sacrificed to industry and farmers were not even going to be thanked for everything that they would have to give up. What was needed instead was equilibrium. Monnet's plans for modernization would amount to nothing if policy continued to pursue productivity for the sake of productivity, rather than "restoring the rural economy by shaping it and giving it the resources it needs to create and maintain the means necessary to ensure a balanced and lasting agriculture."[25] Birre's words rang true for those who believed that under Monnet's guidance, the rural economy would be exploited for the sake of urban comforts. Moreover, state promises to use *aménagement du territoire* to achieve the proper balance between urban and rural France made it clear that their conceptions of equilibrium were not mutual.

In 1948, Birre, along with the agronomist Jean Boucher, began to gather these dissidents together with a new organization called Man and Soil (L'homme et le sol). Boucher had studied at the national horticultural college in Versailles, and after a few more years of training, returned to take a post at its research station (see figure 10). By then he had already begun buying Lemaire bread and was following his efforts to break into the wheat market. In his new position, he had requested to work on pesticides, and when he saw that orchards were being destroyed by spider mites in spite of having been sprayed with DDT, he turned his attention to alternative methods.[26] With Birre, he called on the members of their new organization to launch a "Crusade for the soil."

From Steiner's spiritualist anthroposophy to the conservative Catholicism of Vichy, religious metaphors appeared repeatedly in this early literature on the ills of intensive farming. This discourse surrounding the soil and its metaphorical potential would later be stripped of its religious associations to be co-opted in the 1970s not only by the state but also by the radical Left. In this earlier period, however, it was a language that served well the mix of religious mysticism and science that formed the basis of early anti-industrial critiques. Paradoxically, the Catholic faith was simultaneously providing inspiration for industrialization. Just as the young members of JAC and the CNJA were drawing from a social Catholicism to promote the adoption of chemical inputs and big farm machinery, the adherents of biodynamic and organic methods were drawing from a mystical Catholicism to argue against the very same modernization agenda.

Influenced by a conservative Catholicism and the politics of Vichy that had lauded rural France as the true locus of French authenticity, value, and meaning, Birre looked to the health of the very soil itself as the primary index by which one might read the general health of the nation. The soil, and by extension the French population that it sustained, had fallen gravely ill. In using chemical inputs to kill off every microbe that stood in the way of higher yields, farmers were doing nothing less than abandoning life itself: "We are on the path of death, we are not oriented toward the direction or meaning of life."[27] With their crusade, Birre and Boucher sought to repair the damage and return to health both the nation and the sacred ground upon which it stood.

Together they disseminated these ideas through regular publications and technical demonstrations. Birre created a new journal to advance his crusade, and in the inaugural issue he expressed his goals for the publication: "We give to you *Sol et Vitalité*, a dispatch created to meet the needs of those who are working together for the reconstitution of the deep health of the soil, and of the plants and animals. Their goal is to foster the production of quality foods that will restore the deep health of man."[28] To the same end, he held regular workshops to educate consumers and doctors, and to demonstrate new methods to farmers and agronomists. A report that Birre wrote up following a workshop that he had held in Paris in 1950 reveals that a meaningful interest in organic agriculture was beginning to emerge. Farmers, doctors, consumers, academics, and agronomists—150 in total—came from every corner of the country. Another 120 expressed regret that they would not be able to attend, but offered their support and encouragement. While these numbers hardly make for a national movement, they do suggest that Birre and Boucher were reaching men and women beyond their immediate circle. Workshops like these were instrumental in spreading the word of organic farming. Although those who participated might not have necessarily agreed with the politics of their instructors, their adoption of the new techniques created an embodied afterlife for the ideas of these early pioneers.

While Lemaire operated from Angers, and Birre and Boucher from Paris, a fellow traveler was busy in Bordeaux teaching farmers about the new methods. André Louis was born in the Gironde, just north of Bordeaux, into a staunchly Catholic wine-making family (see figures 8 and 9). For his postsecondary studies, he focused on agronomy, and upon graduation took a post with the Departmental Agricultural Services, first in Gironde and then in several different neighboring departments of the southwest. It was during this time that he discovered the teachings of Rudolf Steiner through the anthroposophist journal *Triades*, and in 1948 he attended a daylong workshop on the soil that had been put together by Birre and Boucher. Having spent most of his career working for the state, Louis felt he could no longer train farmers in its industrial methods once he had discovered biodynamic farming. He left his position for a teaching post at the Lycée agricole de Blanquefort, on the outskirts of Bordeaux, and stayed there until his retirement in 1966. Although he hewed to the mainstream line in the classroom, he worked faithfully on his own time to popularize alternative methods.[29]

Louis's politics are more difficult to pin down than those of Lemaire. Louis converted to Protestantism after the Second World War, but hewed most closely to a deist mysticism than any recognizable branch of Christianity.[30] He was an avid reader of anthroposophy. He admired the eugenicist Alexis Carrel. He shared with Lemaire a devout belief in god, and regularly wrote about the importance of working the land in a state of grace. But his faith did not seem to dovetail with the Catholic anti-Semitism that influenced Lemaire. Nor does anything in his papers suggest that he was necessarily antistatist or politically conservative.

Louis's early activities demonstrate that while opponents to the industrial ideal might have been few in number, they quickly established an informal network that was based on shared training programs, personal correspondence, and a growing body of published materials. Staying on top of new developments, Louis collected Birre's articles, attended his workshops, and maintained ties with Pfeiffer's experimental farm in Switzerland. He also corresponded with farmers and agronomists across western Europe, from managing members of the British Soil Association to individual farmers seeking technical advice. As an expert in biodynamic farming with a rich background in agronomy, Louis was often sought out by farmers seeking advice on how best to adopt the new techniques. In one instance, a German producer of biodynamic apricots wrote to Louis in search of a biodynamic processing facility. In another, a farmer in the southwestern department of Haute-Garonne explained that he had been interested in anthroposophy and biodynamic farming for over a decade, and had experimented a little with these methods on his holdings. He went on to describe Pfeiffer's visit to the area and to list the handful of neighboring farmers who were similarly engaged in biodynamic practices.[31] One letter at a time, Louis was building a community of like-minded producers and consumers.

In one of the most eloquent letters that Louis preserved, a farmer by the name of Frossard, who had read Pfeiffer's *Fécondité de la terre*, expressed concern over how corn was being produced in the Basse-Pyrénées, an area in the deep southwest. The new hybrid varieties that had arrived from the United States required a "large deployment of artificial fertilizers and poisons" to protect against pests. Hoping to convince his neighbors to abandon these poisons and the methods that were being advocated by the state-sponsored agricultural extension service, he inquired whether Louis knew of a more modern text that explained the benefits of biodynamic practices:

> I am myself a farmer (part-time), on a small family property in Orthez. Our primary crop is corn, which is the only crop . . . that currently guarantees a profit beyond our cost of production. But this is achieved with hybrids from America, and with a substantial amount of artificial fertilizer. . . . Is there not something in these methods that is entirely in opposition to Pfeiffer's ideas? What is becoming of the good worms thanks to our poisons? Yet all of this is absolutely encouraged by the Agricultural Services. . . . Without indicting the Services, we could draw the attention of users to the disadvantages of the official methods and look into how we might correct them. . . . Could you tell me if there is a more modern work that expresses the current ideas of biodynamic farmers—if there are biodynamic farmers in France, and in particular in the southwest, and if they are producing corn?[32]

Frossard understood that the lure of modernization, with promises of improved standards of living and diminished toil, exercised a powerful hold on French farmers. The best way to resist the state-mandated version of modernization was to present farmers with a different definition of modernity rather than to abandon it entirely. He likely also understood that the esoteric spiritualism of Pfeiffer's work might alienate the farmers he was trying to reach, and hoped to learn from Louis that there were other texts out there, texts that argued for nonindustrial methods with a language that would appeal to his neighbors.

This letter to Louis is also evidence of how American influence on French agricultural policy informed early resistance to the industrial ideal. Frossard makes no mention of the Marshall Plan or of international politics and trade, but with his mention of the imported American corn varieties, it is clear that his daily life, and the lives of his neighbors, had been profoundly altered by Jean Monnet's plans for economic modernization and American efforts to secure foreign markets for grain surpluses. Faced with an organized state-sponsored network that included the extension service, seed distributors, and powerful international interests, Frossard was trying to establish an alternative network of his own that would foster greater local autonomy.

While Louis was very much a technical and spiritual guide to those interested in the new practices, he was also a student. As part of his ongoing research, Louis kept an active correspondence with Pfeiffer, going straight to the source for information on how best to put Steiner's ideas into practice. In an early letter, Louis expressed his excitement about just having read *Fecondité de la terre*, and then asked that Pfeiffer send him as much material as he could on biodynamic products and their application.[33] In other letters, he inquired about the proper preparation of compost and the best methods for managing pests. He would then relay what he had learned through his extensive network of correspondence, at workshops, and to the degree that he could, in the classroom.

By the late 1940s, there was a dedicated group of farmers, agronomists, doctors, and consumers who shared a common interest in promoting an alternative ideal that was based on small-scale production and quality consumption. Having come to these new ideas by way of their British and German neighbors, these French pioneers regularly reached beyond their national borders for additional training, organizational membership, and inspirational reading material. This regular contact is evidence of the close intra-European network of biodynamic and organic farmers that developed in spite of the recent hostilities that had pitted them against each other. While Franco–German distrust was hampering state efforts at greater European economic integration, French and German proponents of biodynamic agriculture were coming together with a shared purpose and a shared system of beliefs.

In Britain, the development of anti-industrial farming models was likewise proceeding apace. In 1946, Lady Eve Balfour, inspired by McCarrison and Howard at home, and Steiner and Pfeiffer abroad, founded the Soil Association. This was the first organic organization of its kind and included members from France, as well as from throughout the world. Contact between the French, Germans, Swiss, Austrians, and British was regular, through correspondence, workshops, and visits to experimental farms. On occasion, language proved to be a barrier (translations of published works were not always quick to appear). But on-the-ground exchange allowed those who had not yet read these works to learn from those who had. In the wake of what had been one of the bloodiest conflicts that Europe had ever seen, the pioneers of alternative agriculture were forming new alliances with former rivals.

Building a Network

Slowly but surely, these various alternative ideals began to coalesce into an organized movement. Journals were established and groups were founded. Differences were set aside because there was strength in numbers. And the British and German branches were folded into a new language, with the adoption of the term "agriculture biologique," or farming that was based in nature and biology. The first use of the term is sometimes attributed to the medical doctor Pierre Delbet, who in the 1930s became increasingly interested in the role that diet played in human health. In general, the qualifier "biological" (and its non-English variants) was the preferred term to describe the types of nonindustrial farming that were gaining attention through the end of the nineteenth and early twentieth centuries.

In 1946, Henri-Charles Geffroy launched the journal *La Vie Claire* (The Clear Life), a small publication that would later serve as the basis for the first national network of natural food stores. Geffroy came to natural foods not as a producer, but rather as a consumer. According to Geffroy, during the First World War he had suffered mustard gas poisoning and was given just a few months to live by his doctors, but was able to cheat death with a natural and vegetarian diet.[34] The journal became his pulpit, where he could share his story and exhort others to follow him on the path to health and clarity. The goal of the publication, as he stated in an early issue, was "to be the connection between those who suffer . . . to be the means by which we are able to realize that there are more of us than people realize, to think 'clear,' to see 'clear,' to act 'clear,' and to want to live 'clear.'"[35] Geffroy was working to bring consumers together, in an effort to build a critical mass that might begin to challenge successfully the industrial model of food production. But it was not just about diet. Geffroy wanted his readers to be clear and pure in every aspect of their lives.

The wholesomeness of brown bread and the purity of the French (white) race often went hand in hand in the early years of the organic movement. Geffroy, like Lemaire, subscribed to a conservative politics based on national chauvinism. Similarly, Geffroy regularly named as an influence the celebrated surgeon Alexis Carrel, who was also an inspiration for Boucher. Carrel had won a Nobel Prize for medicine, but had also promoted eugenics and had served the Vichy government. In 1958, when Geffroy met Henry Coston, the right-wing journalist who had written anti-Semitic material for Vichy, they became fast friends, and Geffroy began distributing his anti-Semitic writings through his network of followers. In an excellent study of these early years of *La Vie Claire*, anthropologist Christine César has offered a detailed reading of the conservatism that underwrote Geffroy's objectives. Described in her work as a neo-Dorgèrist and archeo-Poujadist, Geffroy bemoaned the laxity and cowardice of the French race and attributed both to an inferior, impure diet. The race was degenerating, and along with it, the power of the nation. Calling for a dramatic overhaul of the entire economic and social system, Geffroy lamented that they were all living in the middle of an "alarming and harrowing social collapse."[36]

In 1948, Geffroy expanded his mission and began a consumer co-op. Pushing beyond the boundaries of print publication and public debate, Geffroy began building a material infrastructure that would go on to outlast his ideas about racial purity and the sanctity of family and tradition. He offered his members fruits and vegetables that had been produced without chemical inputs, as well as whole-grain bread. In 1951, he founded Healthy Food (L'Aliment sain), an organization of shareholders, again drawn from his readership, that would go on to create a nationwide network of natural food stores. By 1952, his readers numbered between forty and sixty thousand.[37] By 1965, there were over eighty stores nationwide, and by the 1980s, in addition to two processing plants (for grains), another one hundred stores had been established.[38] The stores were filled with fruits and vegetables, cookies, dairy products, and wine. And while brown bread continued to occupy space on the shelves, the promotion of the French race had fallen by the wayside. The tainted past of *La Vie Claire* was by then a faded memory.

In 1952, Dr. Jacques-William Bas formed the first of the major organic organizations, the French Research Association for a Standard Diet (Association française de recherche pour une alimentation normale, or AFRAN). Like Geffroy, Bas was heavily influenced by the work of Carrel, and devoted his life to fighting back against the industrialization of French agriculture and the French diet. He was joined at AFRAN by Birre, who was in charge of publicity, and a membership that consisted largely of physicians who were similarly worried that an industrial diet was causing a rise in disease. The public face of the association, as presented by Bas and

Birre, was conservative in its politics and harkened back to Vichy in its emphasis on family, work, and *patrie* (homeland).

Writing in Birre's *Sol et Vitalité*, Bas bemoaned the growing incidence of disease among French men and women. To cure and prevent these diseases, a radically different, nonindustrial approach to the soil needed to be adopted: "When it comes to the soil, one must understand that our modern world, driven by its desire for material output, oriented toward quantity, has proven to be a poor custodian of the fundamental richness of the soil.... Its exhaustion is palpable, its fertility has been squandered like a poorly managed inheritance."[39] In adopting Pfeiffer's biodynamic model for fertilizing the land, French farmers just might be able to save their countrymen, and themselves, from physical degeneration.

The term "degeneration" was central to the early discourse surrounding the organic movement. Geffroy took up this language to link diet and decay: "The real problem is the degeneration of the race.... And the true cause of this evil? All of the toxic products that we have allowed to circulate in the general public, while biologists have for a long time warned of their dangers."[40] Consumers were exposed to poison every day because of industrial agriculture, and it was making them sick. In a letter from Lemaire that Geffroy published in *La Vie Claire*, he likewise wrote of "the degeneration of the French race thanks to the widespread marketing of unbalanced flours."[41] And in his own journal, Bas expressed similar sentiments: "One must recognize that chronic illnesses of all kinds are increasing in number and frequency. A biological mediocrity is establishing itself at all levels of society."[42] Terms such as "biological mediocrity" echoed previous attempts to combat degeneration and to improve the race through a combination of good breeding, diet, and exercise. Even those levels of society that had previously been insulated against this mediocrity and the diseases of a bad diet were at risk. Diet-related illnesses were no longer limited to the poor, who could not afford to nourish themselves properly. As long as food was purchased in conventional markets, no one was safe from the ill effects of a diet derived from industrial agriculture.

Degeneration is a tricky business. Even when these early pioneers of alternative farming used the term to refer to physical processes, ailments, and illnesses, there was almost always a moral quality to their language. The term itself carried with it a sordid history, from its first deployment in the mid-nineteenth century, as part of the emerging field of scientific racism, to later public health discourse surrounding criminality and mental illness. The term was adopted in the early twentieth century by eugenicists, and then in the 1940s by those supporters of Vichy who feared the degeneration of the French race and sought to renew the health and purity of the nation. That the early proponents of organic agriculture adopted it is further evidence of the unexpected political roots in France of what has become a solidly leftist movement.

To combat this decay, subscribers to the AFRAN journal, *Sol-Alimentation-Santé*, were exhorted to change their dietary habits and to support those farmers who were adopting alternative practices. To facilitate the consumption of these natural foods, a list of biodynamic farms, complete with a description of their operations and contact information, was regularly provided with printed material.[43] Readers were encouraged to purchase their food directly from these producers to bypass the poisons on offer at their local shops and on the shelves of the new supermarkets. In seeking these resources out, consumers could improve their physical and moral well-being.

As part of his critique of the quality of industrially produced food, Bas went after the entire system of production and the logic of productivism that underwrote it. Just as Birre had argued that the commercial spirit was squeezing out the small-scale producer of quality goods, Bas similarly critiqued a food system that looked only to the bottom line. With productivity and profit as the end goal, the soil was exploited by intensive production, livestock breeds were selected for yields rather than quality, and industrial processing both robbed food of its nutritional quality and sometimes even made it dangerous with the use of additives: "From the field and the barnyard all the way to the shelves of the grocery store, the food system is dominated by one single concern: productivity."[44] The efforts of political leaders such as Monnet and Pierre Pflimlin to increase productivity during the postwar years were matched in fervor, if not success, by the likes of Bas and Birre, who fought equally hard to supplant quantity with quality.

In addition to publishing the journal, Bas worked in multiple venues to advance his message. He collaborated with various groups that had like-minded interests: the Federal Consumers' Union, Qualité-France, and the Christian Union of Paris. In a dogged attempt to reach the halls of power with his prescriptions, Bas even attended conferences held by such mainstream organizations as the General Association of Wheat Producers.[45] He also gave presentations on diet and disease, and invited others who were active in the movement to speak at AFRAN events. For example, in 1955 Lemaire was invited to Paris to lecture on the inferior quality of French bread and its ill effects on the health of consumers.[46] Lastly, he began to reach out to producers and to market products under the AFRAN label.

These new marketing efforts of the 1950s dovetailed with a rise in mainstream concern about the quality of certain food products, and of bread in particular. The use of adulterated flour during the Second World War led many to clamor for better bread quality. Moreover, producers and professional associations worried that the increasingly powerful association between poor quality, or industrially produced bread, and ill health would hurt sales. Doctors were advising consumers to limit bread consumption, telling them that it caused weight gain, digestive disorders, and possibly even cancer. In an effort to redeem the reputation of French bread, the CNERNA suggested in 1958 that qualifying bread products be labeled with the tagline "made without chemicals."[47] That the AFRAN tag was arriving in stores while a major research arm of the state was trying to establish a label of its own was no coincidence. A certain class of consumer was growing increasingly worried about the industrial food of the new productivist agricultural model and was turning to new organizations such as AFRAN for guidance and solidarity.

AFRAN-approved goods hit the shelves in the late 1950s. As Bas explained in his journal, reorienting the organization toward distribution and marketing was a substantial endeavor, one that required a complete overhaul of the AFRAN mandate and administrative offices. A certification board was set up to review products for approval. AFRAN members had to reach out to potential producers to market their goods. A set of guidelines for what constituted an AFRAN-approved product needed to be agreed upon and formalized. Most important, however, AFRAN had to deliver consumers to these newly recruited producers. The secretary-general of the association, Dr. Lefebvre, made an appeal to their members just as products were scheduled to arrive in stores, pleading with them to use their purchasing power not only to keep the program alive but to prove to other producers and distributors that a viable market for quality goods did indeed exist.[48]

Lemaire tried to have his chocolate sold under the AFRAN label. In a letter to the chair of the certification board, the description of his chocolate serves as a powerful reminder of just how strong the ties were between the alternative ideals of the 1950s and those of the early twenty-first century. Lemaire opened by stating that his chocolate was free of "chemical and synthetic ingredients." He went on to elaborate that it was "made exclusively from cacao beans of the finest origin, cacao butter extract (expeller-pressed, rather than extracted with solvents), sugar, and a light flavoring of natural vanilla." He then wrapped up his presentation by assuring the certification board that his chocolate contained absolutely no additives.[49] When stripped of his quasi-fascist politics, Lemaire sounded more like an average twenty-first-century organic producer than a supporter of Pierre Poujade.

For the most part, the marketing of AFRAN products drew on the standard language of midcentury agrarian conservatism, but some of the terms carried different meanings. While Birre and Bas had previously presented themselves as the guardians of western civilization, AFRAN was selling its new label as the antidote to the ills of civilization and modernity. These statements were not necessarily contradictory, however. Civilization when viewed in one light, referred to ancient traditions of the true (read: rural) France. This was the civilization celebrated by Lemaire. In another light, however, civilization was synonymous with modernity, with a move away from the natural and rural world.

In a flyer explaining why consumers should choose the AFRAN label, civilization was equated with urbanization and a disconnection from the calming influence of rural existence: "Civilized life is upsetting our nervous equilibrium"; and "Our physical and mental well-being are compromised every day by the overburdening that is imposed upon us by our modern existence" (see figure 4). AFRAN eggs, butter, and breakfast beverages (see figure 5) would cure urban consumers of their irritability, fatigue, and depression, just as the clean air of the countryside and the calm of rural life offered an antidote to the ills of modernity and civilization, in this case represented by the increasingly polluted city air.

Two producer-oriented associations were formed in 1958, one biodynamic and one organic. The former would remain active through the postwar period, but it was the latter that developed into a movement and gained the attention of the mainstream. Biodynamic farming remained fairly regional, concentrated in the east, and it did not benefit from the tireless proselytizing of figures such as Lemaire and Louis. To be fair, many of the proponents of anti-industrial farming supported both organic and biodynamic practices, but the workshops and the publications were heavily weighted toward organic methods, which were less demanding (biodynamic compost preparation was both complicated and time consuming) and free of anthroposophist spiritualism. Although the teachings of Steiner had been instrumental in getting nonindustrial farming practices off the ground in France, they were quickly supplanted by a broader, and more straightforward, approach.

The French Association for Biodynamic Farming was founded in Strasbourg, where geographical proximity to German-speaking areas had made biodynamic farming more popular than elsewhere in France. In a letter to

voici pourquoi cette garantie vous concerne

L'avez-vous remarqué ?
Nous sommes tous irritables, fatigués, déprimés.
Nos enfants sont instables, accusent des intolérances digestives dès le biberon.
Le nombre des "maladies de la civilisation" ne cesse de s'accroître : on ne parle partout que de cancer, d'artériosclérose, d'excès du cholestérol sanguin, de défaillances cardio-vasculaires, d'accidents allergiques, etc...

Certes, dira-t-on...
L'air des villes est de plus en plus pollué,
la vie civilisée ébranle notre équilibre nerveux,
les progrès de la médecine ont émoussé les rigueurs de la sélection naturelle.

Tout cela est vrai, mais réfléchissons un instant :
S'il est possible au citadin d'aller respirer l'air de la campagne,
s'il est possible au surmené d'aller se reposer au calme,
Il est **impossible à quiconque d'échapper** aux dangers d'une alimentation mauvaise, car toutes les denrées actuelles ont perdu, en partie ou en totalité, la qualité qui leur permettrait de protéger la santé.

Les progrès de la technique agricole et industrielle,
à l'insu du producteur, n'ont pas été jugés par rapport à la véritable qualité des aliments, par conséquent par rapport à la santé du consommateur. Soumise trop souvent à des forçages chimiques intensifs, la terre ne produit plus des végétaux équilibrés quant à leur constitution. L'industrie aggrave ce déséquilibre : pour augmenter la production et diminuer les prix de vente, pour donner un aspect plus agréable aux denrées, elle raffine, épure, décolore, recolore, désodorise, aromatise, stérilise la matière première alimentaire.

Le résultat est devenu évident.
Nous nous alimentons et nous nourrissons nos enfants avec des aliments qualitativement incapables d'engendrer la véritable santé. Notre équilibre physique et intellectuel est chaque jour plus compromis par le surmenage que nous impose notre existence moderne. Demain, plus encore qu'aujourd'hui, nous aurons besoin d'une alimentation conforme aux impératifs de la vie.

Il faut humaniser la civilisation et la technique,
cette mission incombe à la France.

L'AFRAN EN A PRIS CONSCIENCE ET MONTRE LE CHEMIN.

FIGURE 4 AFRAN (French Research Association for a Standard Diet) advertising leaflet explaining why consumers should purchase AFRAN-label products. *Source*: Fonds Raoul Lemaire, Archives municipales d'Angers, 42J 183 Association française de recherche pour une alimentation normale (AFRAN): Affiche de conférences, bulletins mensuels, correspondance, carte de membre de Raoul Lemaire, 1955–1972.

Louis, Xavier Florin, one of the earliest French adherents of biodynamic farming, discussed the imminent formation of the group. There were approximately one hundred members involved, some of whom had been running a training facility in the department of Yonne for several years already. The goal of the group was "to bring about the purification of sick landscapes and farms that have been exhausted by intensive methods, and, in conjunction, to produce healthy and balanced plant- and animal-based

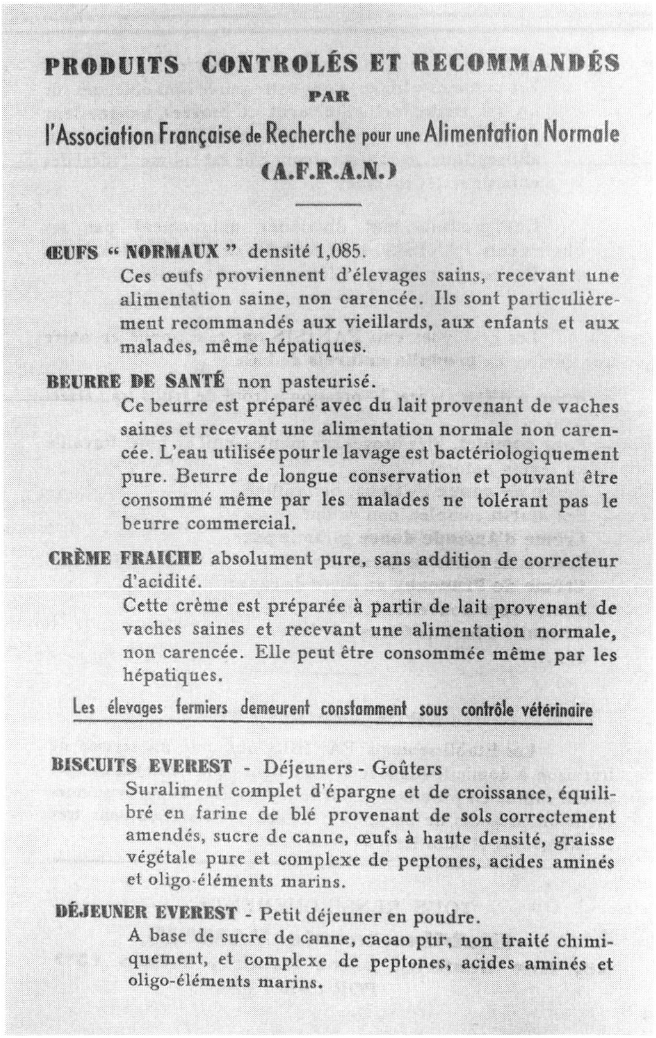

FIGURE 5
Advertisement for AFRAN products, circa 1959. *Source:* Fonds Raoul Lemaire, Archives municipales d'Angers, 42J 183 Association française de recherche pour une alimentation normale (AFRAN): Affiche de conférences, bulletins mensuels, correspondance, carte de membre de Raoul Lemaire, 1955–1972.

foods."[50] Florin and the members of the association clearly shared some points of commonality with the members of AFRAN and the early pioneers of organic farming: the link between health and diet, a critique of intensive industrial practices, and a preoccupation with purity.

Ultimately, however, it was organic farming along the British model that proved more successful with French farmers. There were no labor-intensive requirements for the meticulous preparation of various composts and soil treatments, and while religious belief might have driven many of the pioneers, the *practice* of organic farming itself was free from overt religious

FIGURE 6 Raoul Lemaire, circa 1970. *Source*: Fonds photographique du Groupe Lemaire, Archives municipales d'Angers.

and spiritualist overtones. In other words, British organic farming was much more straightforward: chemical inputs were not allowed; farmers were encouraged to keep animals on the farm to provide manure (though there was disagreement over whether this was an absolute requirement); and intercropping and diversified production, rather than monocultural production, were the standard. Generally speaking, farmers were asked to follow Howard's law of return: whatever nutrients were taken out of the soil, through growing and harvesting, needed to be returned by way of manure, compost, and organic fertilizers.

The consumers and doctors who followed Birre and Bas and the producers who practiced methods promoted by Lemaire and Louis finally came together in 1958 to found the Western Organic Farming Group (Groupement d'agriculture biologique de l'ouest, or GABO). The leadership initially consisted of Louis, Birre, and Mattéo Tavera. Tavera had trained as an architect and worked as an engineer with the national

FIGURE 7 Raoul Lemaire in his fields, circa 1970. *Source*: Fonds photographique du Groupe Lemaire, Archives municipales d'Angers.

railways (see figure 8). But in his spare time he was an avid orchardist and possibly the first producer of organic wines. Through his agricultural research and writings, he became a major figure in the organic world, and in 1966 was awarded the chevalier du Mérite Agricole (Knight of the Order of Agricultural Merit). In his writings, he promoted an esoteric spiritual approach to agriculture and argued that it was the "sacred mission" of humankind to serve the electrical currents of the cosmos. Concrete had created a barrier between urban men and women and these currents. Similarly, rubber boots and rubber tractor tires prevented farmers

FIGURE 8 André Louis and Mattéo Tavera, circa 1965. *Source*: Musée du Vivant, Centre international de recherches sur l'écologie (CIRE)–AgroParisTech, Grignon.

from properly connecting with the cosmos. Tavera advised that as much time as possible should be spent barefoot in nature, to reconnect with the cosmic currents.[51] While anthroposophy was taking a back seat in terms of method and organization, it continued to have a strong presence in the movement.

International aspirations aside, GABO began as a regional association, headquartered in the west of France, which is where organic production was concentrated at the time. Initial membership, which included Lemaire, was largely drawn from the French branch of the British Soil Association, and included agronomists, professors, consumers, and health professionals. The group shared in common with its predecessors a concern over health and an agrarian celebration of rural life and work. Followers were instructed to

FIGURE 9
André Louis
visiting a farm in
Germany, circa
1965. *Source*: Musée
du Vivant, Centre
international de
recherches sur
l'écologie (CIRE)–
AgroParisTech,
Grignon.

follow a simple diet; engage in physical exercise; live life in the fresh country air; work with joy, regularity, and rhythm; and love their fellow man, nature, and God.[52]

GABO differed from earlier organizations, however, in that it was founded as an organization aimed primarily at producers and sought to build a strong farmer base to undergird its membership.[53] Of the original forty or so members who founded the group, just four or five were farmers. But membership rolls reveal that farmer participation increased very quickly—of the sixty-one members listed one year after its founding, a full twenty-nine were entered as farmers.[54]

FIGURE 10
Jean Boucher, 1967.
Source: Fonds
photographique du
Groupe Lemaire,
Archives
municipales
d'Angers.

Many of the farmers who joined GABO did so because they saw their animals regularly getting sick, and attributed this to the new industrial practices that they had adopted.[55] There was in fact very little regulation regarding animal feeds, something that Lemaire had complained about to various ministers and elected representatives, all of whom responded with false assurances that something was being done about the matter.[56] Under industrial methods, animals were pastured less and less to maximize yields, and farmers were feeding them grasses and grains that had been treated with chemical fertilizers and pesticides. One response to the higher incidence of disease in livestock was to treat the animals with antibiotics, a practice that became the standard for postwar agriculture.

Those farmers who joined GABO opted instead to eschew industrial methods altogether.

These early subscribers to alternative practices also tended to be small-holders engaged in polyculture and animal husbandry. They had yet to adopt modern practices and were drawn to a less input-heavy method that would allow them to improve their farms, and possibly even to survive the modernization mandate without having to take on debt.[57] Organic agriculture did not require the expensive inputs that came with industrial farming. Nor did it require large-scale operations and the constant acquisition of new, and expensive, holdings. Small-holders could opt out of the "get big or get out" logic of the industrial ideal by going organic. Joining the community of organic farmers would insulate them against the state's pronouncements on what did and did not qualify as viable.

GABO offered its members a coherent set of principles that formed the basis of organic practice, principles that would persist through the following two decades. A working paper titled "Introducing the Western Organic Farming Group" laid out the general orientation of the organization.[58] The first principle was to denounce any and all practices that destroyed the natural fertility of the soil. These included the haphazard removal of trees, overzealous tillage, and the rash application of chemical fertilizers and pesticides. The second principle was to research and develop methods to restore and foster the natural fertility of the soil. The third sought to provide farmers with guidance on how to practice these methods, and the fourth to test their practices with the scientific rigor required to publish their results.

Once again, the soil was key, just as it had been in the writings of Birre, the treatments of Steiner, and the research of Howard. It was the starting point for both quality production methods and a healthy population, and because farmers were the first line of defense in addressing these concerns, they were put at the center of the group's agenda. As the members of AFRAN had been fond of repeating, the farmer was the first doctor, the first line of preventative care. These priorities were written into the very foundations of GABO.

Attached to this general introduction was a set of guidelines that addressed production directly. Farmers were instructed to improve their soil with manure compost that was fortified with straw and were told exactly how to apply it. The use of marine compost (promoted by Lemaire) was voluntary. The burning of vegetable waste, however, was strictly forbidden, as all products of the farm had to remain within the closed circuit. Farmers were told not to employ heavy tillage equipment and instead to till lightly and on the surface only, to protect the fertility of deeper soil levels. They were instructed to plant cover crops that would provide nutrients to the earth, protect it from erosion in rainy seasons, and aerate the soil. Lastly, farmers were provided with a list of equipment and tools necessary to organic farming: front loader, fertilizer spreader, mechanical excavator, disk pulverizer, cultivator with vibrating teeth, and a subsoiler.[59] With a defined set of practices and tools, farmers could be sure that they were indeed practicing organic agriculture, a guarantee that would become more and more important as foods began to carry certification labels.

In an effort to educate themselves so that they could in turn further educate their members, GABO leadership maintained regular contact with parallel organizations and traveled throughout Europe to visit organic farms, participate in demonstrations, and learn from farmers and agronomists. While the French state was coming up with an industrial agricultural model that was embedded in the international politics and trade of Bretton Woods and European integration, the pioneers of organic farming were establishing an international network of their own. From Steiner's experimental agricultural station in Switzerland and the English fields of the Soil Association, to the Rodale Institute in the United States, GABO was fostering relationships with organic farming groups outside of France to cement its foothold in the farm world.

With this new formal association, farmers interested in alternative practices were able to start building a movement. Farmers used the emerging organic network to situate their own ideas and practices, to educate themselves, and to formulate a critique. GABO held information days for anyone who wanted to attend, and members maintained an active correspondence in which they not only sought to educate themselves in the methods of organic farming but also to build a critique of the modernization program that was being promoted by the French state. In a letter to Lemaire, future member René Juillet, a farmer east of Paris in Seine-et-Marne, expressed his gratitude for having been visited by one of Lemaire's colleagues and for having been shown that he was not alone in his ideas. He asked for reading suggestions, so that he might educate himself even further in nonindustrial practices. And lastly, he took aim at the official agricultural model: "It is a shame to see that most producers don't understand anything at all about wheat. . . . All have but one goal, gladly welcomed by government administrators—to produce, produce, produce—and if I agree with that, it is to say produce well to sell a quality product."[60] Juillet was refusing the industrial model that had compromised on quality. Moreover, according to Juillet, the organic model not only produced high-quality foods but was also capable of challenging the industrial model on yield: "You know, it is very interesting that the farming we practice, without fertilizer, or very little, actually improves the soil, is capable of producing the highest yields, and prevents illness and the invasion of parasites."[61] This kind of correspondence was common. There was strength in numbers and the growing network of like-minded producers and professionals created a space in which they could challenge the productivist ideal.

The Alternative Ideal

In the epigraph that began this chapter, André Birre offered a dystopian vision of the industrial ideal. Profit was everything, and mechanical industrial reasoning was applied to production to maximize yields. Farming no longer had anything to do with nature. It had become an industrial enterprise like any other. The consequences of this transformation were dire. Disease was ravaging the soil, the people of France, and everything in between. Farmers were selling themselves to the banks to keep up with constantly increasing production costs. And to keep the machine moving into the future, to overcome growing resistances in insect populations, and to continue maximizing yields, ever increasingly rapacious methods would have to be implemented.

For Birre and his compatriots, much had gone wrong with French farming, and they spent the better part of two decades coming up with an alternative ideal. The nonindustrial farm would be small-scale, owner-operated, and autonomous. Its soils would never be subject to chemical inputs. Fertility would be supported by organic treatments: compost, manure, and cover crops. Animals would be present on the farm, to provide manure. Insects would be managed by sophisticated planting strategies rather than by toxic chemicals. The ideal farmer would respect the land and the natural rhythms of nature and would respect the law of return, putting back into the soil what had been taken out. He (there were very few women involved in the movement in these early days) would, moreover, be debt free.

Economic autonomy was a major selling point for organic farming. For those with a more libertarian bent, like Lemaire, organic production would allow them to refuse to be part of a market that was subject to constant government intervention. Moreover, given that state plans for expanding the agricultural sector were tied on the one hand to American financial aid and on the other to European integration, government involvement in French agriculture was only going to increase. If these farmers were put off by the notion of having French technocrats dictate their farming practices, they were positively outraged by the prospect that American and European politicians might have a say as well. While the pioneers of alternative agriculture embraced internationalism when it came to sharing ideas and developing methods, they quickly reverted to national boundaries when it came to organizing production, distribution, and consumption.

Autonomy would be more easily preserved if marketing scales remained small. For biodynamic and organic adherents, small was generally better than big, and this applied to market size just as much as it applied to farm size. For instance, André Louis opposed moving into foreign markets with organic French products because of the environmental toll that long-distance transportation would take. And in an article for the Dorgèrist *La Gazette Agricole* (The Agricultural Gazette), Lemaire attacked the common market on several grounds. First, it would cost a fortune for taxpayers. Monnet's presumed ample salary was in fact something to which Lemaire routinely objected. Second, competition with European neighbors would require sacrificing the almost two million small-scale farms that had been deemed unviable.[62] And third, the common market promised to be nothing short of a second occupation, with the French forced to send their wheat and their workers to Germany—the latter because the farmers who would be put out of business would be forced to seek employment within the borders of the industrial powerhouse. Lemaire even suggested that it would be better if the technocrats responsible for the common market, rather than innocent farmers, be sent to Germany to look for work, as they were both inept and a costly taxpayer burden.

Because Lemaire and his proponents of the alternative ideal privileged the rural as a way of life, maintaining as many farmers as possible on the land was a good in and of itself. Moving off the land into the industrial sector was not an improvement to the standard of living. On the contrary, it spelled the death of the soul. Not only would organic farming heal the soil; it would also offer a means of survival for those farmers who were slated to disappear. Expanding operations to include European markets would require farming on a scale that was incompatible with both environmental concerns and an ardent defense of economic autonomy.

"In our youth, we knew class struggle, and now we are living its consequences as we fight for our place" (unfortunately, in this case it is impossible to preserve the cunning of the original French: "Nous avons connu dans notre jeunesse la lutte des classes et nous vivons en ce moment l'aboutissement qui est la lutte des places.")[63] So wrote Lemaire in 1951, expressing a broadly shared view of the postwar world: wealth and political power were distributed according to geography. The days of agrarian power and the Méline tariff were over. Urban France had triumphed over the countryside, and policy and power would now be decided according to the interests of the cities. In spite of having the deck stacked against them, however, Lemaire, Louis, and the others continued to fight for their alternative ideals. Through the 1960s, organic pioneers developed their ideas and grew their ranks. GABO expanded to become a nationwide association, Lemaire began marketing an organic method of his own, Louis founded a publication in support of the movement, and organic goods became increasingly available to concerned consumers. While the productivist state model came to operate at full tilt, renegade farmers and agronomists tilted at windmills, continuing to gather momentum, to build a critical mass, and to formulate a language of critique.

CHAPTER THREE

Operating at Full Tilt, 1958–1968

Gauls for certain; Gaullists not certain; Gaul-ested, it's certain.
(Gaulois bien sûr; Gaullistes pas sûr; Gaulés c'est sûr.)

—PROTESTING FARMERS IN PICARDY, AS QUOTED IN LES
AFFAIRES FRANÇAISES, *L'Express* (January 28, 1960)

In 1962, the community of Montois (Meurthe-et-Moselle) was torn apart by *remembrement*. In a letter to the president himself, Mayor Renauld protested that the redistribution of farmland had clearly favored some over others: "The *remembrement* procedures carried out by the surveyor, Mr. Henquiner, and by the rural engineering department of Nancy were executed in an absolutely unacceptable manner, favoring certain farmers at the expense of others. The commissions did not fulfill their mandate to guarantee the rights of those involved but instead made fools of us all."[1] Renauld claimed that the proper procedures had not been followed—that farmers were not notified of changes to their property holdings in a timely fashion and that the new lines of the cadastral map had been determined in secret.

The mayor then explained that he had written to the Ministry of Agriculture to request that someone be sent to Montois to evaluate the *remembrement*. No one was sent. The mayor, on behalf of those farmers who felt wronged by the land redistribution, then hired a lawyer and filed a petition with the administrative court of Nancy to have the *remembrement* decree annulled. They did not win their case. Barely containing his rage, Renauld exclaimed: "The whole process has been totally arbitrary and illegal from start to finish. We are disgusted by this process, especially now that we understand who benefits from it."[2] Renauld went on to argue, falsely, that the *remembrement* commission and the prefect did not have the authority to require the aggrieved farmers to exchange their holdings and that land could only be ceded by consent. Whether Renauld was stretching his understanding of the truth or was simply uninformed is unclear from the sources. What is clear is that he was railing against what he perceived to be a grave injustice. He then closed his letter by stating that he and his coplaintiffs would do what they could to remain on their farms: "Because those in charge of enforcing the laws that protect our rights have systematically stonewalled us, we will peacefully exercise our right to remain on the lands that provide for the subsistence of our families, and of our descendants."[3] From Renauld's perspective, nothing short of the familial patrimony was at stake.

The mayor's letter was forwarded to the director of the national Office of Rural Engineering, the office responsible for *remembrement*. He in turn sent an officer to Montois to investigate. After inspecting the documentation and meeting with the prefect, the officer determined that the *remembrement* of Montois had been effected according to the letter of the law and that Renauld's claims were in fact without merit: "This proves that either they didn't read or understand the decisions that were explained in the notifications, or they spitefully refused to accept them. I myself have examined the claims of these farmers, both on site and with the assistance of the land allocation files, and not once did the redistributions strike me as being contrary to common sense or the general interest."[4] In an attempt to explain why the situation had grown so acrimonious given that the procedure had been carried out properly, the officer added that the local press had published a series of poorly researched articles that took the vexed farmers at their word, neglecting to mention that many other farmers had been happy with the results and had already taken possession of their new lands.

These farmers, the ones who viewed the *remembrement* as a success, argued that Mayor Renauld had it backward, that in fact he was the one who was abusing his authority to exercise his own interests at the expense of the residents of Montois. In spite of the fact that Renauld and his allies had failed to gain support for their cause with both the local law courts and the administrative offices responsible for *remembrement*, many continued to refuse to leave their lands. In response, thirty-two farmers, frustrated that their neighbors were not complying with the decree, wrote to the prefect to complain about Renauld and his supporters: "This obstinate refusal does damage to the residents and to the interests of the county. Loss of substantial rents. . . . Deterioration of the land, which until now has been well cared for. We are therefore filing a complaint against the mayor and the municipality, for an abuse of power, for misrepresenting the general interest in order to promote his own particular interests, and above all, for the idiotic refusal on the part of a few to accept a process that has clearly led to their substantial benefit."[5] Like Renauld, these farmers argued that the interests of a few were overriding the interests of the community. But in this case, the roles were reversed: the few were the farmers who refused to cede their lands, and the interests of the community were best advanced by the prompt acceptance of the new cadastral map.

For these farmers, the *remembrement* project had improved their situation and the situation of the community as a whole, but definitions of what constituted the general interest when it came to land reform were often contested. When efforts to redraw the map of rural France were stepped up in the 1960s, those farmers who found themselves on the losing side of the modernization battle desperately clung to the language of the general and the particular in an effort to stake their claims.

WITH CHARLES DE GAULLE'S election in 1958 and the advent of the Fifth Republic, the Planning Office put forth a new set of five-year objectives. At the top of the list was preparing for the common market (the other major components of the plan were the war in Algeria, and the coming-of-age of the baby-boomers). With the loss of agricultural markets precipitated by colonial movements for independence, the common market was more important than ever. De Gaulle called on farmers to ramp up modernization efforts: "In order for French agriculture to be in a position to benefit fully from the new export possibilities that the common market will present, it must adapt its production to the consumption needs of the six member-states."[6] In general, productivity was expected to rise by 20 percent before 1961. And in particular, projections for exports focused on wheat, secondary cereals, beef, and fruits and vegetables.

To meet these productivity goals, the restructuring of agricultural land holdings needed to advance with greater intensity. *Remembrement* remained the primary means by which to achieve this restructuring, but it continued to lag behind administrative projections. The Office of Rural Engineering was swamped with requests for *remembrement*, and while the state consistently raised its *remembrement* targets, it failed to provide enough personnel and funding to execute the operations.[7] For example, the third plan called for the *remembrement* of 600,000 hectares per year, and allotted 800 million francs for the full five-year realization of this goal. According to Pierre Coutin, an agricultural economist with the Planning Office, this figure was 2,500 million francs short.[8] In the end, the total for 1959 was 335,000 hectares, and for 1960, just 268,000 hectares.[9]

The failure to achieve the ambitious goals of *remembrement* led to renewed debate on what might constitute a more effective approach to land reform. Union leaders, the minister of agriculture, and media outlets were all discussing the "land problem" (*problème foncier*). The problem was that French farms remained too small to be profitable. In a 1959 Ministry of Agriculture report commissioned by Prime Minister Michel Debré, it was revealed that 56 percent of all French farms were "marginal," meaning they were smaller than ten hectares. "In other words," the reported stated, "one-half of our farms must expand or disappear."[10] The findings of the report prompted Debré himself to declare publicly that improvements to the land reform program were essential in order to increase agricultural incomes and to prepare farmers for the common market.[11] The two major unions concurred. In 1960, the CNJA announced in its monthly publication that *remembrement* was the number one issue for many regions in France. One month later, the FNSEA declared that "*remembrement* must be recognized as the absolutely necessary improvement in assisting the all too numerous heavily parceled operations," and that it was "the necessary precondition for a profitable agricultural sector."[12] To be sure, the FNSEA was ultimately more interested in price supports and market mechanisms, given that its leadership base was drawn from already profitable and well-ordered operations. But the fact that the FNSEA recognized the importance of the land problem as a topic of national concern confirmed the importance of the issue.

Proposals for land reform varied from the conservative to the radical. Those, like Mayor Renauld, who viewed *remembrement* as a threat to property rights in fact wanted to dial back land reform efforts. Moreover, thanks to a lingering Third Republic ideology that posited land ownership as the backbone of social and political stability, many in the National Assembly hesitated to support policies that would diminish rates of ownership in rural France. This association between ownership and stability was not only espoused by certain administrators of the state, but was equally powerful within traditional farming communities. Rural sociologist Henri Mendras wrote that ownership was "the necessary condition of complete social and political independence," and that "whoever worked someone else's soil was always, in one way or another, the debtor—indeed, the servant—of the owner."[13] As Mendras saw it, property in the land was understood to be a means of maintaining political stability as well as economic and social autonomy.

On the other side of the debate, the modernizing members of the CNJA and Minister of Agriculture Edgard Pisani called for a fundamental reimagining of agricultural landholding. One of the most dynamic ministers of the postwar period, Pisani worked with passionate determination to improve the agricultural sector. He put forward plans that ranged from the improvement of tenant farming to the creation of joint-stock agricultural landholding associations, arguing that the best way to address the land problem was to eliminate the need for individual ownership altogether. For many, and especially for the members of the CNJA, investing in land was an inefficient allocation of limited financial resources. The cost of land had tripled during the previous decade and it was becoming increasingly difficult for young farmers to establish themselves on new lands—or for existing farmers to expand their operations.[14] Moreover, given that farmers were required to purchase heavy equipment and costly chemical inputs as part of the industrial ideal, there were fewer financial resources available for the acquisition of new lands. As Pisani later argued, "the capital assets required to purchase land very quickly become intolerable to the farmer who would prefer to allocate his funds toward his business capital rather than toward his land capital." Joint-stock associations would "allow the farmer to avoid devoting the bulk of his resources to buying land."[15] If farmers could redirect those funds toward purchasing updated equipment and chemical inputs, they could improve both productivity and labor conditions.

The land problem was not limited to France. Much of western Europe was attempting to rationalize agricultural landholding structures to one degree or another. In 1959, the OEEC published a report titled *The Small Family Farm: A European Problem; Methods for Creating Viable Units*, in which the land problem was studied in all of western Europe. When compared to regional standards, France, with 53 percent of its farms classified as unviable, was fairly average, and roughly on par with Germany and Ireland. Not surprisingly, Italy topped the list with 64 percent, and the Danes did relatively well with just 15 to 20 percent.[16]

But France was the only western European nation that was building an entire agricultural program around the assumption that it would beat these numbers and succeed in becoming the region's breadbasket. To say that these assumptions were ambitious would be a massive understatement. As a consequence, the stakes were much higher for France when it came to creating profitable farms. As was explained in *La France Agricole*, "The possibility of exporting goods . . . is clearly influenced in large part by production costs. And as part of these production costs, the landholding structures of farming operations determine the degree to which modern agricultural equipment can be employed profitably."[17] Without well-structured farms, France would miss its opportunity to take advantage of the common market, and to use its agricultural sector to buttress a modern and globally relevant economy.

Forcing the Issue

While agricultural policy under the Fourth Republic had advanced in fits and starts, under the newly minted Fifth Republic, industrialization in the farm sector was pursued with a singular determination. In the late 1950s, with the EEC in place and deadlines looming for the removal of trade barriers, French farmers were under added pressure to meet the standards of viability. Fifty-six percent of all French farms were still smaller than ten hectares, the very lowest bar for viability.[18] Farmers called in vain for more vigorous land reform, for more technical training in the new industrial methods, and for better tax breaks on necessary farm inputs such as fertilizer and gasoline. Constrained by lagging incomes, making it impossible to invest in new materials on their own, the only way for most farmers to move forward was to take on even more debt.

The pressure on small-scale producers was particularly intense. The industrialization of the farm sector that had begun a decade earlier called for economies of scale. Moving goods to foreign markets required larger distribution systems, which in turn required larger producers in order to operate efficiently. With the common market promising to provide France with a major opportunity for growth, there was little room in state plans for farmers who failed to expand. Indeed, the price support system that lay at the foundation of the CAP favored large-scale cereal producers, while smaller-scale dairy and poultry operations were left to fend for themselves. As a result, when the common market was lauded as a solution to the farm problem, small producers remained skeptical. The threat of European competition to these growers in particular was the focus of a 1960 article that appeared in *L'Express*. The article stated that whereas hens in France typically produced 110 eggs per year, German and Dutch hens, thanks to the widespread use of artificial incubation, respectively produced 134 and 200, almost twice as many.[19] Small producers in France had been calling for assistance with new methods such as artificial incubation, but the Fourth Republic had consistently failed to provide the financial assistance and educational resources necessary to adopt the new techniques of industrial agriculture. As negotiations for integration progressed, small-holders struggled to survive the stresses of a relentless modernization program that was aimed at dominating European markets.

The state was equally under pressure. With government finances in disarray, and a farm sector that remained overly backward, the newly elected de Gaulle was hoping to force modernization without having to pay for it.

His first move was to eliminate agricultural price indexing, a measure that he hoped would provide farmers with an incentive to get their accounts in order. But the plan failed and the timing could not have been worse. In 1960, violent demonstrations broke out in Amiens (Somme) following the annual general meeting of the FNSEA. Twenty-five thousand farmers filled the streets. Many threw eggs, tomatoes, and rocks at the police. One group of farmers held up a sign that read, "Gauls for certain; Gaullists not certain; Gaul-ested, it's certain."[20] Others called attention to the seriousness of their purpose by drawing parallels between themselves and the insurgent French in Algeria, suggesting that French farmers were prepared to defy the state to ensure their survival.[21] Many chanted "Long live Massu!"— invoking the military leader who at the time was challenging the French state with his insistence on continuing the war in Algeria. Another farmer carried a placard that read, "Do I have to become a *fellagha* in order to get my own Constantine Plan?"[22] Public declarations of solidarity with the militants in Algeria intensified the threat of violence. In the end, the police responded with tear gas. One hundred farmers and fifty-five police officers were injured. And once again the nation was focused on the farm problem.

Social tensions at home were already running high following the escalation of hostilities in the Algerian War and the attendant collapse of the Fourth Republic. With angry French-Algerian extremists and an insubordinate military command on his hands, de Gaulle could hardly afford the kind of social and political disruption that would come with a full-blown peasant revolt. Moreover, as the majority of the protests were local and spontaneous, it was unclear that the FNSEA and CNJA would be able to fulfill their end of the neo-corporatist bargain and control their ranks. Michel Debatisse, the secretary-general of the CNJA, delivered a radio address in the spring of 1960 and declared: "There is a farm problem. This is certain. And this farm problem is the result of a profound crisis in our agricultural sector.... The immediate cause can be summarized in a word: debt. To modernize their operations, many farmers, especially young farmers, went into debt."[23] Farmers had been asked to modernize without being given the proper resources to do so. A decade later, they were struggling to pay the bills.

With the eruption of major agricultural disorder from 1959 through 1961, the state was forced to address the farm problem with a focus that had been lacking under the Fourth Republic.[24] Over the course of the following decade, until the publication of the game-changing Mansholt Plan and Vedel Report in 1968, the French state allocated an increasing number of resources to the agricultural sector. During this interval, the national budget for agriculture *quadrupled*.[25] Export subsidies helped farmers to move their goods to foreign markets. *Remembrement* was intensified, while new legislation was introduced to further land reform efforts. Older farmers were incentivized to cede their lands to ambitious young modernizers with an early retirement package. New loans were introduced. Tax breaks were created. In short, the ambitious plans for agriculture that Jean Monnet had set in motion were finally realized. By mid-decade, the industrial ideal was operating at full tilt and France was well on its way to becoming a major player in global agricultural trade.

Radicalizing *Remembrement*

In Parliament, Debré worked on devising new agricultural legislation that would quell the unrest and lead to long-lasting improvements for French farmers and their families. On April 25, 1960, the deputies gave their first reading of the proposed Orientation Laws, an omnibus package that would cover everything from agricultural education and extension to land reform and improvements to distribution networks. The laws were fiercely debated for months. Because they involved an amendment to property rights, land reforms in particular caused a lot of dissent. Communists, for instance, demanded a provision that would disallow any nonfarmer from purchasing agricultural land, a measure that they argued would keep land prices down and prevent farmland from becoming an instrument for capitalist speculation. Others, however, argued that the new laws threatened to upend the property rights that the revolution had worked so hard to secure.[26] It was not until August and the fourth reading of the proposed legislation that the National Assembly voted it into law, with 295 votes in favor and 175 against.[27]

The most controversial of the reforms put forth by the Orientation Laws was the creation of the Society for Developing and Settling Rural Land (Société d'aménagement foncier et d'établissement rural, or SAFER), a national network of regional land banks. Proposals to introduce an organization of this sort dated back to the early 1950s, when Forget had traveled to Sweden in 1951 to observe similar reforms in action.[28] Upon his return to France, he immediately began to advocate for the creation of an administrative body that would be responsible for managing agricultural lands. This new institution would be like his ANMR in that it would seek to maintain farm families on the land. But rather than being limited to moving families from overpopulated to underpopulated areas, the envisioned organization would have direct control over the real estate market. With the Orientation Laws, his ambitions were finally realized.[29]

That farmland remain affordable was key to the SAFER mandate. Prices rose as pressures to increase farm size mounted, creating widespread concern that only wealthier farmers would be able to acquire new lands. The SAFER was therefore intended "to fight against the all too widespread transformation of peasant and family property into capitalist ownership of the land."[30] Direct influence over the real estate market would enable the SAFER to curb speculation. Moreover, preventing prices from skyrocketing would allow younger and less established farmers to purchase lands. And it was these farmers, young and energetic, that the state assumed would be most inclined to modernize production and to contribute to the growth of the agricultural sector.

It is difficult to assess with any accuracy whether the SAFER ultimately proved successful in its efforts to curb speculation. Many different factors determined agricultural land prices, from crop type and location to the increasing competition from those seeking second homes in the country and farmers from EEC member states with more to spend than their French counterparts. And this is to say nothing of the vast regional differences in which these factors played out. Consequently, the task of assessing whether prices were affected by the SAFER is difficult, if not outright impossible. For while in certain cases it did manage to appeal inflated prices in court, overall land prices continued to rise throughout the boom years of the postwar period. From 1955 to 1980, the price per hectare of land increased at a rate twice that of agricultural revenues per hectare.[31] Looked at another way, between 1953 and 1976, the price of farmland averaged out over all of the departments of France rose by a factor of about ten.[32]

Organized regionally, each SAFER was established by the request of local agricultural representatives. Requests were then approved by the Ministry of Agriculture. Once set up, the regional office, which remained subject to centralized oversight, was responsible for monitoring the local real estate market in farmland. In practical terms, this meant that the SAFER acted as a land bank of sorts, purchasing lands, storing them, and then redistributing them to individual farmers who presented themselves as buyers. Farmers interested in acquiring lands from the SAFER submitted an application for candidacy. By going through the SAFER, rather than directly through the market, farmers were rewarded with a waiver for the fees tied to the transfer of property, and should the land in question require improvements (irrigation, repairs to buildings, etc.), these were subsidized by the state.

Through these redistributions and improvements, the SAFER was expected to advance the agenda for structural reform in the agricultural sector.

Each branch was composed of over a dozen shareholders, drawn from local agricultural associations.[33] These members constituted the general assembly and were responsible for providing a portion of the start-up money required to establish their regional branch.[34] To prevent lopsided decision making, however, no single shareholder was permitted to hold more than 5 percent of the organization.[35] The general assembly elected, from among their own ranks, the twelve members of the administrative council, which in turn oversaw general operations. Lastly, each SAFER was appointed two federal representatives, one from the Ministry of Agriculture and another from the Ministry of Finance. These representatives held veto powers over all SAFER decisions and were consulted on all transactions that involved sums larger than 60,000 francs.[36] Once the SAFER was approved and this administrative structure was in place, personnel closely monitored all real estate transactions involving agricultural lands in the area.

With respect to deciding which lands would be acquired, SAFER administrators were required to follow strict guidelines. The state was anxious about the relationship between land reform and property rights, and wanted to establish a stringent set of rules that would prevent local officials from running roughshod over the market in agricultural properties. Interventions were therefore prioritized as follows: (1) acquisitions linked to a *remembrement* project that was already under way, (2) acquisitions that would put uncultivated land into cultivation, and (3) lands acquired through the state-subsidized program of early retirement for older farmers.[37] Within this hierarchy, administrators would further prioritize (a) situations in which nonintervention would yield results contrary to the public interest, an ill-defined category that almost invariably produced bitter disagreements; and (b) situations in which they would be able to fulfill a previous obligation to a farmer (e.g., to a farmer who had given up holdings to advance the rationalization of lands).[38] Given that the three primary scenarios for intervention accounted for just a small portion of the lands being made available, more often than not committees were forced to grapple with the tricky question of what constituted the public interest and how best to intervene to ensure its fulfillment.

The Orientation Laws and the SAFER would only be effective if implemented widely, and through the fall and winter of 1960–61, the French state was preoccupied with other matters. The Algerian War raged on and an increasingly militant French-Algerian minority, determined to keep the war going at all costs, threatened to interfere with de Gaulle's plans for peace. With energies focused on the crisis in Algeria, the promises of the Orientation Laws fell by the wayside, resulting in yet another wave of agricultural protest in the summer of 1961.

The farmers who took to the streets in 1961 were exhausted by a decade's worth of unfulfilled promises. The failure of the state to follow through on the Orientation Laws was the last straw. In early June, thousands gathered with pitchforks and tractors on the outskirts of Morlaix (Finistère), and then invaded the subprefecture, sparking protests across all of Brittany and the rest of France. The immediate issue was that farmers were unable to sell their vegetables, dairy products, and wine at prices that would cover their costs of production, let alone provide them with a salary. Rather than sell at a loss, many farmers chose to dump their stocks in the streets, resulting in pavements slick with cream and highways jammed by piles of produce. Farmers also cut down telephone lines, parked tractors on major roads, and blocked important rail lines in an effort to disrupt the commutes and travel plans of urban consumers who were ignorant of their plight. Many of these protestors were young men who had just returned from military service in Algeria to take over the family farm. Armed with guerilla tactics and fully cognizant of what violence could achieve in the realm of politics, these farmers posed a serious threat to social and political stability. While the leaders of the FNSEA immediately moved in to control the actions, they nevertheless publicly supported the protestors, declaring that patient lobbying had failed to improve the farm problem and that direct action might prove more successful.[39]

Farmers were angry that they had broken themselves with debt to increase productivity, only to learn that there were insufficient outlets for their higher yields. The state had coerced them into expanding their operations, they had complied, and yet there was no reward. Especially in Brittany, where transportation infrastructure had yet to be updated, it was incredibly difficult for farmers to move their goods to urban, let alone foreign, markets. Bernard Lambert, a rising star on the agricultural Left, explained to L'Express that French farmers were tired of living at the margins of national life and tired of being pushed aside when it came to doling out the financial rewards of postwar economic growth.[40]

With tens of thousands of farmers taking to the streets and military generals taking the Algerian War into their own hands, the Fifth Republic was hovering on the brink of collapse. But as de Gaulle pushed forward with peace negotiations, honoring referenda and dodging assassination attempts, the Ministry of Agriculture fought to meet the demands of its farmers. Wiping the slate clean, Henri Rochereau was replaced by Pisani as head of the ministry. Pisani's first order of business was to bring substance to the Orientation Laws. In late July, just weeks after the termination of the Algerian War, the National Assembly voted 376 to 11 to approve his amendments to the 1960 legislation.[41] With the new amendments, substantial funds and institutional support were finally established to put into action the promises of 1960.

In the discussions leading up to the ratification of the original Orientation Laws, the question that raised the most debate had been whether or not to endow the SAFER with a right of preemption. Under this proposal, the SAFER would be allowed to preempt land sales and substitute itself for buyers on the free market. A challenge to property rights that initially proved too controversial, the right of preemption failed to garner enough votes to be included with the 1960 legislation. But in the first year following the introduction of the Orientation Laws, as protests raged and implementation lagged behind, the newly appointed Pisani began to wonder whether the SAFER had been given enough power to meet its objectives. Given that farmers could generally fetch higher prices for their lands on the open market than they could from the SAFER, advocates for the right of preemption argued that with preemptive powers, the SAFER would be able to acquire all those lands that were necessary to improving the landholding system and not just the lands that were openly offered to them. Without preemption, one of the primary objectives of the Orientation Laws, to improve the distribution of agricultural lands, would not be realized to its fullest extent.

With support from the militant modernizers of the CNJA, Pisani was able to get the right of preemption approved, albeit by the narrowest of margins. To exercise its new powers, each regional SAFER received detailed reports on regional land sales. Forwarded to their offices by local notaries, the reports included the name of the buyer, the agreed price, and information about the land in question. This notification was to be submitted at least two months before the expected date of sale.[42] The SAFER then had thirty days to decide whether it would exercise its right of preemption. If it decided in favor of acquiring the lands, it agreed to purchase them at the asking price listed in the original notification of sale. In some cases, however, if the asking price was deemed too high given market norms in the area, it could ask the courts to lower the price.[43]

Ultimately, the right of preemption was used sparingly. It came with a long list of exceptions, most notably sales within the immediate family and to contiguous neighbors. Moreover, given that acquisitions stemming from preemption frequently resulted in a formal complaint to the Ministry of Agriculture, if not a full-blown legal battle, the SAFER exercised this new right with discretion.

The Local Politics of Property Rights

Depending on one's perspective, the SAFER was either a godsend or a nightmare. While the regional land banks helped many farmers to improve their holdings, they also prevented many farmers from doing the same. Because farmland is a finite resource, the SAFER operated within a zero-sum universe. Deciding to give land to someone necessarily meant deciding not to give it to someone else. Every single decision they made produced winners and losers. As a result, it is impossible to evaluate the SAFER from a moral standpoint. What *is* clear, however, is that the SAFER exercised a tremendous amount of local power. Examining their decision-making processes not only reveals how national policy was put into practice by local actors; it also lays bare the often brutal local politics of backstabbing, one-upmanship, and narrow self-interest.

To argue their own cases, farmers often turned on each other. Unable to comprehend a particular SAFER redistribution or the general objectives of the agricultural reforms, they cited in their letters a particular set of characteristics that they believed made them more entitled—more in tune with the general interest—than their neighbors. Age and family status were the most commonly cited attributions, followed by military service. Farmers between the ages of twenty and fifty were certainly privileged by the SAFER, as it was believed that they would be more amenable to modern techniques than their older counterparts. Some of the plaintiffs, however, took this preference too close to heart. In a case that highlighted the arrogance of youth, Jacques Madalle, a twenty-two-year-old farmer in the Languedoc, complained to a local deputy that he had been traded in for the oldest possible candidate.[44] The chosen beneficiary, however, was forty-two years old, which, the Ministry of Agriculture explained, was hardly the age of retirement. Moreover, he had three children and was the owner of parcels contiguous to the ones in question.[45]

Madalle and the thousands of farmers who protested the decisions of the SAFER all shared a similar sense of entitlement. As French citizens, they believed that the SAFER existed to protect their rights and to further their interests. When these expectations were not met, they experienced a profound sense of betrayal. But the SAFER did not, in fact, exist to protect their rights and further their interests. The SAFER existed to curb speculation, to improve landholding patterns, and to facilitate access to lands for young farmers.

While most farmers, along with Madalle, felt powerless when up against the SAFER, others brazenly tried to game the new system. In 1966, the SAFER of Aveyron-Lot-Tarn sold thirty-six hectares to Mr. Guglielment for 87,906 francs. In 1972, just six years later, Mr. Guglielment attempted to sell the same lands for 180,000 francs. Locals and SAFER administrators alike were outraged by the sale. Guglielment, who had benefited from the lower prices and reduced administrative costs available through the SAFER, stood to make a hefty profit. Legally, there was no restriction after a preliminary five-year period on selling lands that had been purchased through the SAFER. The only recourse left available was to preempt the sale. The SAFER then sent the case to court to have the price reviewed, having appraised the property at just 140,000 francs. The director of the SAFER wrote to the Ministry of Agriculture to explain his decision to preempt in spite of the financial burden it would impose on the organization: "We decided to preempt and to request a revision of the purchase price to prevent a SAFER beneficiary, who had previously benefited from the financial advantages attached to our transactions, from profiting through speculation."[46] The director made it clear to the ministry that he would not allow beneficiaries to use the SAFER for their own financial gain.

Local union representatives regularly lent their weight to individual farmers seeking assistance from the SAFER. When the Ministry of Finance told the SAFER of Franche-Comté that it could not preempt a particular sale because of an exorbitant asking price, the departmental branch of the CNJA sent a letter of complaint to the local deputy. In the letter, union representatives stated that it was unacceptable that prices on the real estate market had prevented the SAFER from setting up a young farmer on new lands.[47] This complaint eventually made its way to the secretary of commerce, who wrote to the minister of agriculture that the SAFER had already been endowed with as much leeway as it could be given and that it simply could not preempt sales at such prices because doing so would be a tacit acceptance of speculative practices.[48] This circular reasoning certainly leaves something to be desired. If the SAFER was to curb speculation by interrupting sales and reviewing prices, disallowing such an action on the grounds that the prices were too high carried with it a certain amount of contradictory reasoning.

A similar case, in which the SAFER and local union representatives also resisted speculation, demonstrates how sellers quickly adapted to the new rules and discovered how to circumvent them. In Brittany, a small parcel of six hectares was slated to be sold for 154,000 francs, a price that local farmers, along with the SAFER, quickly decried as excessive. Upon receiving notification of the impending sale, the SAFER immediately requested that the local courts review the price. The seller, upon hearing of this, retracted the sale. Shortly thereafter, he put the land back on the market, but this time added a number of qualifications: the land would be sold at auction, which meant that the sale price would remain unknown until the final moment, every bidder would be required to submit to the notary a certified check in the amount of 20,000 francs to participate in the bidding, and lastly, the full price of the sale was to be paid in cash immediately after the auction.[49] The seller knew exactly to whom he wanted to sell his lands and organized the sale accordingly, making it virtually impossible for area farmers or the SAFER to purchase the lands instead.

In response to these conditions, members of the departmental chapter of the FNSEA stormed the sale in protest. When asked to comment by local media, the president of the union stated, "We are protesting the conditions of sale and are reaffirming our resolve to defend the principle that land ought to be sold at a price that corresponds to the economic value that it holds for farmers."[50] In full support of the FNSEA and the SAFER, the minister of agriculture expressed his anger over what had happened: "The case to which you have, quite rightly, drawn my attention, and which I especially deplore, illustrates the rise of this practice in certain regions where prices reached at auction hold no correspondence with the actual value of the soil, and in some cases, with the actual sum ultimately paid by the buyer."[51] Those in charge of the SAFER, along with local unions and the minister of agriculture himself, were all committed to preventing speculation on the market in farmland. But sellers were equally determined to maximize their profits—and as the final statement in the minister's letter suggests, often fudged the terms of sale, inflating prices at auction to keep the SAFER at bay, and then adjusting prices later.[52] In this particular instance, there was nothing the SAFER could do. The lands in question were acquired by the originally intended buyer—a nonfarmer with no intention of using the lands for agricultural purposes.

For many, the SAFER was an affront to the sanctity of the property rights that had been established with the revolution and with Napoleon's Civil Code. In a front-page article in *La France Agricole*, the SAFER was attacked for its favored position in the market: "As a privileged buyer, paying prices that are not freely determined, [the SAFER] eliminates not only the freedom of sellers, but also the freedom of buyers who might be willing to pay an equal, or even higher price."[53] The article went on to discuss the various rights and restrictions that the SAFER brought to the real estate market in agricultural lands, and while the ancien régime was not named outright, the constant references to "privilege" suggest that the SAFER was seen as a ghostly manifestation of the system of property rights that had predated the revolutionary abolition of feudalism.

Similar arguments were put forth by those buyers and sellers who were thwarted on the market. For example, plaintiff René Meyer wrote to the Ministry of Agriculture to protest the preemption of a recent purchase. He explained that he had been caring for an elderly woman of seventy-seven and had done favors for her and her family over the years. As a show of gratitude, and "above all because she was counting [on him] to watch over her in her final days and to care for her," she offered to sell him her lands at a very reasonable price. The SAFER preempted the sale. Outraged, Meyer protested that the preemption "served to deny the aged Madame Thevenot the means to ensure the effective care that she needs," and then concluded by stating, "if the law permits it, it would seem that the honor of French society does not."[54] Because, however, the SAFER had acted within the confines of the law, and had fulfilled its mandate by transferring the lands from a nonfarmer to a farmer, there was nothing that Meyer could do to appeal the case. His understanding of honor was irrelevant. As far as the SAFER was concerned, this transaction was about nothing more, or less, than guaranteeing access to agricultural lands for local farmers.

Even those farmers who were trying to sidestep the modernization mandate altogether were subject to the whims of preemption. Antistatist organic pioneer Raoul Lemaire purchased a nine-hectare parcel knowing that the adjacent farm of twenty-seven hectares was soon going to be put on the market. He had planned to combine both purchases into a single well-structured medium-sized farm.[55] When the larger parcel was brought to market, however, the SAFER preempted the sale and sold the land to someone else. Lemaire was furious. As an owner of an adjacent plot of land, he had thought that he could not be preempted. Indeed, legally speaking he should have been safe in this assumption. But the SAFER countered by arguing that Lemaire was too old to purchase the larger parcel, irrespective of his intentions to leave it to his sons. Local politics often played a decisive role in SAFER activities, and given Lemaire's high profile and his vocal opposition to state-mandated modernization, it is entirely possible that the SAFER thwarted his attempts to expand his organic holdings to make a political point.

Lemaire, characteristically, would not go down without a fight. In his letters to various authorities, he argued that as a family farmer who was trying to set up an inheritance for his sons, he should have enjoyed privileged status as a buyer. He was helping to keep young people on the land and to stave off the rural exodus.

Further complicating matters, because the two parcels had once previously been joined, there was no good access for the larger farm. Knowing full well that this was the case, the SAFER expropriated a portion of Lemaire's original purchase to build a road. Needless to say, if Lemaire was furious at the preemption, he was apoplectic at the expropriation. He had paid double the market rate for the nine-hectare plot, thinking that he would make up for the loss with the purchase of the larger parcel. Given that it had no access road, it would sell on the cheap. When the SAFER remunerated Lemaire for the expropriation, they paid him at the market rate, rather than at the rate he had actually paid.

Outraged that the state held the authority to suspend property rights and to interfere with his economic liberty, Lemaire immediately initiated legal proceedings. In a letter to his notary, he lamented his situation with his usual verbal flair: "I had at first believed that after buying this isolated farm . . . I would live a happy and quiet life, with nothing more to occupy me than my biological and phytogenetic research. Instead, I find myself in a viper's nest, relentlessly pursued by the technocratic monster, endowed with a power of diabolical force."[56] Lemaire tried in vain to fight the case, from the preemption to the expropriation. He even wrote to Minister of Cultural Affairs André Malraux, who had once expressed interest to a third party about a health organization to which Lemaire belonged. Using this connection as a justification to appeal to his authority, Lemaire pleaded his case and asked Malraux to intervene. Desperate letter-writing campaigns like this were all too common. Lemaire just happened to be better connected than the average farmer who fell victim to the right of preemption.

Thousands of letters were written by distressed farmers to the SAFER, the Ministry of Agriculture, senators, deputies, and often the president of the Republic himself. Most of them described devastating circumstances, and most of them fell on deaf ears. For example, Mr. Rives, a grape grower in Hérault, hoped that the SAFER would intervene in a local sale to help increase the size of his holdings. When he was refused, he wrote in protest to the Ministry of Agriculture: "Grape producer, married, the father of two small boys, this is for me and my family an essential question of vital importance to our future."[57] Mr. Rives captured in this one sentence what many farmers were feeling across the countryside—a sense of profound vulnerability.

While preemption was certainly the most publicly controversial of the SAFER actions, the routine operations of land redistribution were similarly met with regular complaint. The problem was that the SAFER needed to determine who, among a pool of applicants, would be deemed the priority candidate for receiving land. While there were guidelines for this process, more often than not, the final decision was based on more subjective criteria.

The technical committee of each regional SAFER was, like the shareholding base, composed of departmental administrators and representatives from the major agricultural organizations, and was charged with the task of meeting on a regular basis to decide how to redistribute the acquisitions. Serving as liaisons between the farmers and the superstructure of the SAFER, they then made recommendations to the administrative council. Determining who qualified as a priority candidate involved a complicated, though usually standardized, calculus. Farmers whose land had been expropriated by the state for public works (e.g., highways, airports, and urban expansion) were usually given first consideration. Next were those farmers who agreed to trade in their own lands in exchange for new consolidated farms. This scenario typically involved having a farmer give up dispersed plots, which could then be used to improve the distribution of several neighboring farms, in exchange for an already well-structured operation elsewhere in the county. The final two priority recipients were (1) tenants who lost their farms due to the owner's right of repossession, which could be exercised at regular and predetermined intervals; and (2) young farmers who were working as paid labor, but who wished to set up their own operation.[58] If, however, several candidates from the above priority situations emerged, or if there were no priority cases, which accounted for the vast majority of the transactions effected by the SAFER, a more subjective set of criteria were then used to determine which farmer would be the beneficiary. For instance, the technical committee would discuss which candidate had the best chance of success with the new lands. This could come down to a professional distinction (e.g., the land in question was well suited to barley and of the three candidates, one farmer already produced barley). It could, however, be decided according to the farmer's personal situation. The technical committee might decide, for example, that one farmer had a better work ethic than another farmer, a decision that generally prompted an official complaint from the farmer who was passed over.

In one case, a farmer in the Alps wished to acquire lands in Languedoc and submitted an application to the SAFER. Given that those administering the land he wanted to purchase did not know the farmer personally, they contacted the SAFER offices in the farmer's home region. What they learned quickly put an end to the farmer's candidacy: he was apparently a well-known polygamist. When later asked by higher authorities, with whom the reported polygamist had filed a complaint, why he had not been chosen, the SAFER of Languedoc-Roussillon replied that he "did not possess the required moral characteristics (his polygamy being too well known)."[59] That the SAFER insisted on finding out about the character of this applicant, rather than simply evaluating his candidacy based on the facts presented in his application (e.g., farming experience, family situation, age), suggests that deciding who would have the best chance of success was sometimes based on subjective moral judgments rather than professional merits.

What is clear from the archives, however, is that these decisions were almost always carried out according to a strict and precise interpretation of the SAFER mandate. Complaints, while understandable and often emotionally compelling, were very rarely justified by the letter of the law. Jean-Maurice Duvernoy, for example, a tenant farmer in Burgundy, found himself without a farm when his landlady passed away and, several years later, SAFER administrators set their sights on her former holdings. Duvernoy had begun working the widow Delechenault's land in 1965, and when she died in 1970 without an heir, her title was passed to the Public Lands Administration. Duvernoy continued to work the land and settled his yearly tenant accounts with its local office. Once the SAFER decided that it was interested in the land, however, Duvernoy was asked to produce a copy of his lease. It was then revealed that Duvernoy did not have a lease, but rather had relied on a verbal agreement with the widow Delechenault, which prompted the SAFER to declare that Duvernoy's occupation of the land was "precarious and liable to annulment." The farm was subsequently purchased. Duvernoy put himself forward as a candidate, but was passed over in favor of someone else. After seven years of investing his labor and resources into this farm, it was given to someone else because of a legal oversight—he had entered into a verbal agreement rather than an official lease. Legally, the SAFER was perfectly within its rights to transfer Duvernoy's farm.[60]

The act of choosing one farmer over another, however noble the intentions, necessarily ended for many in heartbreak. But saving individual farmers from the cutthroat demands of modernization was never part of the agenda. Saving the agricultural sector as a *whole*, and preparing it for global domination, was the real objective. Some politicians tried to paper over this reality by promising to protect small producers, or more strategically, by promising to protect the ill-defined "family farm." Others were more honest about the war of attrition that was taking place in the countryside. The CNJA, for example, was straightforward about the fact that many farmers would have to be put out of business to free up enough land to make the surviving operations viable. The SAFER, more so than any other vehicle for modernization, embodied this ruthlessness. It was a radical institution endowed with the power to determine at the local level who would and who would not be granted access to the most fundamental of agricultural inputs— the land itself.

While almost eleven million hectares had undergone *remembrement* by the end of the 1970s—one-third of all agricultural lands in France—the SAFER necessarily traded in smaller numbers. For while each act of *remembrement* affected an entire county, each act of redistribution effected by the SAFER involved just a few parcels. This is perhaps one of the reasons the SAFER has been neglected as an important factor in the postwar industrialization of French agriculture—the statistical results of its efforts, when read out of context, appear less impressive than those of *remembrement*. But the SAFER dealt only with lands that found their way to the real estate market—a small fraction of the total. Typically, roughly 600,000 hectares were put on the market every year, but the SAFER did not have access to all of them. Because of its limitations, it could not interfere with sales involving family members, neighbors, or expropriated farmers, to cite several of many exceptions. By the end of the 1970s, however, the SAFER had nevertheless managed to acquire roughly one million hectares, installing 6,800 new farmers and expanding the holdings of an additional 100,000.

While high hopes at the start of the 1960s had expected more, one can hardly argue that such results were insignificant. Moreover, beyond the statistical results, the impact of the SAFER on individual lives and communities ought not to be underestimated. Farmers lost their lands; inherited traditions were interrupted by new models of land tenure; and with *remembrement*, the property lines of entire counties were redrawn.

Safeguarding French Soil

Adding to these anxieties over who and who did not have access to farmland was the increasing porousness of borders within the EEC. When the Treaty of Rome was ratified in 1957, there were approximately fifty thousand foreign farmers living in France, cultivating an estimated one million hectares.[61] By the end of the decade, a steady increase in those numbers caused many in the agricultural sector to worry that native French farmers would be priced out of the real estate market, and that the identity of true France would be compromised by the arrival of foreigners. While agricultural land was increasingly scarce in France, the situation was much worse in neighboring member-states. The average hectare in France was typically three to four times less expensive than the average hectare in Germany, Belgium, and the Netherlands.[62] Moreover, France was much less dense than its neighbors, with just 81 inhabitants per square kilometer, compared with 205 in Germany, 296 in Belgium, and 358 in the Netherlands.[63] With its comparatively affordable prices and abundant supply of land, France provided an opportunity to continue farming when options at home had run out.

Agricultural interests were quick to express concern about the presence of these foreign buyers. In a letter written in 1962 to Prime Minister Georges Pompidou, syndical leaders Debatisse and Marcel Deneux urged the state to defend the interests of its native farmers: "Finally, the population-density map of the common-market countries makes evident that France is a pseudodesert, to which our densely populated neighbors have turned their eyes. It seems to us, therefore, that you ought to do for French farmers what our neighbors will do for their own nationals when they send them over to our land."[64] Characterizing the political leaders of fellow EEC member-states as opportunists plotting to send off their farmers to invade rural France, Debatisse and Deneux lobbied for increased state aid to the agricultural sector. They pointed out that farmers in neighboring EEC countries could rely on loans that were ten times the size of those offered to French farmers.[65] With such a disparity in levels of start-up capital, French farmers simply would not be able to compete with member-state buyers. The social desertification of rural France had rendered the nation vulnerable to invasion. But rather than an attack of cannon fire or trench warfare, this incursion would be mounted on the open market.

While full EEC citizenship was not established until 1992 with the Maastricht Treaty, intracommunity movement was first mandated by the Treaty of Rome. Title 3 (Free Movement of Persons, Services, and Capital) included provisions for the right of establishment of member-state citizens, and article 43 of chapter 2 stated, "Restrictions on the freedom of establishment of nationals of a member-state in the territory of another member-state shall be prohibited."[66] The removal of obstacles to intracommunity movement within the agricultural sector proceeded apace. In 1962, member-state farmers were granted the right to establish themselves on French agricultural lands that had been abandoned or uncultivated for at least two years. In 1966, they were given the right to take up agricultural leases, and by 1968, they had been given access to credit, cooperative membership, and French agricultural subsidies.[67] This steady elimination of hindrances to intracommunity border crossing caused an equally steady disquiet within the agricultural sector.

Objections to the arrival of non-French farmers dovetailed with an ongoing discourse that raised questions about citizenship, the boundaries of the nation, and the meaning of the French landscape. The provision in the Treaty of Rome that denied the priority of French citizens to occupy French territory threatened the stability of the physical landscape, as well as the cultural and political systems that mediated it. As the EEC developed and as "Europe" became an entity unto itself, the specificity of what constituted "France" became increasingly important. At its most basic level, France, as a meaningful signifier, referred to the territory occupied by French citizens and administered by French government.

This problem of definition was further exacerbated by the war in Algeria and by decolonization more broadly. While European integration conceptually altered national borders, the end of empire physically transformed the borders of France. Moreover, arrivals from North Africa similarly threatened to increase competition for farmland. French Algerians were repatriated to the metropole, and as many of them were farmers, they settled in rural France. With repatriation benefits from the state, they were often able to outbid locals for agricultural land. While the arrival of a French Algerian was certainly greeted with less hostility than the arrival of a German, this new presence on the landscape was nevertheless a source of concern. Native French farmers worried that they would be priced out of their communities by these outsiders who benefited from superior state assistance.[68]

This political context, in which the sovereignty of the nation-state was in flux, when coupled with rural depopulation, led many to question the very meaning of what constituted France. Could the French landscape still be French if it was farmed by Germans or Belgians? And how would French farmers imagine their relationship to the state if non-French farmers were equally entitled to benefits that they had in the past held exclusively? Surely, understanding the rights and responsibilities of citizenship has something to do with preferential entitlements meted out by the state. What happens to this understanding when such entitlements are shared across national lines?

In an early example of this discussion, *Paysans* featured a discussion of European integration and the free movement of member-state citizens.[69] The article, published in 1959, looked upon the recent creation of the common market as yet another obstacle to the ideal occupation of the French landscape. Given that the journal's treatment of European integration had otherwise been almost entirely positive, with articles emphasizing the economic possibilities that an expanded consumer base would bring to French producers, its unequivocal stance against the free movement of member-state farmers was all the more arresting. Although Europeans were more than welcome, in fact encouraged, to buy French agricultural products on the common market, they were decidedly not welcome to install themselves on French soil.

Anxious about the availability of farms for the next generation of young farmers eager to establish their own operations, the article expressed concern that competition from foreign buyers with larger pocketbooks would price out local candidates. The article went on to quote Forget, who had devoted most of the decade to fighting to keep French farmers on French land, and who therefore expressed a profound disquiet at the prospect of having non-French farmers labor on French soil: "We, and many more along with us, must be concerned about the adoption in our country of all measures aimed at settling French people and French families in our underdeveloped regions, and we must declare this problem as urgent, which if left unresolved, risks inciting an unreasonable and worrisome influx of foreign families and workers into France."[70] For Forget, the occupation of French land by anybody other than the French themselves was construed as "unreasonable" and "worrisome"—a threat to the very survival of French farming. And given the opportunities for land acquisition that were being opened up by the rural exodus and "la France du vide," he sought to use the ANMR to fill these gaps with French families.

Forget's approach to the ownership and occupation of French farmlands was complicated. As one of the architects of the SAFER, he argued that ownership of the land ought to be understood in economically rational terms. Land was a tool of production, intended to service the needs of farmers, rather than a material embodiment of ancestral heritage. Thinking in these terms would allow farmers, freed from emotional attachments to the land, to exchange lands to maximize efficiency. At the same time, however, his remarks regarding the occupation of French lands by non-French farmers suggest that his understanding of farmland did indeed extend beyond the economically rational and into the symbolic.

Established in the midst of growing apprehension regarding European integration, and conceived of by Forget, who openly expressed deep-seated fears that French lands would be occupied by non-French farmers, the SAFER was very much the product of nationalist designs to maintain control over the French landscape. Better *aménagement du territoire* at home would provide protections against the greater purchasing power of member-state citizens in search of farmland. It would also reinforce the sovereignty of the state over its own territory. At a time when both colonial wars and European integration questioned the territorial authority of the metropole, the SAFER provided the state with an arena in which it could exercise this territorial authority with unrestricted power.

While devising the rules and regulations that would govern the SAFER, policymakers worried openly about how the dissolution of borders between EEC member-states would affect their plans.[71] To be sure, the policymakers behind French land reform could not legally discriminate against EEC farmers, but there was an unmistakable commitment to safeguarding French farmland for the French. Indeed, when asked during a press conference whether the right of preemption that had been bestowed upon the SAFER would come into conflict with the common market and its provision for the free circulation of persons and capital, Minister of Agriculture Pisani responded that the primary objectives of the SAFER were twofold: to prevent wealthy buyers from monopolizing the land market and to guarantee access to well-structured holdings for family farmers.[72] With respect to EEC citizens seeking to buy property in France, stated Pisani, they would be treated in the same way that French candidates from outside the region were treated.[73] Given that nonlocal candidates were actually treated quite poorly—or at least were at the bottom of the list in terms of priority— Pisani's statement suggested that while France would do everything to abide by the letter of the law as established by the Treaty of Rome, the SAFER would in fact attempt to make it very difficult for foreign buyers to acquire agricultural lands.

Complaints regarding the acquisition of farmlands by member-state buyers emerged as soon as the SAFER was operational. German buyers in particular were singled out as threats to the French market, both in letters of complaint and in the press. Yet given that Italians and Belgians were purchasing lands at three and five times the rate, respectively, singling out German buyers likely had more to do with the memory of the occupation than it did with actual rates of acquisition.[74] In a letter to the Ministry of Agriculture, one farmer, who was having trouble acquiring lands of his own for lack of financial resources, wrote, "What angers me most is that the Germans, who destroyed my family, can buy land on our soil, and me, the father of six children, I will have to work as a servant for them in their new homes."[75] For this farmer, the horror of the occupation was being reenacted all over again, as he envisioned being forced to work for Germans on French lands because he could not purchase holdings of his own. This farmer was not alone in harboring resentment toward Germans who sought to relocate to France. In all cases regarding foreign buyers, there was a sense among French farmers of being entitled to French lands. Any loss of land to non-French buyers was construed as a breach of this entitlement. In cases involving German buyers, these claims were all the more forcefully articulated, as any suggestion that a German might reside on French soil immediately called to mind memories of the Second World War and the occupation.

Within the first year of its existence, the SAFER of Centre faced numerous complaints that lands in the region were being bought up by Germans. Jean-Paul Jaloux, owner of the Ferme Frutière de Montrésor in Indre-et-Loire, expressed concern over the number of Germans in the area and wrote that one in particular had managed to acquire an especially attractive holding. He then asked why the SAFER had not intervened to preempt the sale and that in this case, surely, the right of preemption would have been justified.[76] Similar letters were sent to the SAFER by the departmental offices of the two major agricultural syndicates—the letters were actually identical copies printed on the respective letterheads of each union, suggesting the development of a concerted campaign to keep Germans from acquiring lands in the region. The syndicates cautioned that farmers in the area were angry about the acquisition of large holdings by German buyers, who were routinely paying twice the market value for these lands. Such practices were driving land prices up and making it more difficult for French farmers to compete.[77] Given that one of the mandates of the SAFER was to prevent speculation in the agricultural land market, it was assumed that the organization should step in to prevent member-state buyers from distorting the market.

Unsure of how to handle these complaints, the director of the SAFER of Centre wrote to the Ministry of Agriculture to ask for guidance. Writing that the agricultural syndicates, as well as the ANMR, had all expressed concern over the presence of Germans in the area, the director explained that the SAFER simply could not preempt sales at the prices being paid by German buyers. He then explained that in one instance, the SAFER had assessed a holding at 1.5 million francs and had made an offer accordingly. A German buyer, however, had offered twice that. It was therefore no surprise to the director that he had yet to hear from the seller.[78] The response of the Ministry of Agriculture is absent in the archives. But from the continued incidences of complaints regarding German buyers, one can surmise that the ministry failed to address the issue adequately.

Agricultural leaders such as Debatisse, Forget, and the administrators of the SAFER presented the threat of foreign buyers most immediately in economic and material terms, arguing that foreign buyers would drive up prices and make it harder for French farmers to expand or acquire holdings. But their words gestured beyond the scope of the market. In this respect, anxiety over land prices, prices that would have presumably risen at comparable levels should the competition have been limited to French buyers (for there was no shortage of wealthy large-scale producers in search of expansion), functioned more as a symptom of a larger crisis than as a direct reflection of reality. The common market had arrived, and while the nebulous process of political negotiations that took place hundreds of miles away remained distant to the daily lives of most French farmers, the arrival in their counties of a German or a Belgian provided a concrete target for their fears and worries. In this respect, their discourse extended past the limit of strictly material concerns, and toward a more ephemeral, and somehow infinitely more troubling danger. Bound up in this discussion was the suggestion that nothing short of national sovereignty and the basis of citizenship were ultimately at stake.

The Broken Dreams of European Integration

As policy changes were put into place and the common market slowly came into being, the results of the Orientation Laws and European integration were laid bare. Far from having fulfilled earlier promises to benefit the agricultural sector universally, the big changes of the 1960s, just like the small changes of the 1950s, tended to favor disproportionately those who were already ahead of the competition. Once again, the majority of farmers were unable to put their hands on the financial and material resources necessary to meet the standards of viability. From 1960 through 1967, a full one hundred and sixty thousand French men and women left the countryside every single year.[79]

Looking back on the Orientation Laws, the president of the Crédit Agricole of the Loire lamented that state promises had fallen short. Not enough had changed compared with what had been envisioned. At the beginning of the decade, with sweeping legislative changes, there was a hope that structural reforms would help smaller farmers to survive the modernization process, by way of expanding or retraining. But in the end, not enough financial assistance had been given to those institutions such as the SAFER that were charged with the task of carrying out these reforms.[80] And so the small-holders were no better off at the end of the 1960s than they had been a decade earlier.

A similar opinion, this time applied to the common market, was put forward by the CNJA at its 1968 congress. With agricultural revenues predicted to rise just 1 percent in the following year, it was clear that integration was not providing the dividends that farmers had been guaranteed: "One of the objectives of the Treaty of Rome was 'to assure a fair standard of living for the agricultural population.' But the results of the Common Agricultural Policy have not been equal to these propped-up hopes."[81] The gap between viability and nonviability persisted. Revenues for the large-scale producers of cereals and sugar beets continued to climb, while revenues for the small-scale producers of poultry and milk stagnated. The unrelenting focus on price supports, the number one policy priority of the all-powerful FNSEA, undermined any benefits that the SAFER and its peer organizations might have realized for the farmers who needed them most.

As individual farmers continued to struggle, however, agricultural exports had in fact grown so lucrative that the French began to refer to them as their "green gas." While OPEC (Organization of Petroleum Exporting Countries) dominated the global oil market, France was staking its claim in the global food market. Between 1962 and 1967, French agricultural exports, as a percentage of total exports, had risen from 14 to 20 percent, while agricultural exports to the common market had risen by a factor of eight.[82] In comparison, the increase for Belgium had been a factor of just 4.2 and for the Netherlands a mere 1.9. Pierre Pflimlin and Monnet had been right. Western Europe was hungry for French food products, and the French farm sector proved capable of meeting the demand. The ambitious objectives of postwar planners had actually been realized.

The disparity between this general success and the intensity of individual failures drove farmers back into the streets in 1967. While some protests were peaceful gatherings designed to garner the attention of both the state and the wider public, other protests turned violent. Across Ille-et-Vilaine, farmers protested that the small-scale producers had been left behind, sacrificed to the common market. Farmers carried banners representing dead pigs. Some carried the slogan "Dead in Geneva and buried in Brussels!" A local FNSEA representative explained: "Who did we sacrifice in Geneva and Brussels? The weak, the small-scale producers."[83] Protestors called for higher prices on pork and for better controls on the poultry market. In Redon, they marched to the subprefecture and started hurling eggs and dead chickens, products not subsidized by the CAP, and the police responded with tear gas grenades. Escalating the violence, farmers turned to rocks and beer bottles, and the police hit back with their truncheons. Widespread injuries were sustained on both sides.[84] Reporting on the violence, well-known journalist Jean-François de Virieu wrote in *Le Monde*: "It has all been a dream, carefully maintained for years by the government and the syndical leaders, and now it is falling apart: a dream that the commercial conquest of the common market would magically resolve the marketing problems of French production."[85] Realizing that they had never really been part of the plan, small producers throughout the country began to turn their backs on the state that had falsely promised to distribute its rewards across the entire sector.

How could it be that the small producers had been so wrong in placing their faith in the state and in their syndical leaders? As de Virieu rightly pointed out, agricultural leaders had been fudging the truth for decades, selling French farmers on a dream of prosperity that would be limited to the few who managed to survive the rigors of modernization. Although those formulating policy certainly knew the truth, they very rarely spoke about it in public. Because the FNSEA had opted at its founding to represent the farm sector as a whole, it spoke throughout the 1960s of how the Orientation Laws and the common market were going to rescue *all* French farmers from ailing incomes and insufficient outlets. And doubtless many of the leaders who made these promises hoped that they would be fulfilled. But the truth of the matter was that state policy encouraged a brutal war of attrition in which farmers were forced to battle each other for survival. Occasionally, political leaders would admit as much. In 1964, while engaged in a public debate with farm union leaders, Minister of Agriculture Pisani admitted: "However much this saddens me, we will not save all of the farms.

For decades, we went weeping all over the place that we would save the small farm, and in fact, we didn't. We didn't save the small farm and we haven't had the courage to admit it."[86] Pisani was always more ready than most officials to present the truth. That said, he is also on record for celebrating the family farm and the need to protect it at all costs. Political expediency sometimes interfered with transparency. In 1966, secretary-general of the CNJA Raoul Serieys made a similar statement to the press: "It is unreasonable to hide the small- and medium-sized farmers from the truth with dazzling solutions that will never be anything but mirages. It would be wrong to foster false hopes in those who are duty-bound to modernize."[87] Tacitly pointing the finger at his FNSEA colleagues who told their constituents that all would be saved, Serieys argued that it was better to prepare those who were going to lose than to let them unknowingly soldier on in the vain hope of success.

By the late 1960s, the truth was out. Neither the state nor the syndicates continued to speak of saving everyone. Operating at full tilt, the French agricultural juggernaut could no longer be sold as an equal-opportunity enterprise. Farmers consequently began looking to alternative means to maintain their livelihoods, from rural tourism to niche markets in quality and organic goods. Through the 1960s, both options developed substantially, the former as a state-sanctioned safeguard against the predicted fallout of agricultural modernization, and the latter as a grassroots response to the failings of state promises. By the end of the decade, the rebellious youth of the May uprisings were retreating to the countryside to take up organic farming, a life option that very well may not have presented itself if not for the continued efforts of their conservative forefathers.

CHAPTER FOUR

Tilting at the Windmills of Modernization, 1958–1968

> In France (and the problem is not limited to France), the chemical
> fertilizer industry, along with producers of other noxious chemicals,
> and especially synthetic pesticides derived from DDT and parathion,
> have unfurled, with the support of official agricultural channels,
> a growing propaganda campaign. But in the face of this official
> encouragement to use these poisons, so harmful to the life of the
> earth and all that it bears and nourishes, has emerged a veritable
> awakening of consciousness.
>
> —MATTÉO TAVERA, speech to the Soil Association, England
> (October 12, 1965)

Dreaming of owning his own farm, long before he became a major figure
in the French environmentalist movement, Pierre Rabhi moved from Paris
to the Ardèche in 1960. Born and raised in Algeria, Rabhi had married a
Parisian woman, Michèle, who shared his bucolic aspirations. But dreams
of farming were difficult to realize, even in an area that had been hit hard
by the rural exodus. Rabhi needed land, and to acquire land he needed either
money or credit. But he was poor and as a man with no experience in farming, he had no access to loans through the Crédit Agricole. Undeterred,
Rabhi saved up the money necessary to enroll in agricultural classes, and
then began work as a farmhand. With a certificate from the local training
center and three years of work experience, he would qualify for a low-
interest loan from the Crédit Agricole (3 percent over thirty years).[1]

While many Algerians were moving to France at the turn of the decade,
fleeing the war, most of them were settling on farms in the south, where
the climate was familiar. Moreover, the vast majority of these new arrivals
were *pieds-noirs*, the descendants of French colonial families. Rabhi, however, was born a Muslim to an Algerian family. He had dark skin. While he
did have contacts and supporters in the area, most notably Pierre Richard, an
early ecologist who had encouraged Rabhi to take up farming, he was nevertheless an outsider. As Rabhi himself recalled, he stood out in his classes:
"I am a stranger to them [his fellow students] in three different ways: by my
race, my age, and my origins." But Rabhi's status as a stranger provoked

curiosity more than enmity. As he explained: "I like them very much, and I am touched by the kindness that they have shown me. It is true that the head of the program sets the tone, and he seems to view my undertaking as a tribute to his rural way of life."[2] Rabhi's commitment to the land, and to rebuilding a community that had been decimated by out-migration, enabled him to build a life for himself in his new home.

Where Rabhi did come into conflict with the locals was on the subject of industrial farming. While disenchanted revolutionaries would flee to the countryside in droves after the collapse of the rebellion of 1968, in 1960 Rabhi belonged to a small band of outsiders, tilting at windmills, trying to farm organically when everyone else around them was practicing industrial methods. In his training courses, Rabhi was instructed in productivist methods, told to apply chemicals to the soil, and to treat animals with antibiotics. When Rabhi protested to one of his instructors that agriculture should be grounded in nature, the response was: "Nature is the insects, the caterpillars, the mushrooms that you scrape together for a harvest. You starve if you don't manage to order everything properly. As for chemical fertilizers, they have increased agricultural productivity by a factor of ten, and have surely proved their worth. It is not by conforming to the laws of nature that we will feed the millions of people who are dying of hunger."[3] The Malthusian counterargument to organic claims that only industrial agriculture could feed a growing population became a familiar refrain by the end of the decade, when the public media fretted about Paul Ehrlich's "population bomb." This fear of hunger in a growing world would persist through the end of the century and was often cited as a reason for why organic farming could never be anything more than a supplement to industrial production.

It would take Pierre and Michèle several years to establish themselves as farmers. He took on extra work restoring old houses, while she often stayed with family in urban areas where jobs were more abundant. Eventually, they became goat farmers and cheese producers, selling their goods at the local market. The revenue was meager. Rabhi continued to supplement his income with construction work, something that small-scale farmers across France were doing with increasing regularity. But by Rabhi's account, they were happy, happy to have realized their dreams of becoming farmers.

Rabhi's story is both exceptional and exemplary. It is exceptional in that he moved to the Ardèche with no farm experience long before the disillusioned youth of '68 followed suit; he was North African, and he chose to farm organically. Moreover, his story is exceptional because Pierre Rabhi, alongside Pierre Richard, went on to become one of the most well-known advocates of organic farming in France, publishing books detailing his experiences, speaking at the United Nations, educating future generations of organic farmers, and working as an activist to promote organic methods in North and West Africa.

These differences notwithstanding, there is much to Rabhi's story that is also exemplary. First, it demonstrates just how difficult it was to acquire land, even in areas that had suffered massive out-migration. Funds were hard to come by and the requirements at the Crédit Agricole were often hard to meet even for those who came from farm families. Moreover, Rabhi's poverty as a small-scale producer in a mountainous region was all too common. Just as both he and Michèle had to supplement their farm income with various other employments, it was becoming increasingly common for farm families to build multiple streams of income.

While Rabhi was a forerunner—a back-to-the-lander *avant la lettre*—by the end of the decade there would be thousands more like him. In the aftermath of the rebellions of 1968, young men and women fled the cities of France in search of an antidote to the evils of mass-consumer society. Together, they would rewrite the history of organic farming, transforming it into a leftist story of anticapitalist resistance.

WHILE THE MODERNIZATION machine was operating at full tilt through the 1960s, a countermovement continued to take shape. Organic farmers grew their numbers, expanded their organizations, and increased their presence on the market. Biodynamic producers likewise continued to expand, but they remained concentrated in the east and failed to gain the momentum of their organic counterparts. While the nation at large was contending with the consequences of European integration, from the in-migration of land-hungry neighbors to the continued financial hardship of the small-holders, the world of French organic agriculture continued to build connections across the globe. Workshops sponsored by both GABO and AFRAN were held throughout France. Visits were organized to tour organic farms abroad. Like-minded farmers the world over shared ideas through new publications and correspondence. A new national organization, the French Association for Organic Agriculture (Association française d'agriculture biologique, or AFAB), was created to replace the regional GABO.

As organic production continued to grow, mainstream press and agricultural organizations began to take notice. While it was not until the 1970s that the industrial and alternative ideals came into sustained contact, they slowly began to converge in the 1960s. Established agricultural publications were far from endorsing organic methods, but they did provide limited coverage of those farmers who had chosen to convert their operations. For instance, as early as 1960, a regional paper in western France published an article with the subheading "A New Method: Organic Farming," in which readers learned about a farmer who had converted in 1949. He maintained that organic farming required less water, reduced the incidence of disease among livestock, and nevertheless produced yields comparable to those of conventional agriculture.[4] By the end of the decade, another regional newspaper, this one in the southwest, was openly discussing reader demands that the paper devote more coverage to organic practices.[5]

Striking out on their own, Raoul Lemaire and Jean Boucher joined forces to codify an organic method and market the inputs necessary to its practice. For Boucher, coming up with a specific practice that organic adherents could follow would improve the ability of French farmers to resist the industrializing ethos of the state. Reflecting on the ills of industrial farming, he wrote: "An agriculture of profit is being realized, rather than an agriculture of health and prosperity. The great disaster of French agriculture, and the mistake of France in Africa and elsewhere is a 'nonfunctional' agricultural production that absolutely does not meet the needs of mankind. This agriculture is likewise incapable of guaranteeing the health of the urban consumer and the peasant family, and of assuring the long-term prosperity of the peasantry and the fertility of its land. This agriculture carries within it the seeds of its own destruction."[6] For Boucher, the stakes of coming up with a new method and reaching a wider audience with organic agriculture could not have been higher. State-mandated industrialization was harmful to the health of French consumers, financially burdensome for farmers, and toxic for the land. Boucher believed, perhaps naively, that these evils would eventually be made obvious and that the industrial farm system would collapse.

The Lemaire-Boucher Method became the most popular organic practice in France and the business boomed. Small producers in particular were keen to adopt the method as a means of bypassing state-mandated modernization and its increasingly stringent standards of viability. Lemaire's fierce antidirigisme and his public run-ins with the authorities appealed to smallholders who felt betrayed by the state. Extension agents for the new method explained to farmers that organic production could be just as profitable as industrial farming. Producers might witness a small dip in yields in the first few years after conversion, thanks to the rebalancing of the soils.

But the higher prices fetched for organic products would offset the lower yields. Moreover, after two or three years, productivity would start to rise and would continue to do so as the soil became richer and richer.

As business boomed, Lemaire sought to expand his commercial empire. His sons, Jean-François and Pierre-Bernard, grew the family business with the creation of La société de diffusion des produits Lemaire and the société des moulins de Jarry. The former was established to market organic products such as chocolate, crackers, and vegetables, whereas the latter was devoted to the production and marketing of flours based on the Lemaire-Boucher Method. The roster of Lemaire products would continue to grow through the 1960s, eventually including everything from bread and wine to cookies and juice.

This push to commercialize organic practices led to a split within the movement. André Louis and Mattéo Tavera wanted to keep commerce out of the program and strongly objected to the efforts of Lemaire and Boucher to expand their business through the channels of AFAB membership. Seceding from the newly established national organization, they established a national organization of their own: Nature and Progress (Nature et Progrès). While the Lemaire-Boucher Method accounted for the bulk of organic practitioners through the 1960s, Nature and Progress would go on to form the basis for the back-to-the-land movements of the following decade. The end result was a divided organic community with competing visions of how to bring alternative production and consumption practices to the nation, but a community that was nevertheless expanding in new directions.

Reaching a Wider Audience

The health of both the soil and of the consumer remained at the top of the organic agenda. With its expansion into marketing, AFRAN upped its efforts to sell consumers on the health benefits of organically produced food. In an open letter to the medical community, published in the association's *Sol-Alimentation-Santé*, Bas once again decried the fatigue, food sensitivities, and digestive trouble that were the result of the "application of technological progress to food production." He then added, "Once again, our civilization is at present subject to the laws of a 'politics of quantity' that seeks by all means possible to increase productivity at the deliberate expense of quality."[7] The industrial ideal, in its pursuit of productivity at all costs, was compromising consumer health. While calories were abundant, nutrition was inadequate. Turning instead to AFRAN-approved products would increase energy and digestive function, while improving overall well-being. Taking his message beyond the pages of the journal, Bas regularly evangelized in person with workshops on everything from healthy eating to how to make your own flour and bread.[8]

Similarly, when invited to give a talk at the national college of mechanics in Nantes, Boucher used the opportunity to argue that cancer rates were on the rise due to the increase in chemical farm inputs. Taking on an institution of mainstream higher learning, Boucher worked to convince his audience of the superiority of organic methods: "Organic agriculture is a doctrine of agronomy that is founded upon a respect for the laws of vegetable and animal life, and upon a reasoned approach to work that allows man to remain in accord with Creation, and to provide for his descendants a better land."[9] If the nation's farmers adopted organic farming, and aligned themselves with nature and with its creator, diseases such as cancer would subside. He closed his address by calling on the students and professors in the audience to join him in fixing the problems of industrial agriculture, by using their training to build new machines tailored to the needs of organic farming.

Drawing a link between cancer and chemically intensive food production was a common trope that persisted through the twentieth century. In an open letter to the minister of agriculture, published in his *La Vie Claire*, Henri-Charles Geffroy bitingly wrote: "Dear Mr. Minister, While you read this letter, two people in France will die of cancer and four of cardiac arrest. . . . A tragic situation for these six families. But even more tragic for *you*, because you are responsible for these six deaths, as you are for those that have preceded them and those that will follow in another ten minutes, and another, and another."[10] Holding the state responsible for the lives of its citizens, Geffroy then called on the minister to regulate the use of carcinogens in agriculture and to encourage the consumption of cancer-fighting foods. Highlighting the 20 percent tax on wholesale whole-wheat bread, Geffroy argued that consumers were forced to choose cancer-causing white bread because it was less expensive. The brown bread lining the shelves of his three hundred Vie Claire stores was inaccessible to consumers on a budget. A change in food-tax policy on the part of the state could remedy this situation and make healthy choices available to French citizens.

With a graphic portrayal of how animals were treated in industrial farming, a 1962 article in *Alimentation Normale*, the organization's new publication, attacked mainstream farming from a different angle altogether (see figure 11).

FIGURE 11 Industrial versus organic poultry production. *Source*: Fonds Raoul Lemaire, Archives municipales d'Angers, 42J 183 Association française pour une alimentation normale, 1955–1972, *Alimentation Normale*, no. 5 (October 1962): 7.

Rather than focusing on the health benefits of organic food, which is what the vast majority of the literature did, this article instead appealed to the sympathies of consumers, entreating them to make choices that would lead to better conditions for farm animals. The byline asked if the chicken of 1962 was a machine or a living animal. Using imagery to answer the question, photographic images of industrial and nonindustrial poultry production were shown in juxtaposition. In the left column, the life of a cooped-up factory hen was depicted in all of its caged misery, while in the right column her organic cousins frolicked in the open air. The text supplemented these images by revealing that factory-farmed chickens were medicated in order to withstand their unhygienic living quarters, and that to maximize productivity, the chickens were "doped" with artificial light and housed in such crowded conditions that they lived in a constant state of panic.[11]

What is most striking about this full-page comparison is the relevance that it would continue to carry into the twenty-first century. While the language of degeneration and civilization would slowly but surely fade from organic discourse, replaced by such terms as "natural" and "whole," this kind of imagery would remain. It is all too easy to read these early arguments for alternative agriculture in a sly ironic mode, laughing quietly at the magical elements of anthroposophy or taking objection to Lemaire's support for right-wing extremists. Similarly, it is tempting to dismiss these men as neo-fascist kooks, as interested in the purity of the French race as they were in healthy eating habits. But these pioneers were building a language and a set of images that would travel down through subsequent generations of critique. Moreover, much of what we find unsavory in the thinking of these pioneers has not disappeared as thoroughly as we would perhaps like to believe. The organic movement of the twenty-first century has been criticized for its elitism and for its lack of racial diversity. Anti-Semitic texts might have disappeared from the shelves of health food stores, but white people constituted the vast majority of organic consumers at the start of the new millennium.

The renegade ideas of organic pioneers were, in fits and starts, being adopted by a mainstream that was beginning to question the politics of productivity that had driven the machine of postwar economic growth. Drawing public attention to the potential dangers of industrially produced poultry, the widely read French daily *Le Figaro* revealed that an industrial producer who raised chickens in a battery farm to earn his living kept a separate clutch raised in the open air for household consumption. As he himself explained: "I produce free-range chickens and battery chickens.

Naturally, the battery chickens are for the market and the free-range are for my table."[12] That a producer of factory-farmed chickens refused to eat himself what he was sending to the market was a serious blow to conventional agriculture. The author of the article then expressed regret at having ridiculed those who warned against industrial farming: "We made fun of the consumers. We disputed the producers by maintaining that the removal of the wheat germ did nothing to diminish the organic content of our bread. We reoffended by arguing that it was possible to produce excellent affordable chicken in highly concentrated operations that relied on purchased feeds. And so were born veritable factories of poultry production."[13] Slowly but surely, the organic critique migrated to the mainstream press.

In an effort to get out in front of these public attacks, the Federation of Agricultural Industries (Fédération des industries alimentaires, or FIA) established a commission on healthy food and requested a meeting with AFRAN to determine whether the two organizations might be able to work together. In May of 1959, the producers' delegate to AFRAN met with the secretary-general of the FIA. Needless to say, the FIA had a lot of complaining to do about how industrially produced food was being portrayed by proponents of organic agriculture. The secretary-general accused AFRAN of taking just a few bad examples from the industrial sector and then presenting them to the public as emblematic of the whole of industrial food production. He also argued that AFRAN relied on the opinions of a few doctors and then presented these opinions as medical fact. The secretary-general finished by saying that he hoped the two organizations could work together, and that in doing so, AFRAN could prove itself to be a "scientific organization and not a movement of mystics and demagogues." Backhanded insults aside, the FIA was willing to forge a relationship with the proponents of organic agriculture to mitigate the damage of public attacks against industrial farming.[14]

As AFRAN continued to grow, and as interest in organic products increased, the organization stepped up its earlier efforts at marketing. In 1959, research into consumer awareness and preferences was conducted in the small northeastern city of Nancy (Meurthe-et-Moselle).[15] Researchers entered several area grocery stores that carried AFRAN products and interviewed forty female and ten male shoppers. Of these, forty-eight had heard that industrially produced food could be dangerous, and forty worried about the quality of their food. When asked about what specifically worried them, respondents named liver disease, cancer, and heart disease.

To be sure, these respondents had self-selected into a small group of French consumers who shopped at stores that sold organic goods. The goal of the study, however, was not to measure the general awareness of organic products. Researchers were interested rather in the degree to which AFRAN specifically was on the radar of concerned consumers. They were trying to judge how successful they had been in marketing the AFRAN brand. Of the fifty interviewed, only fifteen had heard of the label. Disappointed by this lack of brand familiarity, AFRAN engaged in a local publicity blitz. An informational meeting was put together and attended by one hundred local doctors and pharmacists. The regional press covered the meeting and published several follow-up articles on the subject of organic food and farming. Survey numbers rose after these efforts. But AFRAN continued to worry that the label risked failure if its public profile did not dramatically improve.[16]

In a similar effort to reach consumers, in a 1963 issue of the AFRAN bulletin, readers were exhorted to vote for organic at the grocery store. In language that would have resonated with twenty-first century foodies, the editors at AFRAN drew parallels between the marketplace and democratic politics: "Every purchase on the part [of the consumer] is analyzed, dissected, interpreted, classified, and registered on a punch card. Specialists then produce studies, publications, reports, films, television programs, publicity slogans, and consumer guidelines.... Whether we like it or not, whether we know it or not, our purchases will always be interpreted as the expression of a preference.... It is not just a sum of money that we are putting on the counter, it is a ballot indicating which candidate gets our vote."[17] AFRAN wanted to ensure that consumers understood their power, that the decisions they made at the grocery store were not just about consumer choice, but were likewise about national politics and agricultural policy. The article went on to warn readers that the stakes of this marketplace election could not be higher, that consumers held the power to make or break businesses and to determine the future of food production. This is precisely the sort of language that would survive the mainstreaming of the organic movement.

These early years of the association's existence reveal a keen awareness of what it would take to make the movement for organic agriculture work. Success would require cooperation between producers, distributors, and consumers. Internally, there was a lot of discussion about how to get the word out and about how to get products into stores. If French men and women did not buy these alternative products, for lack of awareness or for budgetary reasons, the AFRAN label would never make it. In other words, while the leaders of AFRAN often pedaled a dreamy idealism, informed by a Catholicism that valued purity, they also had a solid understanding of how to spread these ideas to the general public.[18] Their tactics were in fact so successful that they would persist through several social and food movements and survive into the twenty-first century.

Finding Method in the Magic

Lemaire operated according to a similar blend of ideological dogmatism and marketing savvy. Through the 1960s, the last full decade of his long life, he continued to agitate against the technocratic dirigisme of the French state and to develop his own brand of organic farming. His travails with the Fraud Bureau were far from over, and in addition to defending the integrity of his wheat varieties, Lemaire was now forced to answer for his new composting products. Lemaire was in such regular correspondence with the authorities, either to voice his dissatisfaction with the status quo or to respond to an accusation, that his archives include an entire series devoted to this correspondence: "Interactions with the authorities." His queries, however, were rarely met with a response, aside from the occasional form letter assuring him that the appropriate authorities were looking into whichever matter he had raised in his complaint: "Thank you very much for your letter. Rest assured that I am very much interested in the agricultural issues you have outlined and will give them my closest attention."[19] In spite of these stock responses, Lemaire forged on, convinced of the righteousness of his convictions.

In a letter to a like-minded colleague, M. G. Raquet, the director of the conservative agricultural journal *Le Progrès Agricole*, Lemaire likened his struggle against the government to that of the Dreyfusards, who in his youth had taken on military corruption and state-sanctioned anti-Semitism. Taking issue with the lopsided state support for conventional farmers, he borrowed from Emile Zola and penned his own "J'Accuse": "I accuse the totalitarian-technocratic dirigisme of being the cause of all of our hardships."[20] From keeping his wheat off the market to subsidizing the farmers who produced approved wheat varieties, the state interfered with Lemaire's ability to produce and market his goods. That Lemaire, whose own record on racial politics was far from unquestionable, would call upon the language of Zola in his case against the anti-Semitic persecution of Alfred Dreyfus, is yet another testament to both the omnivorousness of his politics and his

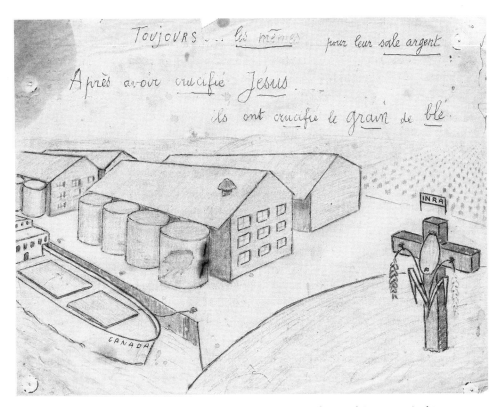

Toujours ... les mêmes pour leur sale argent ;

Après avoir crucifié Jésus ...

... ils ont crucifié le grain de blé.

FIGURE 12 Crucifying the grain of wheat. *Source*: Fonds Raoul Lemaire, Archives municipales d'Angers, 42J 250 Dessins à caractère politique de Raoul Lemaire mettant en scène la sacrifice du grain de blé, l'action du SVB Lemaire contre l'INRA, l'ONIC, et l'AGPB, n.d.

single-minded conviction that nothing short of personal freedom was at stake in the battle against the machine of industrial farming.

Lemaire regularly added colorful marginalia to magazines, correspondence, and advertisements. He also had his son Jean-François draw several sketches that visually represented his deep antistatism. In one of the more striking examples of this work (see figure 12), Lemaire contradicts his appropriation of Zola's "J'Accuse" by drawing on an anti-Semitic trope, tacitly accusing the Louis-Dreyfus wheat conglomerate (no relation to Alfred Dreyfus) of being no better than the Jewish moneylenders who crucified Jesus. While Louis-Dreyfus is not named directly in the drawing, Lemaire railed against his power throughout his writings and correspondence. For Lemaire, Dreyfus and the French importation of wheat from abroad were synonymous. In the drawing, storage houses for grains stand alongside a barge marked "Canada," nodding to the fact that France imported high-quality wheat rather than producing its own. In an adjoining field stands a cross on which a sheaf of wheat has been crucified. In the background lies a planted field with a sign that reads "INRA," which is both the acronym for the wheat variety–regulating National Institute for Agricultural Research and a play on the usual "I.N.R.I." that one finds in depictions of the crucifixion. Across the top of the image, Lemaire Sr. himself brought together his religious faith and his thwarted commercial ambition: "Always . . . the same ones for their dirty money, after crucifying Jesus, they crucified the grain of wheat." The grain of wheat is here both literally the wheat that Lemaire could not sell *and* metaphorically the pure-of-heart Christian peasant producer crushed by capitalist Jewish moneylenders.

There is nothing subtle about this drawing. Lemaire had been angry since the 1930s about how wheat was regulated in France. His own varieties were barred from sale, while the incredibly successful Louis-Dreyfus company held a virtual monopoly, importing high-quality wheat from Canada and elsewhere and then selling it on the French market. A notoriously secretive company, Louis-Dreyfus was founded in the mid-nineteenth century alongside its American counterpart, Cargill, and rose to become one of the largest players in the global grain trade. Given the genuine lack of transparency in its dealings, and in the global grain trade more generally, Lemaire's anger and frustration must be read as something more than monomaniacal ravings. He was in fact never entirely off base. Instead, he was close enough to the industrial machine to know how it operated, but not close enough to bring it to a halt. That lack of agency drove him to ideological extremes.

Undaunted by his continued run-ins with the authorities, in the late 1950s Lemaire once again expanded his reach into the world of organic agriculture by developing a new soil treatment. Both he and Boucher had grown interested in lithothamnion, a natural compost harvested from the sea. Lithothamnion, also known as maerl, is a variety of lime-rich red algae. To use it as a fertilizer, which farmers in Brittany and in the British Isles had done for centuries, it was dredged from the sea floor, dried out, and then pulverized into a powder that could be applied to the soil. By the time of their discovery, Boucher was already in trouble with his superiors in his position as a plant inspector for the Ministry of Agriculture, largely because of his role in the founding of GABO. He had been transferred to Bordeaux shortly thereafter, where he spent a miserable year before resigning. Free from his government position, Boucher could pour all of his energies into this new project with Lemaire.[21] For several years, the two partners conducted experiments and gathered data, eventually coming up with what they called the Lemaire-Boucher Method.

Lemaire and Boucher viewed lithothamnion as nothing less than the miracle product that was going to free farmers from the chains of chemical inputs. In a letter to Boucher, Lemaire referred to lithothamnion in rapturous terms, writing that it was "the heaven-sent antidote that God has placed in our hands to combat the poisoning of the earth . . . and of mankind."[22] The calcified algae was already being sold on a small scale by a company in Brittany, but Lemaire and Boucher had bigger plans. By the early 1960s, Lemaire and Boucher had successfully scaled up the production of lithothamnion fertilizer, drying and pulverizing this "miracle" seaweed in commercial quantities at a factory in Morbihan. What they failed to appreciate, however, is that because it takes millennia for lithothamnion to form, it is a nonrenewable resource. Scaling up its extraction in the interest of organic farming would have deleterious environmental effects, as habitats for sea animals were destroyed and coral resources depleted.

It was not long before state regulators challenged Lemaire and Boucher.[23] In 1961, Lemaire was taken before the District Court of Angers by the Fraud Bureau for allegedly selling lithothamnion under false pretexts. The prosecution argued that Lemaire was at fault for claiming that it was "the remedy of remedies" and that it offered natural immunity against a host of ills. The defense argued that Lemaire had never stated that lithothamnion was a miracle remedy, that it would heal sick animals, or that it was a medicine in the medical sense of the term. The court acquitted Lemaire and declared that he had not defrauded anyone with his advertising claims about the quality of his merchandise.

Buoyed by the win, Lemaire and Boucher soldiered on. As business expanded, they dropped the price from sixty francs per ton to forty-five. Because Lemaire and Boucher viewed lithothamnion as the key to organic farming, and organic farming in turn as the key to national health and to winning independence from the state, making the product more affordable was essential to their broader struggle. They argued that farmers who found it difficult to modernize according to the state mandate had a sustainable alternative in the Lemaire-Boucher Method.[24] They broadcast this message throughout the countryside with a growing team of converts, many of them old Poujadist contacts, who worked on commission to spread the word. Lemaire and Boucher tended to attract small- and medium-sized farmers, most of whom worked in livestock-based polyculture, and whose operations were ill suited to modernization without huge investments of capital.[25] These types of operations tended to be located in the west, where Lemaire was based, and in the mountainous regions of the Jura and Massif Central. By 1964, there were 220 adherents, and their numbers continued to grow until peaking at 1,500 in 1971.[26]

In *La culture biologique et ses applications* (Organic agriculture and its applications), a small booklet published in 1965, Lemaire and Boucher laid out the new method in full.[27] They started with a Socratic question, "What is organic agriculture according to the Lemaire-Boucher Method?" And then answered: "A new agricultural method that is based on the latest and most promising discoveries in biology . . . that proscribes the use of all toxic substances . . . that brings together the goals of fertility and of health . . . that gives to the forces of Life a boundless faith." Colored by their shared Catholic devotion, the Lemaire-Boucher Method was presented as a mix of old-world purity and contemporary science. It respected the sanctity of the soil and of God's creation, but it was also new and modern.

That said, the science that Lemaire and Boucher deployed to argue for the superiority of lithothamnion was sometimes questionable. Particularly suspect was their belief in the process of biological transmutation, a process then recently "discovered" by the French outsider scientist and engineer Cotentin Louis Kervran. According to Kervran, one substance could become a different substance by way of a series of continuous internal nuclear reactions:

> After many observations, some of which go back to my childhood, I have come to the conclusion that a major property of matter has until now remained unrecognized, namely that in nature the phenomenon of transmutation occurs. One natural element can change into another. Such transmutation, once the derided dream of the old alchemist, is common practice today through the application of atomic energy. Atomic transmutation, however, requires enormous energy . . . and is incompatible with biological energy. Yet the evidence for biological transmutation is so overwhelming that it cannot be rejected.[28]

A biological science for the atomic age, transmutation was presented as evidence that the current science on molecular and nuclear forces could not alone explain the building blocks of life. The current science, however, begged to disagree. Kervran was summarily dismissed as a quack.

Not too far afield from Steiner's vitalist principles, Kervran's theory of transmutation found a natural home in the world of organic farming. Kervran became a regular contributor to Geffroy's *La Vie Claire*, and exercised a keen influence over the organic pioneers. Lemaire and Boucher believed that lithothamnion underwent a process of biological transmutation, transitioning from calcium into fertilizing potassium. As they explained to their prospective clients in their guidebook, "The membrane of the algae Lithothamniun Calcareum is mineralized and calcified and becomes very hard. The limestone that it contains is a form of dry solidified Magnesium that is dissolved by the sea water after a biological transmutation. . . . This transmuted substance then adapts to produce what is needed by the soil microbes and vegetable foliage."[29] While it was unlikely that lithothamnion would transmute into other nutrients, the notion that it would was hardly a far cry from Steiner's directive "to put manure into cow horns and bury them for an entire winter so that the manure could capture the Earth's etherizing and astralizing rays and be transformed into a powerful fertilizing force."[30] The early years of organic farming were as much about outlandish scientific theory as they were about practicing agriculture without the benefit of chemical inputs.

In the Ardèche, Pierre Rabhi experimented with all kinds of alternative approaches. The language that he used to describe his experience of trying out Steiner's methods with a friend sounds much like the language used by Kervran to describe transmutation: "Olivier and I were like two alchemists, at once sorcerers and Cartesians. We gathered the materials on a field: manure, organic waste of all kinds, all of which would be subjected to the *mutation*. The materials must be arranged in a trapezoidal formation with a two-meter base. The length can vary according to how much material you have. The pile must always be in direct contact with the earth. It can neither get dried out nor soaked by the rain."[31] Rabhi then added that he and Olivier created a control, gathering a separate pile of compost and not subjecting it to Steiner's guidelines. Yes, they carried some skepticism into the process, but they were nonetheless open to the possibility that vitalist forces could create superior fertilizers by drawing on the cosmic energies of the universe. It was a small step rather than a giant leap to accept that the soil was changing at an atomic level.

The leap of faith into transmutation notwithstanding, the actual practice of the Lemaire-Boucher Method was simple enough. Farmers would use the lithothamnion-based fertilizer, purchased through Lemaire and Boucher, as well as composts prepared at home with the manure of their livestock. They would not use any chemical inputs. In addition, they would partition their operations as follows: 20 percent forest, 35 percent pasture, 45 percent planted fields. The section of their guidebook on application was therefore short on practice and long on theoretical orientation. Farmers were told that the sea was a source of life and that while they were free to prepare their own organic composts, derived from manure, the Lemaire-Boucher compost was superior in every way. Lithothamnion would solve all of their problems. When applied to pastures, grasses and plants regrew more quickly; when fed to ailing animals, their illnesses abated; and when applied to manure, it not only deadened the smell and kept flies at bay, but also augmented its nutritive properties.[32] Yields would rise 15 to 30 percent. Fruits and vegetables would be more flavorful. Pests would disappear. Clearly, Lemaire and Boucher had not been intimidated by the original 1961 charge of false advertising.

While the sales pitch might smack of snake oil to twenty-first century readers, the method went on to become the most widespread organic practice in 1970s France. Lemaire and Boucher and their miracle compost from the sea were in fact responsible for converting a great many farmers to organic production. In 1972, one of them, Antoine de Saint Henis, published a practical guide to the Lemaire-Boucher Method. By way of introduction, he told his own conversion story. He had farmed 450 hectares in Morocco from 1950 to 1958, and during this time he became increasingly wary of the primary role played by chemical inputs. In 1958, his farm was visited by a blight "against which modern agronomy was powerless," and his entire harvest was damaged. Several years later, farming coffee plants in the Central African Republic, de Saint Henis was visited by a bark beetle infestation. To address the problem, a crop duster was used to spray the fields with the insecticide endrin. Seven of the fifteen cows that pastured on the edges of the coffee plant fields fell ill later that evening. The following morning, they were dead.

Upon returning to France in 1965, de Saint Henis found a position with the agricultural department of a petroleum company near Blois. His job was to market a product designed to prevent blights in strawberry plants. The product was harmful to humans and the packaging clearly indicated to farmers that their strawberries were not to be sold to consumers until after a sufficient period of time had elapsed since the application of these chemicals. But de Saint Henis suspected that the farmers ignored this warning, and the crisis of conscience that had begun the previous decade in Morocco finally came to a head.

Shortly thereafter he discovered the publication *Agriculture et Vie*, a monthly magazine that Lemaire's son, Pierre-Bernard, had founded in 1964. De Saint Henis quickly made arrangements to visit several organic farms in the area around Angers, where the Lemaire family was located. He then quit his job for the petroleum company and devoted himself to organic production. His *Guide pratique de culture biologique: Méthode Lemaire-Boucher* (A practical guide to organic farming: The Lemaire-Boucher Method) was therefore not simply an advertisement for the Lemaire-Boucher Method. It was a personal reckoning, a conversion narrative: "I have come a long way since, and it is with all of my heart that I offer this work for the consideration of organic farmers."[33]

De Saint Henis repeated much of what Lemaire and Boucher had written in their 1965 guide, but expanded on each point with greater detail. He argued that organic farming was a new method and not a traditionalist return to the past. He delved into the transmutation process and lauded Kervran for demonstrating that "life on Earth was connected to cosmic forces, and that these forces could be used to improve the vitality, the blight-resistance, and the yield of plants."[34] He appealed to farmers who were having trouble keeping up with the financial demands of industrial production: "The Lemaire-Boucher Method also has the advantage of being cost efficient, which in turn increases the profitability of your business."[35] De Saint Henis's conversion experience had turned him into a true believer and enthusiastic proselytizer for the Lemaire-Boucher Method.

Most significantly, de Saint Henis established an intellectual lineage for organic farming by offering short biographies of the men he deemed to be the major figures in its historical development. He began with the celebrated nineteenth-century physiologist Claude Bernard, who was a founder of experimental medicine and who, ironically, was very vocal in his disavowal of Steiner's vitalism. He was, however, very much interested in the human diet and its effect on health and well-being. De Saint Henis then moved on to the other nineteenth-century titan of French science, Louis Pasteur, before moving into the twentieth century with the vegetarian and naturist physician Paul Carton, Steiner, Howard, Kervran, and Lemaire and Boucher. Bridging the gap between mainstream and fringe science, de Saint Henis's genealogy of organic agriculture challenged the critics who dismissed the practice as reactionary. Lemaire, Boucher, and their followers believed that they were following in the footsteps of the greatest scientists that France had ever produced, and that their lithothamnion fertilizer was a revolutionary new product that would forever change the practice of farming.

The Movement Splinters

As the reach of organic agriculture continued to expand, the leadership of the previously regional GABO decided to reinvent the organization in 1961 as the national French Association for Organic Agriculture (Association française d'agriculture biologique, or AFAB). The association was led by the usual suspects: Boucher, Louis, Tavera, and Lemaire. A new journal was established, *AFAB*, to provide farmers with both practical and intellectual resources. By the end of the year, there were 141 members, and by the end of 1963, that number had more than doubled to 300.[36] Initially, membership was concentrated in the areas around Paris, the west, and the southwest. But with the new national scope of the association, informational meetings and farm demonstrations held throughout the country served to expand membership both numerically and geographically.

One such meeting took place in Saint Aubin (Côte d'Or) on the 17th of June in 1962, when twenty-nine people gathered at the farm of Mr. Pozzer. Ten of these twenty-nine were new to AFAB. Mr. Pozzer had converted his sixty-hectare farm to organic agriculture two years prior. He produced seventeen hectares of wheat, five of corn, and held fifteen milking cows, seven calves, and one bull. In the account of the meeting that appeared in *AFAB*, it was emphasized that his animals were in "perfect health." It was also revealed that the only off-farm fertilizer that Mr. Pozzer used was guano from Peru (otherwise, he prepared his own with manure and composted materials). But Mr. Pozzer was not without his own set of challenges. Earlier in the year, a section of alfalfa that had been treated with liquid manure was visited by an infestation of leaf beetles. The magazine used this opportunity to remind readers that "liquid manure is full of potassium oxide, which is a growth stimulant, unstable and pathogenic (we saw this before in 1961 on J. Lebastard's fodder beets). Liquid manure is made for compost, not for direct application."[37] Without extension agents in the field to explain these things to farmers who were converting to organic methods, missteps were bound to occur.

These informational meetings, as well as their summaries in the *AFAB*, were instrumental in building a knowledge base for organic farmers. While the new journal still featured the odd spiritual rant on the life forces of the soil, much of its content was devoted to the technical ins and outs of organic practices. Tips on everything from fertilizer to integrated pest management appeared in the *AFAB* pages. Different producers were profiled to discuss how they made the conversion, what challenges they faced, and how they fared with an alternative production model. On occasion, these methods were additionally contrasted to those being mandated by the state. In an early issue, Louis counseled readers on how to deal with an armyworm infestation with organic methods and took the Ministry of Agriculture to task for its recommendation that farmers rely on chemical treatments alone to eradicate the bugs.[38]

Through the 1960s, Louis continued his efforts to build organic farming in France. In addition to his involvement in AFAB, he dutifully responded to letters from interested farmers across the country with technical suggestions, workshop information, and words of encouragement.[39] But national boundaries hardly defined his efforts. In a letter to fellow traveler and friend Rich Hediger, Louis wrote, "I believe in effect that it is indispensable that we make contact with those abroad who see things as we do."[40] Letters came from as far afield as Brazil, Iran, New Zealand, and Madagascar, written by a wide variety of farmers seeking technical advice on how to convert their holdings to organic production.[41] Regionally, Louis continued to travel throughout western Europe, making regular trips to Italy, Switzerland, Germany, the Netherlands, Denmark, and Great Britain. He often traveled alone, driven by his own desire to learn everything that he could about these new methods, but he also made several trips as part of larger groups and organized tours, serving as a guide and instructor for traveling AFAB members.

In 1963, Louis helped to organize an AFAB trip to England to tour organic farms and to meet members of the Soil Association. It must be noted that these trips shared much in common with the state-mandated productivity missions to the United States. Large groups of delegates were sent abroad to tour successful farms and then shared their experiences with the wider agricultural community upon their return to France. Just as French corn producers visited Iowa to learn from the best, French organic farmers visited England to see how the Anglo-Saxon pioneers had deployed the discoveries of Howard and McCarrison to develop their own organic practices. In the *AFAB* write-up, coauthored by Louis and another participant, we learn that nineteen AFAB members, including Lemaire and Pozzer, participated in the trip. The group included farmers, engineers, agronomists, and strangely, one decorator. And while the group complained about the road food, they found the farm visits to be enlightening. The write-up included details on the farming practices of the three operations they visited and reflections on such things as the proper balance of cereals, animal husbandry, and the use of off-farm fertilizer.[42]

Ultimately, a major difference in approach between Louis and Lemaire caused a rift in the movement. The two did not see eye to eye on how best to approach the expansion of organic farming. Louis and Tavera were more committed to the intellectual foundations of the practice and devoted much of their time to corresponding with like-minded believers around the world. Lemaire and Boucher, however, were more committed to spreading the practice through France as quickly and as thoroughly as possible. If Louis was the intellectual idealist, Lemaire was the tireless pragmatist.

Specifically, Louis and Tavera criticized Lemaire and Boucher for being too focused on marketing lithothamnion. To be sure, the appearance of articles in *AFAB*, penned by Boucher, on the miraculous properties of lithothamnion constituted a conflict of interest. On the one hand, Boucher had a business stake in its market performance; on the other, AFAB was supposed to be an open organization in which members were free to practice a variety of methods. Moreover, Lemaire and Boucher had plans to expand their market beyond French borders, a move that angered many for its ecological implications—shipping long distances would require more fossil fuels and expansion would risk permanently depleting the supply of lithothamnion off the shores of Brittany.[43] Louis and Tavera argued that the AFAB should be free of the profit motive, that it should instead be a community of like-minded supporters of organic farming, brought together by common interest rather than commerce. While Lemaire and Boucher placed economic autonomy and freedom from the dirigiste state at the top of their priority list, Louis and Tavera believed instead that ecological balance should hold the place of primary importance in the movement.

These differences led Louis and Tavera to leave AFAB in 1964 and to found their own organization: Nature and Progress. They were then joined by André Birre and Dr. Jacques-William Bas. In a letter to a friend explaining his decision to secede, Louis made damning statements about Boucher and his "arrogant and intransigent" character, before adding that he suffered from a "total lack of rationality."[44] His words for Lemaire were no less biting:

> I can assure you, I have no sympathy for the Maison Lemaire, which I (having no commercial interests) reproach for pilfering its technico-commercial approach from that of its competitors [i.e., industrial agriculture], and for indiscriminately pushing the sale of its own [organic] products derived from pulverized lithothamnion. This is why, after initially finding ourselves in the same boat as the Maison

Lemaire, as part of AFAB, my friends and I have decided that we prefer to chart a course on our own with Nature and Progress and to spread the message of pure organic agriculture, free of all commercial interests.[45]

With little love lost between the two camps, the organic movement splintered in two.

Under Boucher and Lemaire, AFAB espoused a more conservative politics, while Nature and Progress evolved into an organization that appealed more to the liberal base of white-collar professionals and environmentalists that would go on to form the core of the organic market in the following decades. With the absence of the moderating force of those who went on to found Nature and Progress, AFAB took on the character of earlier organizations and emphasized the importance of fighting for physical and spiritual purity. In the first issue of the AFAB journal put out after the split, the goals and origins of the association were reinvented to come closer into line with these ideological leanings: "Our association of practicing farmers, founded in its original form in 1958, studies the deep-rooted causes of present-day degeneration: decreasing fertility; increasing parasitism in agriculture and in man; increasing production costs; economic disorder; and the rural exodus." Degeneration was once again a primary concern. And the solution to this ongoing problem was once again to be found in God. The end goal was articulated as a "genuine human development, inspired by the Christian faith, that will give rise to a new peasant elite, capable of defending rural life and liberty in the face of an invasive and destructive collectivism."[46] The importance of Catholicism to the organic movement was widely shared. Even Louis spoke of God in his correspondence. But for Lemaire and Boucher, a staunch Catholic, religion was at the center of their mission, a spiritual counterbalance to the institutional power of the state.

Louis and Tavera set Nature and Progress apart by emphasizing its noncommercial profile. In a promotional leaflet in which the differences between organic and industrial agriculture were explained, Louis and Tavera made a not-so-subtle point of distinguishing their own organization from that of Lemaire and Boucher: "Nature and Progress has nothing to sell you. This is concrete proof of its TOTAL independence. It is a totally impartial not-for-profit association. It has nothing to sell, but everything to give. Its only concern is the common interest of agricultural producers and the health of consumers."[47] Given how acrimonious the split within the organic movement had become, as evidenced by Louis's private correspondence, it is perhaps not a surprise that backhanded criticisms of Lemaire and his business ventures appeared in the new association's promotional material.

In addition to being adamantly noncommercial, Louis and Tavera wanted to make sure that anyone and everyone would feel welcome to join their new organization. Religion was still important to Louis and Tavera, but it hewed closer to a universalist spiritualism than a traditional Catholicism. Tavera wrote in the pages of the first issue of *Nature et Progrès* that the association would "welcome equally its friends regardless of political, religious, or ideological affiliation. . . . These things do not concern Nature and Progress, should not concern Nature and Progress. We want everyone to feel comfortable here: Muslims, Jews, and free thinkers, Christians of all denominations. . . . All of us have the same need for a natural organic agriculture."[48] This kind of inclusion was absent from the writings of Lemaire and Boucher. This is not to say that they might not have supported it, but this was not their focus. Their focus was on the rehabilitation of France and its race. For Louis and Tavera, national borders were arbitrary. If the French suffered from an inferior diet as the result of chemically intensive agriculture, so too did the Americans, the Japanese, and the Germans. The problem existed on a global scale. For Louis and Tavera, so too did the solution.

The emphasis on nature further set Louis and Tavera apart from Lemaire and Boucher. As Louis explained in the opening issue of *Nature et Progrès*, he and Tavera had chosen the name for their organization very carefully. They wanted the public to understand first and foremost that organic farming was not a return to the past, that organic farmers were of their own time, and possibly even ahead of their time. Real, sustainable progress, however, could not be had without respecting the laws of nature. Industrial agriculture had tried "to dominate nature with violent methods." But Nature and Progress would instead "see in nature a mother and a friend," and "try to understand its infinite and awe-inspiring teachings."[49] Organic agriculture would have to work with nature rather than against it. That was the future of farming.

Developing their own model of organic agriculture, Louis and Tavera appealed to prospective Nature and Progress members by telling them that organic methods would be both more profitable and better for the health of their plants and animals. In a leaflet distributed at a workshop, Louis and Tavera started by highlighting the ills of industrial agriculture: "After several years of this practice, your soils mineralize and . . . become less and less responsive to fertilizer, so in order to maintain your yields, you must constantly increase the dose. Your yields are good, but the quality of your product has diminished . . . your plants are increasingly vulnerable to pests; your livestock contract new illnesses; human consumers are slowly poisoned by chemicals and toxins, leading to increased rates of cancer . . . and finally, the profitability of your farm is more and more compromised by the number of chemical inputs that you are forced to purchase."[50] For many farmers in France, this experience was all too real. Once producers adopted chemical inputs, it was very difficult to abandon them. Many carried debt levels that made the conversion to organic farming seem like a risky, if not reckless, decision. Purchasing more chemicals or acquiring more land to amortize the costs of inputs would have seemed like a safer bet.

Those farmers who were willing to risk conversion tended to be smallholders who had not industrialized in the first place, who had been unable to raise the funds necessary to achieve state standards for viability. To these farmers, Louis and Tavera offered the promises of organic agriculture: "It improves the structure of the soil, improves the vitality and the health of plants and animals, improves output and quality of harvests, and improves the overall profitability of the farm."[51] By joining Nature and Progress, farmers would have access to a community of organic farmers who could share their knowledge and offer their support.

One of the major selling points of Nature and Progress was that its model of organic agriculture was indeed more flexible than the Lemaire-Boucher Method. While the latter required the purchase of lithothamnion, the former was open to a variety of organic and biodynamic practices, and had no set requirements for fertilizer usage, provided farmers met the more global standards of organic farming by not using any chemical inputs or antibiotic treatments for livestock. Farmers could make their own organic fertilizer or they could buy it on the open market from one of several sources. This flexibility in method also allowed Nature and Progress to expand beyond French borders. By 1974, there were forty groups abroad. This model of international cooperation was harder for Lemaire and Boucher to realize given that their method required the use of their own lithothamnion fertilizer.

By the 1970s, the Nature and Progress model of alternative agriculture proved to be popular with back-to-the-landers, environmentalists, and those who preferred to excuse themselves altogether from national markets, opting instead to establish local distribution networks, and to focus on sustainability rather than profits. By the end of the decade, Nature and Progress boasted 8,000 members, though roughly 80 percent were urban consumers rather than rural producers. There were just 900 farmers on the membership roster, and of these, 100 to 200 did not practice organic farming (as compared with 1,500 at the peak of the Lemaire-Boucher Method). Those farmers who did engage in organic methods tended to be orchardists and vegetable growers, and most belonged to the back-to-the-land movement.[52] While Lemaire might have done more to grow the numbers of producers through the 1960s and 1970s, it was Louis's version of organic farming, supported by an urban white-collar intellectual base, that ultimately came to dominate the conversation.

The conflict, however, between these two strains within the organic farming community continued to shape the status of organic farming in France well beyond the initial rift. With the movement split between a right-wing antidirigisme and a more liberal-leaning protoenvironmentalism, it was all but impossible for the leaders of the community to create a coherent platform, a failure that would haunt the movement into the 1970s and 1980s as it sought recognition from the state. The Lemaire line alienated potential allies with its resolute Catholicism, anti-Semitism, and ties to the eugenicists of Vichy, while the Louis line failed to increase the market share of organic products because of its hardline stance against commercialism.

While French farmers initially outpaced their European counterparts in converting to organic production, by the end of the century they lagged well behind their neighbors. The number of French farmers practicing organic methods went from roughly 3,000 in 1985 (one-fifth of a percent of all French farmers) to 9,300 in 2000 (1 percent of the total).[53] But when compared with its neighbors, France in fact was falling behind. In 1985, France was at the forefront of organic production in Europe, producing 60 percent of the total share. Just one decade later, that share had fallen to 10 percent.[54] French demand for organic goods had increased, but that demand had risen much faster and much more steeply in places like Germany, Austria, and Great Britain.

The breach of 1964 between Lemaire and Louis was a pivotal moment in this history, one that shaped the future outcomes of the French food industry. In the late 1970s, when it first came time to negotiate with the state for official recognition and development assistance, the movement lacked a strong center that could lobby for its interests. While neighboring members of the EEC (and then the European Union after 1993) allotted new environmentally oriented funds toward their organic sectors, the French state instead invested the bulk of this assistance elsewhere. What had begun in the 1940s as a pioneering movement had fallen behind by the end of the century.

The Mainstream Takes Notice

The environmentalism that would eventually dovetail with the organic movement was in its early stages in the 1960s. French scientists and conservationists championed environmental causes, while the state commissioned reports on farm pollution and introduced legislation creating national and regional parks.[55] At the European level, the Committee for the Protection of Nature and Natural Resources was formed, and a French delegate attended regular meetings that brought together the member-states of the EEC to discuss such issues as pesticides and public health.[56] It was a far cry from national environmental regulation, but it was a start.

The budding of environmentalism in France had everything to do with the "silent revolution" that was taking place in the countryside.[57] As the nation raced to modernize at breakneck speed and rural residents fled the countryside, French men and women could actually see the farms disappearing before their very eyes. A process that was often slow and piecemeal in other countries was happening within the space of a lifetime in France, an experience that produced a profound sense of loss. As city dwellers looked with growing nostalgia to the countryside, they likewise became increasingly interested in the natural environment.

By the end of the 1960s, environmentalism as a mass movement began to emerge, the result of a combination of man-made natural disasters, growing disaffection with consumer capitalism, and the radical politics of the antinuclear and student movements. Wanting a connection to an authentic nature, French consumers turned their interest to the rural landscape and sought out organic products as totems of natural purity. The cleanliness that had once stood for racial integrity began to lose its eugenicist beginnings and would by the 1970s be associated instead with a countercultural authenticity that stemmed from an environmentally conscious and anticapitalist approach to production.

As organic farming and organic products became more popular through the 1960s, the industrial and alternative ideals slowly began to converge. Or rather, the proponents of the industrial ideal began to decipher how to absorb and co-opt those parts of the alternative ideal that might further their cause. The pioneers of organic farming had always placed a premium on nature. Functionaries therefore began to call for the protection of nature and to advertise how agriculture could benefit the environment. By borrowing from organic farming, the champions of the industrial ideal were able to expand opportunities for growth.

In 1965, as part of these new efforts, the High Commission on Quality (Commission supérieure de la qualité) was established by the Ministry of Agriculture. The president of AFRAN was invited to consult on the commission and later reported on his experience in the pages of *Documentation AFRAN*.[58] Meetings were held by the commission in which participants labored to come up with a set of standards that would apply to products bearing a new "label of quality." As part of this process, the commission evaluated applications from different producers to have their goods included in the program. At the first meeting, there were six different applications: several for cereals, one for wine, and one for poultry.

It was this last application that served as a harbinger of things to come. The poultry was marketed as "Yellow chicken of the Southwest" and was found to be superior in quality to standard industrial poultry because "the chickens had access to a larger living space, and their feed, which was hardly that of chickens raised in the open air, was nevertheless carefully monitored and consisted primarily of cereals." Somewhere between the open-air and factory-farmed chickens of the *Sol-Vitalité-Alimentation* article that had appeared in 1962, this "quality" chicken was the perfect marriage of the industrial and alternative ideals. It could be produced on a large-enough scale to take advantage of national and foreign markets, but at the same time carried with it the value-added cachet of a quality product, something that was typically associated with small-scale artisanal production. This convergence of the industrial and alternative ideals would not be complete until the 1980s with the resurgence of terroir, but these early moments in its development reveal that the reputation for quality that came to be enjoyed by the French farm sector was deliberately manufactured by the very same institutions that were pushing for its industrialization.

CHAPTER FIVE

Greening the Mainstream, 1968–1980

> The advantage to this concession is to allow area farmers to
> increase their cultivated surface area, mainly for carrot production.
> Apparently, it is impossible to weigh this gain against the loss of
> one of the last sections of Cotentin coastline.
>
> —Letter from the Ministry for the Protection of Nature and the
> Environment to the Ministry of Agriculture (October 1, 1973)

In 1973, a case involving the draining and reclamation of a wide tract of sea-side in Normandy put the SAFER directly into conflict with the relatively new Ministry for the Protection of Nature and the Environment. In 1952, a thirty-year concession on 427 hectares located in Havre de Lessay (Manche) was granted by the state to the Society of Neo-Polders.[1] By 1973, the society had drained and put under cultivation eighty hectares. When local farmers learned that the majority shareholder in the society was trying to transfer his rights to a real estate developer in Caen, they worried that the development of a new large-scale agricultural operation on these lands would put them out of business. The departmental chapter of the FNSEA approached the SAFER of Basse-Normandie and asked that it intervene on their behalf.[2]

Upon further investigation, the SAFER determined that its intervention into the sale would be justified as the current farming situation in the area was bleak, with most farmers working small operations of four to eight hectares that were broken up into disparate holdings. It was deemed that the creation of a few hundred hectares of usable farmland would be a boon for the local agricultural economy. Moreover, the SAFER saw opportunities for growth in the vegetable market, this land being particularly well suited to carrot production. The official SAFER report on the projected intervention stated that as a net-importer of vegetables, France could stand to increase production in this area. Even more important, however, England and Germany were huge importers and were purchasing only a small fraction of produce from France. The report suggested that if handled properly, the development of this land could lead to the capture of a large portion of this market.[3]

The Ministry for the Protection of Nature and the Environment was less enthusiastic. In a letter to the Ministry of Agriculture, regarding the above-mentioned report, it was stated unequivocally that the needs of agriculture were incompatible with those of the ecological well-being of Havre de Lessay. Juxtaposing the needs of area farmers to those of the natural environment, the ministry went on to state: "The advantage to this concession is to allow area farmers to increase their cultivated surface area, mainly for carrot production. Apparently, it is impossible to weigh this gain against the loss of one of the last sections of Cotentin coastline."[4] The ministry then suggested acquiring the lands from the Society of Neo-Polders to ensure the protection of those lands that had not already been drained and to impose limitations on the farmers working the eighty hectares that had already been put under cultivation. In this particular instance, the interests of agriculture and the environment were at odds with one another and the Ministry for the Protection of Nature and the Environment clearly stated that there was no comparison to be made between the two.

Ultimately, the project was approved by the Ministry of Agriculture only to be vetoed by the Ministry of Finance, given the high costs involved in acquiring the land and then reclaiming it for agricultural purposes. While President Pompidou had seen fit to establish a ministry devoted to the environment, its powers were limited in its early years. In spite of its inability to challenge the Ministry of Agriculture in this instance, however, the fact that it had been consulted at all marked a significant shift in how decisions regarding land use policy, and agriculture more generally, were handled.

THE 1970S MARKED a major turning point in state-mandated modernization. By the end of the decade, the state had not only tempered its exacting demands of French farmers to make room for niche-oriented small producers; it had also begun the process of co-opting the organic movement. The first indication that the productivity-oriented status quo needed revising was the release of two landmark agricultural reports: the Mansholt Plan and the Vedel Report. Both called for drastic reductions in the number of farmers, both in the EEC and in France. Both suggested that the viability standard be raised yet again. And both drew attention to the inefficiencies of a subsidy system that encouraged overproduction. Paid for their output, farmers were incentivized to produce as much as they could, regardless of whether or not there was sufficient demand. The production of serious surpluses led the state to question its emphasis on quantity over quality and to consider whether the two might not work together to address the enduring farm problem. The oil crisis that hit in mid-decade served to intensify this questioning. As gas prices rose, the option of farming with fewer chemical inputs became increasingly attractive both to farmers and to the Ministry of Agriculture. Moreover, a less fossil fuel–dependent farm sector was in keeping with the rising tide of environmental awareness. As citizens became more concerned about the toll that industrial capitalism was taking on the natural world, it became incumbent on the state to incorporate their concerns into policy initiatives. Gaining access to the halls of the Ministry of Agriculture, environmentalism pushed for a greener approach to farming, from a decrease in the use of chemical inputs to the recognition of organic methods.

This is not to say that the productivist model was abandoned in favor of a more holistic approach to farming and the environment. On the contrary, industrial agriculture continued to develop at breakneck speed. Farms grew larger, the application of pesticides and fertilizers increased, and the productivist ideal continued to govern the overall structure of French farming. By the early 1970s, France was the world's second largest exporter of agricultural goods. While exported grain had earned the French economy 332 million francs in 1959, that number had risen by a factor of almost twenty to 6.1 billion francs by 1972. Increases were likewise significant for wine and fruits and vegetables.[5] Overall, French agricultural exports grew by 390 percent between 1963 and 1974.[6] Given that exports in other sectors were falling in the same period, a thoroughly modernized French agriculture was propping up the balance of trade just as Jean Monnet and Pierre Pflimlin had hoped it would. The green gas of the French economy had become a global success.

Environmental considerations in the farm sector and a growing interest in quality production were supplements, not substitutes, to industrial agriculture. In this respect, the greening of agricultural production mirrored the greening of consumption that historian Michael Bess has masterfully analyzed in his *The Light-Green Society*. State administrators were hardly ready to accept the possibility that the productivist model they had been pushing on the farm sector might have been a mistake. It was a major moneymaker for the French economy, and the wealth generated by this model ultimately trumped any of its harmful environmental or social consequences. Organic farming and environmental regulations were therefore only cautiously incorporated into the agricultural sector.

The 1970s equally marked a new era in the management of the French landscape, in which an emphasis on agricultural productivity was moderated by the new agendas of rural development and environmentalism. As France moved closer to its position of global dominance in the agricultural realm, the French landscape was freed up for the commercial and recreational habits of the consumer capitalist world. Agricultural productivism continued to drive policy. But the very notion of productivity had begun to change. Whereas productivity had at first been more or less synonymous with yields, by the early 1970s the definition had expanded to include all manner of human activities that furthered the development of the countryside. As a result, rural France became less and less synonymous with farming. Urban inhabitants, for example, exhausted by the pace of city living, came to see the countryside instead as a site for rest and recreation. Just as AFRAN eggs and butter would cure urban consumers of their irritability, fatigue, and depression, the clean air of the countryside and the calm of rural life offered an antidote to the ills of modernity and civilization, in this case represented by the increasingly polluted city air. Realizing that the money these weary urban souls were spending in rural communities could be used to buttress the ailing incomes of those farmers who were having trouble keeping up with modernization, the state began to grow the national and regional park systems and to develop the infrastructure that urban vacationers and second-home buyers would require (e.g., sporting centers, alpine resorts, campsites).

While profits in the countryside had previously been sought exclusively through agricultural commodities, by the end of the decade profits were also identified in the preservation of the environment, fresh air, and the romanticized urban visions of the rural landscape. Urban residents could look to the countryside for escape from the hustle and bustle of economic growth, and to stay on the map, rural communities could turn to the development of tourism and recreation. As a consequence of this expanding definition of what constituted productivity in the French countryside, the claims on rural lands put forth by city dwellers and emerging environmentalists were weighed alongside those of local farmers—a development that just twenty years before would have been unthinkable.

It is no coincidence that regional parks were being established at the same moment that small producers had once again taken to the streets. While European integration and rigorous modernization had been kind to a minority of farmers, many of whom had started the process ahead of the game, the majority continued to struggle. A full half of all French farms were still classified as unviable, and were therefore slated to disappear. As state officials became more transparent about this fact, small producers became more enraged. Rural development was an answer to this rage. State officials hoped that by supplementing the incomes of small farmers with rural tourism, they might find a way to survive. Rural development was meant to be a palliative to the cutthroat war of attrition that was being waged in the countryside.

This transition ultimately benefited organic farming in that increased interest in maintaining viable rural communities along with increased interest in more environmentally sensitive farming methods both pointed in the direction of organic agriculture. Linked to a growing commitment on the part of the state to ecological concerns, rural development approached the land as a natural environment rich with resources that should be used to benefit all citizens, both urban and rural. To cater to this new approach, policymakers in the agricultural sector began to present French farming in a new light. The French farmer had already been called on to occupy the increasingly empty spaces of the landscape to maintain social stability through the flux of the rural exodus and to maintain the identity of true France in the wake of the invasion of land-hungry member-state farmers. In the 1970s, the role of the French farmer as guardian of the national territory was extended beyond the concept of mere occupation to include the language of the emerging environmentalist movement, for it was relatively easy to move from the ideal farmer who guaranteed the survival of French civilization by occupying the soil to a slightly modified version of the same who would ensure the well-being of the natural environment.

The notion that the farmer, the guardian of true France, served the interests of the environment ultimately relied on a romantic vision of French agriculture that was largely divorced from actual practice. While farmers were trained in chemically intensive methods, newly urbanized populations made efforts to reconnect with a pastoral French landscape that had largely ceased to exist. For many of these French men and women who sought out a stronger bond with their rural past, through a summer vacation or through the purchase of organic products, the countryside had become a distant abstraction onto which they could map their own desires and assumptions. And it was this nostalgia and this longing for connection that fed the growing niche markets of the 1970s and 1980s. The resurgence of terroir was still a decade away, but the emergence of a powerful longing for a cleaned-up rural past set the stage for its eventual triumph.

Meanwhile, a new generation of organic farmers saw in the state the possibility of legitimization and access to resources that would foster more research in alternative practices and support for producers and distributors. In 1970, André Louis and Mattéo Tavera were killed in a car accident while traveling home from a naturopathic conference. Two years later, Raoul Lemaire passed. As the pioneers were succeeded by new leaders, the culture of organic farming began to change. Lemaire's stringent antistatism gave way to a more flexible attitude toward government regulation and assistance, while Louis's anticommercialism yielded to a pragmatic realization that if organic farmers were going to make it, marketing their goods effectively was essential. Perhaps most strikingly, the degeneration of the French race was no longer a part of the organic discourse. Purity remained a central category, but it was no longer associated with racial politics, eugenics, or national chauvinism. Instead, purity was tied to the rising environmentalist movement and its conception of nature.

Modern Agricultural Enterprises

In December of 1968, Sicco Mansholt, the Dutch vice president of the European Commission and a key contributor to the original CAP, submitted a report on the state of agriculture in the EEC. Known as the Mansholt Plan, the report called for a massive restructuring of European agriculture, including the replacement of family farms with "modern agricultural enterprises."[7] Mansholt was concerned about both the problem of overproduction and the soaring costs of maintaining an inefficient agricultural sector through price supports. Surpluses in cereals, sugar, and dairy had already begun to appear in the early 1960s.[8] By 1968, they were out of hand. In 1955, for instance, the average French cow produced roughly 2,000 liters of milk per year. By 1972, that same cow was producing roughly 2,900 liters.[9] In large part due to the subsidies paid out for such productivity gains, the CAP had come to account for a full 95 percent of the community's total budget.[10] To remedy these problems, Mansholt suggested a radical reduction in the amount of farmland and in the number of farmers: "The rapid diminution of the agricultural population is a feature of the times. But if the living standards of farmers are to rise enough within ten years to make good the present leeway, then the rate of decrease in the agricultural population must be greatly accelerated." Between 1970 and 1980, it was recommended that five million farmers be eliminated and that 12.5 million hectares of land be removed from cultivation. He also insisted that the minimum size for a viable farm ought to be raised to forty hectares, a standard that at the time was met by just 40 percent of all French farms.[11]

Needless to say, the plan was met with hostility by farmers and with apprehension by member-states. Farmers throughout the EEC protested the plan and no member-state was willing to put its recommendations into full effect. Given the recent events of the summer of 1968, social stability was at the forefront of state concerns and unrest in the countryside was to be avoided at all costs. That said, while the French state hesitated to publicly endorse the Mansholt Plan, it nevertheless understood that his recommendations were necessary. In the pages of *Le Monde*, François-Henri de Virieu wrote that while the French state paid lip service to wanting to protect its farmers from the more extreme recommendations of the Mansholt Plan, in reality it would continue to pursue policies that favored large-scale industrial production: "For the first time in the history of our long-standing Western nations, a man of power, charged with political responsibilities ... dares to say openly, and with a certain solemnity, to the small farmers, the cold truth about their future, or rather more precisely about their lack of a future. It was to be expected that after the conspiracy of silence of recent years, orchestrated by state officials, politicians, and union leaders to minimize systematically the gravity of the situation ... the voice of Mr. Mansholt cracked like thunder."[12] Mansholt said nothing in his plan that French policymakers had not already been saying themselves behind closed doors. If put into practice, his recommendations were political suicide, but they were also economically necessary.

While Mansholt was preparing his findings, the French government commissioned a study of its own, the Vedel Report.[13] Concerned about the failure to increase agricultural incomes in spite of enormous progress in terms of productivity, French policymakers worried about how to devise the 1969 budget in such a way that would effect positive changes in agriculture without further bankrupting state coffers.[14] It was estimated that for every one hundred francs that a French farmer took home, the state spent thirty-three francs to subsidize that income.[15] Moreover, in the eight years prior to the release of the Vedel Plan, spending on agriculture had risen a full 240 percent. Stated in other terms, by the mid-1970s, state spending on agriculture totaled 16 percent of the total value of the entire sector, whereas in the 1950s, it had totaled 9 percent of the sector.[16] It was of primary importance that the state curb expenditures on agriculture.

The results of the study were made public in September of 1969. While its recommendations were less severe than those of the Mansholt Plan, it nonetheless called for a substantial reduction in farmland and in the number of farmers. Land under cultivation was to be cut by one-third and the farming population further reduced by three hundred thousand. The ruthless war of attrition was far from over and farmers were being called to yet another ferocious battle.

Violent demonstrations ensued throughout the French countryside.[17] The FNSEA called for a special congress in an attempt to rein in its members and return stability to rural France. Union president Gérard de Caffarelli pleaded with his members to stop protesting and to work instead on developing mechanisms that would ease the transitions called for by Mansholt and Vedel. The secretary-general of the CNJA, Raoul Serieys, was less acquiescent. In an editorial in *Le Monde* explaining why so many farmers were furiously rioting in the streets, Serieys wrote that the Vedel Report was an act of betrayal. Farmers felt as though the state had broken its promise to them—to protect them, to increase their revenues, and to improve the quality of their lives and their labor.[18] The state had once promised that the common market would solve the farm problem by providing consumers with French surpluses. But surpluses were an EEC-wide problem by the mid-1960s and the common market could no longer absorb French agricultural products. Moreover, extreme inequality in the farm sector persisted. One-half of all agricultural revenue went to just 10 percent of French farms, while at the other extreme, 46 percent of all farms took home just 5 percent of all agricultural revenue.[19] Most farmers were already at risk of going under. The Mansholt Plan and Vedel Report only confirmed that they were indeed expendable. While the common market had been promised to them as a panacea, many were beginning to see it instead as the very root of their problems.

In the end, the EEC arrived at a compromise between Mansholt's suggestions and the protests of member-state farmers. In 1972, it agreed to lower the age of retirement in the agricultural sector to fifty-five to persuade more farmers to accept retirement subsidies in exchange for giving up their lands. This would both reduce the farming population and free up holdings to increase the size of existing operations. It was also agreed that rural development plans (and no longer only *agricultural* development) would benefit from low-interest loans, agricultural land would be made available to rural development purposes, and the creation of new farmland would be strictly prevented.[20]

Even though the suggestions of Mansholt and Vedel were never fully put into practice, their proposals did change the tenor of the debate over agricultural policy. For instance, in a meeting of the national office of the SAFER, held shortly after the release of the Vedel Report, representatives discussed the recent turn in policy discussions and asked themselves whether the SAFER would have to reconfigure its own operations in order to adapt. Addressing the Mansholt Plan directly, they stated in their final report that the decision of the EEC concerned the SAFER "to the highest degree," and that given the plan's emphasis on transferring agricultural lands to other purposes, the SAFER needed to consider extending its services to nonagricultural areas.[21] By 1973, the SAFER had transferred twenty thousand hectares out of agricultural production and into tourism and second homes, a change that would have been unimaginable in 1960 when the organization was first created.[22]

Making matters worse was the global financial crisis, which made it harder for farmers to set aside funds for buying lands because of the rising costs of their industrial inputs—gasoline for the machinery and chemical fertilizers for the earth. In addition, land prices continued to climb throughout the decade. This likewise made it harder for the SAFER to redistribute holdings—while it received a modest increase in state funding, the increase trailed behind rising prices, which meant that every year the SAFER was able to do a little less on its budget.[23] As one farmer put it to Le Monde: "Peasants expected a miracle from the SAFER. But instead of a magic wand, the government gave them nothing but a branch of dead wood."[24] In the aftermath of both Mansholt and Vedel, while policymakers struggled to redefine the role of agriculture, not only within the economy, but within the nation as well, morale was at an all-time low.

With the writing on the wall, farmers did what they could to adapt, opt out, or resist the modernization machine. One aging farmer in the department of the Loire took a hard-line stance against this latest round of impossible demands and simply refused to participate in the market. Profiled in Le Monde in 1974, this eighty-seven-year-old farmer was hanging on to his 200 hectares and his 150 head of livestock in spite of the fact that he was operating at a 20 percent deficit.[25] While he admitted to being at the "bottom of the barrel," he refused to give in, pointing out that in the last thirteen months he had not sold a single animal because "rather than ceding [his] herd to the cabals," he preferred "to let them starve." Refusing to allow any portion of his farm to be transferred to a "modern agricultural enterprise" had also prevented him from selling his house and some of his holdings. Lands in the Loire were too expensive for the sorts of farmers to whom he would be willing to sell. So instead he set up something of a cooperative with a handful of his farmworkers, which he humorously referred to as his "kolkhoz." In the face of state-sponsored cutthroat competition, he had opted instead to sacrifice himself to maintain his sense of community. Defiant to the last drop, this rebellious country squire would not be going gently into that good night.

Environmentalism Enters the Halls of Power

The Torrey Canyon oil spill, which took place off the coast of Brittany in 1967, is often cited as a turning point in popular concern for the environment.[26] Further contributing to the rise of environmentalism in France was the growth of popular social movements in the late 1960s: the student and antinuclear movements, feminism, and anticonsumerism. Not only did the general spirit of contestation lend itself to the new environmentalist sensibility but the protestors' rejection of consumer society came to dovetail naturally with criticisms of industrial and urban pollution, as well as demands for a better quality of life.[27] In 1969, protests against the development of a ski resort in the Vanoise National Park (Savoie) offered the movement an opportunity to put its ideas into practice, the end result of which was a major victory with the decision on the part of the state to disallow the development. National news media coverage of the construction plans and the protests likewise offered the general public a crash course in the environmentalist agenda.[28] Together these events worked to create a coherent understanding of what constituted the "environment" and how it should be cared for.

In light of the Mansholt and Vedel recommendations, along with the rise of environmentalism, the Ministry of Agriculture was beginning to reimagine its role. Farming was becoming just one of several essential rural activities, along with recreation, tourism, and conservation. Given the new claims being made on rural lands, the ministry slowly adopted a new model of intervention that would focus on rural, rather than just agricultural, development.

Land use policy in particular underwent profound changes as a result of this reorientation toward a more holistic approach to the rural landscape (see figures 13–15). Prior to the emergence of rural development and environmentalism, much of the *remembrement* that was carried out disturbed the natural systems that had previously managed water and wind. Banks and hedgerows were destroyed while rural engineers implemented massive irrigation and drainage projects: "*Remembrement* overturned the old inherited

order of the fields, substituting it with the real-world checkerboard of the surveyor. The commanding banks and hedgerows of Brittany were cleared, at times to excess (Morbihan), and came to look like the neighboring plains."[29] Agricultural productivity was pursued at all costs and rationalizing the landscape was a means to achieve that end. By the end of the 1960s, however, such measures were being challenged. Environmentalists argued that such practices disturbed local ecosystems and rural development boosters maintained that banks and hedgerows rendered the landscape more appealing to tourists and second-home buyers.

When Mayor Nicolas Peneff brought *remembrement* to Cadours (Haute-Garonne) at the end of the 1960s, an ecological assessment was required before any changes in the landscape could be effected. Consequently, the entirety of the county's land-based interests were to be taken into account when redrawing property lines and altering the landscape.[30] As Peneff understood the new provision: "This relatively new study required that we earmark trees to be preserved, and pushed us to protect as many of them as possible."[31] But the preservation of trees was only one component of the new approach to *remembrement*. Elaborating on the purpose of this new model of engagement, the departmental representative of the Ministry of

FIGURE 15 Removal of trees as part of *remembrement*. *Source*: © DR/Min.Agri.Fr.

Agriculture explained to Peneff that ecological safeguards would "preserve the quality of the landscape and the recreational function of rural areas" and would therefore "ensure a lively agricultural sector as well as an inviting landscape."[32] On the one hand, incorporating environmentalist concerns into *remembrement* would maintain the productive quality of the landscape by maintaining natural structures that served as built-in irrigation systems and worked to prevent erosion; on the other, it would maintain the aesthetic quality of the landscape, which was essential to providing tourists with an escape from urban living.

The rise of environmentalism was given an institutional boost in 1970 with the creation of the General Directorate for Environmental Protection (Direction générale de la protection de la nature), housed within the Ministry of Agriculture. While a separate ministry was created one year later in 1971, the fact that the environment was originally treated as the responsibility of the Ministry of Agriculture demonstrates just how closely these two worlds were linked in the early days of French environmentalism. Upon the creation of this new branch of government, Minister of Agriculture Jacques Duhamel sent out a memo to all of the prefects to explain that agriculture and the environment were related, and offered advice on how to resolve differences when the two came into conflict. He then made a point of reminding the prefects that *remembrement* in particular needed to be carried out with respect for the environment. The ministry had produced a pamphlet to this effect and Duhamel exhorted the prefects not only to study it closely themselves, but also to distribute it to every single elected official in their department.[33] Memos from the same period covered a variety of environmental problems, from the polluting waste of large-scale industrial pork production to the threat of water contamination at the hands of industrial farmers.[34]

Surely memos like these should be read with a grain of salt. The archives are replete with stories about ministry-mandated policies not being carried out at the local level. Moreover, the marriage of agriculture and environment in fact often made it easier for the Ministry of Agriculture to dismiss environmentalist concerns. For instance, in 1970 the ministry commissioned a report on the environmental aspects of *remembrement*, and while an environmentalist contributor argued that agriculture could have a negative impact on the land, the representative from the ministry fiercely maintained that because of their natural connection to the land, farmers could be nothing but good for the environment. Arguing that farmers cared about the land because it was in their interest to do so, he wrote that "farmers are especially well situated to know the possible advantages and disadvantages of *remembrement*—for they are its first beneficiaries. And similarly, they are the first victims should it fail."[35] The suggestion that their actions ought to be monitored in any way generated deep indignation, as it disregarded the immediate connection that farmers had to their lands, a connection that was presented as proof that farmers were better judges than conservationists when it came to the natural environment.

Environmental regulations on *remembrement* were expanded in 1975, a development that demonstrated the Ministry of Agriculture's commitment to rural development as both a concession to popular ecological concerns and as a means to extract profit from the countryside by means other than agricultural production.[36] Reporting on the changing priorities of the state with respect to land management, an article in *Le Monde* highlighted efforts to "integrate ecology" into land use policy.[37] The text made reference to efforts on the part of the SAFER to work with the Ministry for the Protection of Nature and the Environment in the acquisition of lands in the Sologne (Loir-et-Cher, Loiret, and Cher)—lands that would be put to multifunctional purposes. In addition, the article introduced readers to a new form of *remembrement*——*remembrement écologique*—as it had been carried out in the Vendée and Creuse. It then discussed proposals for claiming lands for environmental preservation and recreational needs. In reference to a project underway in Seine-et-Marne, the article stated that there were plans to establish an improved system for monitoring environmental pollution and to develop a winter sport station, riverside bicycle paths, and pedestrian walkways.[38] In short, rural land use policy was no longer what it used to be. While agriculture continued to play an important role in the countryside, rural France had come to serve a variety of interests.

The acceptance of environmentalism set a powerful precedent that paved the way for the acceptance of organic agriculture, another fringe movement that was growing increasingly popular with concerned citizens. While the recognition of the environment on the part of the Ministry of Agriculture might not have led to an immediate reorientation of farm policy, it was nevertheless important in that it demonstrated that what had started out as a fringe movement, supported by scientists and a handful of concerned citizens, had entered the halls of power. Moreover, the arrival of environmentalism at the Ministry of Agriculture moderated the longstanding exhortation to "get big or get out." To be sure, this remained the dominant imperative. But a parenthetical "try not to pollute while you're doing it" became a standard addendum. Again, this shift did not produce a tidal wave of change, but it certainly led to significant ripples.

In conjunction with this reshuffling of the Ministry of Agriculture, *La France Agricole* began running a regular column on environmental issues, bringing new kinds of ideas to farmers all over France. In the wake of the announcement that the ministry would house the Office for the Protection of Nature, the paper published a front-page editorial on the relationship between agriculture and the environment. Walking the line between the agricultural status quo and growing concerns over agricultural pollution, the editorial both pointed the finger and went on the defensive. At first conceding that *some* farmers remove too many trees, use too many chemical inputs, and abuse the soil, the editorial concluded by arguing that while agriculture might be partially responsible for air and water pollution, the key problem was in fact urbanization: "The grievances we might hold against French agriculture are absolutely minor when compared to the harm done by the absurd distribution of human activity and population in our territory, by urban density, by the abandonment of a way of living and working that is more compatible with the natural demands of men!"[39] While the mainstream was able to admit that farming could be harmful for the environment, it was quick to argue that agriculture was a minor player when it came to pollution. Industry, the consumer capitalism of urban living, and the rise of the automobile were held to be the real culprits. Readers of *La France Agricole* were exposed to the new ideas being espoused by the environmental movement, but they were also able to distance themselves by pretending that rural production was completely unrelated to urban consumption.

It was during this time that urban French men and women were moving to the countryside in greater numbers, which might in part account for why farmers had targeted them in discussions regarding environmental pollution. The arrival of new and transient populations, most notably second-home buyers and tourists, created new tensions between production and consumption in rural France. For instance, farmers often complained that second-home residents drained local resources without contributing to the community—outsiders were often criticized for bringing food and supplies with them from the city rather than shopping at local establishments.

Relations with part-time residents grew even more strained when they decided to get involved in local politics. Typically blessed with more free time than the average farmer, these residents ran for posts on the municipal council and were often elected as mayors. It was usually only a matter of time before they passed a motion that incited the anger of local pro ducers.[40] Conflicts often erupted over livestock odors, the aesthetic integrity of farm buildings, and rights and privileges regarding the gathering of mushrooms.[41] The clash between locals and second-home buyers stemmed from contradictory relationships with the landscape. While the former argued, when it was in their best interest to do so, that they relied on it to reproduce themselves, the latter viewed it as a site for leisure and relaxation.[42]

In light of both the rising tide of environmentalism and the arrival of part-time urban residents, the SAFER was likewise obliged to adopt a new mandate. In the 1970s, the organization began handling cases that involved the transfer of farmlands to nonagricultural purposes, from sports complexes to second homes.[43] It is remarkable that an institution created for the sole purpose of guaranteeing access to land for farmers could, in less than a decade, begin removing lands from agricultural production. This massive departure from its original mandate was evidence of a widespread sea change in both French politics and culture.

To be sure, farmers remained the priority of the SAFER, and regional offices fought to hang on to the original mandate to protect the interests of farmers on the real estate market. Indeed, as competition for lands increased, the SAFER worried that not only would farmers be unable to expand their operations to remain economically viable, those who did would face mounting debt levels as competition drove land prices even higher.[44] At the 1971 general assembly of the SAFER of Burgundy, the president provided an exhaustive list of threats to agricultural land: "suburbanization, new residential developments, second homes, vacation spots, industrial infrastructure, airports, highways, high-speed rail, natural parks, protected historical sites, etc." He then concluded: "All of these infra- or supra-structural phenomena and their inevitable amputation of soil will be carried out in the name of rural space, but always at the expense of agricultural space. We must coldly face reality."[45] The SAFER did not necessarily want to get involved in the attribution of lands to nonagricultural buyers, but given the already existing state of things, it was determined that trying to maintain some semblance of order in the face of what was deemed to be an anarchical appropriation of agricultural lands was better than ignoring these new buyers out of principle. So while the SAFER begrudgingly agreed to conform to a changing political and cultural terrain, the bulk of its energies remained devoted to defending farmers against their new competitors.

A case that pitted the SAFER against an ardent conservationist demonstrates that the local chapters of the organization were often able to maintain their original mandate in spite of changes that were being pronounced by national agencies. In the county of Garric (Tarn), Maurice Clemente purchased some land in 1972 that he wanted to use to create a bird sanctuary. He was quickly preempted by the local SAFER. Clemente protested by arguing that draining these lands to turn them into farms was a waste of resources given that France was hardly in need of more wheat, while the birds of Garric were absolutely in need of a home: "It is now more or less decided that this microcosm of refuge inhabited by game and birds, notably aquatic game and birds, will be handed over to the bulldozers in order to harvest a few hundred kilograms of cereals, which France does not really need."[46] For Clemente, how this land would be used was a question of what was best for the environment as a whole and not just what was best for the agricultural sector. The SAFER proceeded with its plans nonetheless.

That Clemente was so easily defeated might be read as a sign of the failure of environmentalism to interrupt the productivist ideal. But letters such as the one authored by Clemente simply were not written prior to the 1970s. Its mere existence signals a massive shift in how French men and women understood their relationship to the rural landscape. After the institutionalization of environmental protections and as the environment began to capture the imagination of the wider public, these sorts of letters, addressed to local officials and the Ministry of Agriculture alike, began to appear with greater frequency.[47] As the decade progressed, the environment came to occupy an important position within the constellation of factors that made up the general interests of both the countryside and the nation.

The inclusion of the environment was a radical transition for the rural land use policy of the postwar period, for no longer, as Forget had argued, was land in the service of men. In other words, land was no longer strictly a tool of production for French farmers. Under the laws governing the protection of the environment, this relationship was in fact reversed, and humankind was placed in the service of the land. Setting French land aside for any purpose other than that of agricultural production would have been unthinkable to the majority of the population in 1960. That it was in fact mandated by the state just ten years later was a testament to how quickly and how thoroughly the emergence of competing claims on the French countryside altered ideas about how land use policy could best serve the economic and social needs of the nation.

The agricultural productivism that had ruled the land reform agenda from liberation through the first part of the 1960s gave way to a multipurpose approach to rural land use policy. This is not to say, however, that rural lands ceased being productive or that productivity, as an economic objective, lost any of its saliency. Rather, there was a shift in how productivity was understood and pursued. Second-home buyers and regional parks were not increasing agricultural yields, but they were productive in the sense that they fostered economic growth in rural areas. Especially after the recommendations of Mansholt and Vedel, it was no longer held that it was in the best interest of the nation to reserve the countryside for agricultural production. The setting aside of as much land as possible for agricultural purposes would no longer be the guiding principle of agricultural reform. Instead, the allocation of farmlands would have to be reconciled with other development initiatives, initiatives that would rectify the agricultural surpluses that had begun to appear on the common market in the mid-1960s, and which Mansholt and Vedel had highlighted as being detrimental to broader economic development.

Worlds Collide

The new social and environmental movements of the late 1960s and early 1970s led to a greater interest in organic agriculture. The Lemaire company and Nature and Progress continued to expand. The latter reached out beyond France to strengthen ties with the Soil Association and to form an international federation of organic farmers. The former continued to expand its brand, selling everything from bread and flour to jams and cookies. These goods and others like them were sold in 180 Vie Claire stores, processed in two factories, and promoted by four hundred employees, all of which constituted by the end of the 1970s the largest distribution network of organic foods in France. In addition, organic food co-ops emerged as a means to distribute new organic products to interested consumers who were either having trouble finding organic foods in their local grocery stores or were reluctant to pay the higher prices for goods on offer at health food stores like Vie Claire (for instance, organic bread typically cost twice the price of nonorganic bread).[48] Co-ops also appealed to those members of the counterculture who preferred to operate outside of the established markets of French consumer capitalism. Just as producing organic food became a means of resistance for the disenchanted youth of '68 who moved back to the land and swelled the ranks of organic farmers, consuming organic food through these buying clubs similarly offered French men and women the means to opt out of the society that the radicals of '68 had rejected.

In a seminal study of former sixty-eighters who moved to the Cévennes (Ardèche, Gard, Hérault, and Lozère) to take up farming and artisanal trades, sociologists Bertrand Hervieu and Danièle Léger argue that while many of these neo-ruralists were quickly divested of their pastoral fantasies, others were able to make ideological adjustments to remain on the land. Their experiences were very much like those of Pierre Rabhi, who had moved to the region almost a decade earlier. The initial attraction for the disenchanted students of urban France was twofold: the deserted landscape of the Cévennes promised a tabula rasa devoid of all societal conventions and state controls, while the land itself promised a connection to an "ancestral civilization that opposed at every turn the urban and industrialized society" that they refused.[49] Feared by the vast majority of French men and women for its lack of human settlement, *la France du vide* offered these thwarted radicals political and spiritual asylum. As Hervieu and Léger discovered, however, those who refused to adapt their romantic visions of the countryside—those who shunned state aid and participation in the rural communities that surrounded them—by and large failed to sustain themselves. Of the approximately one hundred thousand who moved to the countryside in the aftermath of the student revolts, 90 percent gave up within a few years.[50] On the other hand, those who reconciled themselves to state interference and approached the SAFER and Crédit Agricole for aid in acquiring and developing farmlands, managed to succeed.

For the locals, the arrival of these outsiders was met with mixed reactions. While some were designated by the pejorative terms *espélourdis* (long-haired) or *loqueteux* (those wearing rags), others were more easily integrated into local communities,[51] for those who managed to remain on the land did much to buttress the demographic and economic decline of the Cévennes, a region that had been especially hard hit by rural out-migration. Moreover, many rehabilitated certain traditional production practices that had been on the wane, such as raising local varieties of livestock and maintaining local distribution networks for their products.[52]

Demographic desertification, which had previously caused concern for its lack of generative power, both economic and cultural, had become the very means by which the countryside was able to recover its productive potential. One young farmer by the name of J.-F. Vallot produced fruits and vegetables, as well as honey, for local markets. When asked why he practiced organic farming, Vallot responded that organic practices required less expensive inputs, such as chemical fertilizers and machinery, while the yields were comparable to those obtained by conventional farming. Moreover, for those crops that produced smaller yields, such as potatoes, he was able to make up the difference by fetching higher prices for a premium organic product. In Vallot's experience, organic agriculture was not only in keeping with his political beliefs, it was also a savvy marketing strategy that allowed for the survival of small-scale production: "Because of the additional human labor that is required for organic agriculture, and because of direct sales, the rejuvenation of the small-scale farm is helping to promote the repopulation of the countryside. This development runs counter to those policies that have been adopted by the public authorities, policies designed to liquidate the small-scale producer."[53] In addition to providing small-scale farmers with alternative markets and distribution networks, organic farming would ensure the survival of rural communities threatened by demographic decline and the modernizing agenda of the state, for while empty landscapes proved difficult to sustain by native farmers alone, when marketed to those in search of either a temporary or permanent escape from urban living, these areas of France were able to reconfigure themselves as spaces of both consumption and alternative production practices.

The director of the SAFER of Lozère, which administered this region, echoed the sentiments of Pierre Rabhi's agronomy instructors when he explained to Hervieu and Léger that the young families that had arrived in the area would guarantee the survival of the area, and its patrimony: "These young people are an asset. For twenty years, we looked for a way to revitalize this area that was dying. They have allowed for the safeguarding of the patrimony, and their sensitivity to the local aesthetic has given a big boost to the restoration of the patrimony and the landscape."[54] Eager to escape the confines of social convention and state control, these neo-ruralists in fact helped to solve a problem that both Paris and local government had tried to address for decades.

It was not just the disenchanted youth of '68 who turned to organic agriculture as a means to combat the perceived injustices of the state. In the aftermath of the Vedel Report, de Virieu, once again writing for *Le Monde*, similarly presented small-scale niche production as a strategy for surviving the ruthless capitalism of the French state. While de Virieu emphasized the quality of the product over the methods of production, the end result was largely the same—the development of alternative markets and local distribution networks. De Virieu began by describing how the situation for farmers had grown so difficult: "The generous notion that most farmers would quickly be able to integrate themselves into economic development, thanks to structural reforms, is today abandoned by the facts. The mobilization of the entirety of this section of society had two disastrous effects: productivity-based income supplements led to surplus production, while the excessive amounts of debt—carelessly encouraged—prevented farmers from benefiting from these gains in productivity."[55] The situation as a whole, however, was not without hope. The problem, as de Virieu understood it, was that agricultural modernization was being sold to all farmers in the same way, namely, as a means to take advantage of the common market. It was simply assumed that those who could not take advantage of this new mass of consumers would be unable to survive. But de Virieu, along with those farmers who were taking up goat cheese production and bee-keeping in the Cévennes, saw an alternate path for those who could not produce on a larger scale. De Virieu concluded by suggesting that these small-scale farmers begin producing expensive, quality goods for consumers who were themselves beginning to react against the industrialization of agriculture and the degradation of the natural environment.

Reiterating the sentiments of Vallot and de Virieu, an article in the weekly *France Catholique* similarly suggested that small-scale organic production could not only ensure the survival of rural communities but could also cater to consumers, who "for philosophical and dietary reasons, will be ready to pay a lot more for organic products."[56] State-mandated modernization was focused on the average, price-sensitive, consumer. Food costs had to remain low to drive economic growth—because keeping food costs down meant that employers could keep wages down, which in turn meant that investors could spend their money more productively. But a different kind of consumer was emerging in the 1970s—a white-collar urban consumer who valued quality over cost, who was willing to subsidize indirectly the survival of small-scale producers and the protection of the environment.[57]

With this increasing interest in the environment and in small-scale niche production, the mainstream agricultural media began to pay more attention to organic producers, albeit with a critical eye. The editorial board at *La France Agricole* was prepared to accept that farmers should be working in concert with the environment, but continued to draw the line at an endorsement for organic practices. In an article typical of the time, a farmer, who wrote in the first-person about how he viewed himself in relationship to the natural environment, concluded that his intensive methods were in fact *good* for the environment. First, the increase in agricultural production meant more photosynthesis. Moreover, French farmers were not

American farmers, and were not using chemical inputs irresponsibly (a false assumption on his part): "I honestly believe that it must be stated that in a country like France, pollution and misuse are in reality very limited."[58] In conclusion, he responded to claims that DDT was poisoning the earth, a message that had been popularized by Rachel Carson's *Silent Spring*, which had been translated into French in 1963.[59] He argued, just as the Ministry of Agriculture would continue to argue in the years to come, that while farmers and scientists certainly needed to work together to ensure that agriculture remained a positive force in the environment, on balance, farmers practicing intensive methods were good conservationists.[60]

It was not until 1973, in an interview with an organic farmer, that *La France Agricole* represented organic production in a more positive, or at least neutral, light.[61] Mr. de Monbrison, the article explained, had started farming with industrial methods in Aquitaine in 1961. He grew cereals and heavily fertilized his soils. But he was nevertheless unhappy with his yields. In 1964, he attended a conference on organic farming, and convinced by the successes of other farmers in attendance, converted his own operations. He moved from industrialized cereals to organic livestock production and began exporting his meats at a decent profit. The reporter described de Monbrison as a modern young farmer who kept up with new methods but was quick to caution that de Monbrison's success alone was not sufficient cause to believe that organic methods were superior.[62]

By the end of 1973, mainstream agriculture had become much more receptive to organic methods. The oil crisis that hit in October, and continued to wreak havoc on the global economy through the middle of the decade, prompted many to consider more seriously farming practices that relied less on industrial inputs. The production of synthetic fertilizers, the operation of farm machinery, and the manufacture of pesticides all required the consumption of fossil fuels. When oil prices spiked, production costs followed suit. Farmers, agronomists, and the Ministry of Agriculture all tried to come up with new approaches that would minimize oil consumption. For example, in the mid-1970s, INRA embarked on a new research agenda that sought to reduce the dependence of farmers on industrial inputs. They named it "maximum value-added organic agriculture" (*agriculture à valeur ajoutée biologique maximale*). In speaking to the press, general director Jacques Poly said that his goal was a "reasoned agricultural production" (*agriculture raisonnée*) that would benefit the bottom line by reducing the inefficiencies of unnecessary inputs, while simultaneously benefiting the environment and improving quality of life.[63] Several years later, Poly published a report in which he stated that this less fuel-intensive agriculture would allow farmers both greater autonomy and greater economy, while producing less environmentally harmful waste. But he never questioned productivity and he never made specific mention of organic farming.[64]

The state was ideologically and politically incapable of fully embracing organic agriculture. Doing so would have required calling into question the entire edifice of postwar productivism, founded on scientific research and economic principles. Organic farming, thought to be the stuff of alchemists and cranks, was therefore only very slowly accepted into the mainstream and was never turned to as a replacement for productivist agriculture.

In Search of Legitimacy

While the state was slowly warming to the idea of organic farming, the leaders of the movement were likewise slowly warming to the mainstream. Knowing that further expansion would be impossible with existing ad hoc research and distribution networks, cooperation with the state would open new opportunities for development and marketing. The Lemaire-Boucher method began to occupy a stand at the Agricultural Salon in Paris, while the leaders of Nature and Progress began giving radio and press interviews to the mainstream media. By the mid-1970s, Nature and Progress began to minimize the importance of vitalist principles and to play up the scientific basis for organic agriculture.[65] And by the end of the decade, the president of Nature and Progress was invited by the state to sit on an information-gathering committee on nuclear energy.[66]

The 1970s proved to be a decisive decade for the split that had formed between the Lemaire and Nature and Progress camps. Raoul Lemaire passed in 1972, leaving his sons to run the family business. Georges Racineux, a longtime member, used this opportunity to secede and found his own organization, the French Union of Organic Farming (Union française d'agriculture biologique, or UFAB). The politics of UFAB were Poujadist, Racineux himself having run for office on a Poujadist ticket in 1958 (alongside Lemaire).[67] In keeping with these politics, UFAB maintained that family farms ought to remain free from the grip of industrial capitalism. The group remained small, with roughly just two hundred members throughout the decade, but the impact of its formation was significant. With the most extreme elements siphoned off into their own organization, what was left of the Lemaire group was free to pursue a more moderate agenda, and as a result, to appeal to a broader swathe of the agricultural population.[68]

The Lemaire sons grew their ranks and expanded their roster of products, spinning the company out into several different branches. By 1980, there were 1,500 farmers practicing the Lemaire-Boucher method, up from 1,290 in 1970 and 220 in 1964.[69] The company that their father had started with a loaf of organic bread was now selling everything from breakfast cereal to cooking oil.

Nature and Progress similarly grew its membership base considerably over the course of the decade. By the late 1970s, the organization boasted six thousand members, though just one thousand of these were producers.[70] The rise of environmentalism and an urban nostalgia for a cleaned up rural past contributed heavily to the group's success. Nature and Progress took a serious interest in the leftist political questions of the day, from third world poverty and nuclear power to the ills of industrial capitalism and environmental degradation. For a counterculture that came into its own through the 1970s, Nature and Progress provided an already existing network of like-minded citizens.

In a mid-decade publication of their quarterly journal, *Nature et Progrès*, the association offered a succinct list of timely reasons readers should support organic farming. Covering health, the livelihood of small producers, and the environment, these arguments carried contemporary resonance with a wider public that was growing increasingly sensitive to these issues. In answer to the question "Why organic agriculture?" the editorial board of the journal responded: "1) to produce foods of high quality both in terms of taste and nutritional content . . . 2) to allow farmers to live from their labor . . . 3) to put an end to the enormous waste of energy and primary materials . . . and 4) to protect the environment."[71] Together, these four points rallied white-collar professionals concerned about the chemicals used in conventional agriculture, members of the counterculture who opposed the excesses of consumer capitalism, and early environmentalists.

In an effort to appeal more to producers, Nature and Progress tried to sell them on the financial benefits of farming organically. In an article titled "Organic Farming: The Solution to the Economic Problems of Small Producers," an agricultural engineer explained how conventional agriculture trapped farmers in a vicious cycle of debt, from the extra costs associated with heavy machinery and the weakened health of industrially raised livestock, to the downward pressure on prices that was the result of subsidy programs that encouraged surplus production. By converting to organic methods, those farmers who were feeling the squeeze of modernization could return their finances to the black while improving the health of both their animals and themselves.[72] Similarly, in a pamphlet advertising a three-day conference in Tours (Indre-et-Loire), farmers were reminded of the dire recommendations of the Vedel Report before they were provided with the usual reasons for taking up organic agriculture: "If you do not want your farm to be one of the 1.5 million agricultural operations that have to disappear in the next twenty years; if you are having increasing difficulties with parasitism and disease in your livestock; if you are mindful of the fact that you are producing food that is more and more adulterated and poisoned."[73] Diverting from the usual practice of leading with health and nature, Nature and Progress instead spoke to the financial anxieties of small producers to spread the word. With organic agriculture gaining a higher profile in widely read publications such as *La France Agricole*, Nature and Progress was trying to reach a new audience, one that was not necessarily interested in anthroposophy or the sanctity of the natural environment, but was instead trying to survive the ruthless world of state-mandated modernization.

By 1978, it was estimated that there were three thousand farmers in France who were practicing organic or biodynamic methods. With roughly one million farmers in total, the organic population accounted for less than one-half of one percent of the whole.[74] Roughly two-thirds of these farmers were located in the west and in the south, where polyculture was most common. They produced wheat, rye, spelt, peas, soybeans, lentils, and potatoes. Vegetables, as well as beef and dairy, were likewise well represented on organic farms. The production of fruit, however, was fairly limited given how hard it was to scale without the assistance of chemicals.[75]

That the number of organic producers remained low said more about the dominance of postwar state-mandated industrialized farming than it did about preferences on the ground level. For instance, one farmer wrote to André Louis in the late 1960s to express his frustration at not being able to convert to organic agriculture because the financial incentives all pointed toward conventional farming. He wanted to know, in advance, what kind of premium he could expect for carrying a Nature and Progress label on his products and whether that would be enough to offset the costs of converting his farm and allow him to turn a profit.[76] In spite of promises on the part of Nature and Progress that organic farming would solve the financial difficulties of small producers, for most of them the stakes were simply too high. With livelihoods in the balance, it was difficult for farmers to accept the risks associated with converting their operations.

The influx of new blood through the 1970s led many to push for a new organization that would be more inclusive than those of the early pioneers.

In 1978, they founded a nonpartisan association for organic practitioners, the National Federation for Organic Agriculture (Fédération nationale d'agriculture biologique, or FNAB). Rather than having to choose between the conservative Lemaire-Boucher Method and the eco-leftist Nature and Progress, French producers could now belong to an organization that sought only to advocate for organic agriculture, rather than to advocate for a particular lifestyle or politics. Moreover, these new organic farmers were fresh on the job and needed a community that would provide them with the support they needed if they were going to be successful and remain on the land.

With greater legitimacy in the eyes of both the state and agricultural research organizations, organic farmers could benefit from the forms of assistance that had been profiting their conventional counterparts. To that end, in 1978 organic farmers also established the Association of Independent Organic Agricultural Advisors (Association des conseillers indépendants en agriculture biologique, or ACAB). Challenging the hegemonic position of both the state's agricultural extension agents and the Lemaire-Boucher technical advisors, these new consultants would advise on any and all organic practices, regardless of method. ACAB also facilitated the push toward greater uniformity in organic agriculture. If organic goods were going to be successful as a niche market, their quality needed to be standardized to assure the public that an organic label would guarantee certain conditions of production. With an independent and less politically charged wing of technical advisors, organic agriculture could present itself to the state and the wider public as a legitimate practice that was backed by science.[77]

The vice president of FNAB, Philippe Desbrosses, proved instrumental in negotiating with the French state. In 1969, his parents converted their family farm in the Sologne (Loir-et-Cher, Loiret, and Cher) to organic production. He immediately returned home, from a European tour with his band, and began a lifelong project of advancing the place of organic farming in France. In 1979, the Ministry of Agriculture was preparing a new Orientation Law and the National Assembly had begun deliberating over just how to include organic agriculture, if at all. To sway the debate, Desbrosses wanted to present organic farmers as a united front. The founding of FNAB and ACAB had already gone a long way in this endeavor, but Desbrosses wanted a formalized show of unity.

In June of 1980, Desbrosses gathered the various organic organizations together in the city of Blois (Loir-et-Cher), not far from his farm, and persuaded them all to sign a charter.[78] Prior to the charter, organic practices ran the gamut. There were twenty-odd different organizations representing organic farmers by 1980, from Nature and Progress and FNAB to Biobourgogne and UFAB. There were, of course, general principles largely based on Howard's law of return that were followed by everyone positing the farm as a closed system in which all organic waste was fed back into the soil. But beyond that, there was little standardization in what constituted organic farming or an organic product. The Charter of Blois provided that uniformity by supplying key definitions and standards for organic production. For instance, the charter provided guidelines for distinguishing between chemical and natural products as well as for such practices as pest management, animal husbandry, and food processing. The charter also included strict instructions on how to convert a conventional farm into an organic farm and what it would take after the conversion to be recognized as an organic operation. In short, the Charter of Blois provided a clear picture of what exactly constituted organic agriculture.

As a result of Desbrosses' efforts, organic farming was included in the new Orientation Law of 1980, marking a major turning point for organic agriculture in France. This inclusion initiated a process of institutionalization that would continue through the end of the century. Commenting on his success to his regional daily paper, Desbrosses championed the various advantages of organic farming: "The agricultural model that has prevailed in recent years has been superseded. In terms of yields, we have obtained with organic agriculture considerable increases, and the nutritional content of our products is absolutely superior to that of the products of traditional agriculture. All of this plays to our favor."[79] But the process of greening the Ministry of Agriculture was slow. The Orientation Law of 1980 did not even use the term "organic agriculture," opting instead for "an agriculture that does not use synthetic chemical inputs." The championing of organic agriculture was simply too politically controversial for the majority of legislative representatives, many of whom relied on the rural vote and the major agricultural unions to mobilize that vote. Moreover, a wholehearted acceptance of organic practices was tantamount to questioning the wisdom and virtue of the postwar productivity drive and the industrial farming that it had fostered, and so the Orientation Law tread lightly.

This new legislation, however, was not simple lip service. For those who supported the recognition of organic farming within the halls of state power, the objective was twofold. First, by recognizing it, they could control it. Organic farming had developed in a largely haphazard fashion, with eugenicist Poujade supporters farming alongside hippie back to the landers. The new Orientation Law would impose some order and coherence on the practice, which would in turn make the marketplace a safer and more legible space for both buyers and sellers. Consumers would no longer have to wonder what an organic label meant, while purveyors could rest assured that the state backing of their value-added organic labels would guarantee their products a distinct position on supermarket shelves.

Second, organic agriculture presented market opportunities that the state could not ignore. It was clear that there was a niche market here to be developed and exploited, one that would generate revenue for the French economy and improve the situation of politically volatile small producers. The Ministry of Agriculture had already begun experimenting with these markets. For example, the Red Label (*Label Rouge*) had been operational for roughly a decade and signaled to consumers that products carrying the label were of a superior quality. Everything from charcuterie and cheese to fruit and vegetables were eligible for the label, though chicken was by far the most popular item on the market. Red Label chickens were free from growth hormones, raised on a higher quality feed, containing a minimum of 70 percent grain, and were subject to stricter sorting rules at the slaughterhouse.[80] Between 1973 and 1980, the consumption of Red Label chicken rose every single year by a whopping 15 to 25 percent.[81] With this kind of success, it was reasonable to assume that consumers would be receptive to other kinds of value-added goods. Organic products therefore held the promise of not only expanding markets for high-quality French food items but also promised to grant small producers new streams of badly needed revenue.

Moreover, the rest of Europe was beginning to take greater notice of organic production and France did not want to be left behind. The German Ministry of Agriculture had in fact been spending significant sums on research into organic farming since the early 1970s, and in 1975 the European Community had recommended to its member-states that they study and evaluate the role of organic agriculture in their respective farm sectors. Even Sicco Mansholt, the late harbinger of doom, had been forced to amend his policy prescriptions by the rise of environmentalism and the economic shocks of the oil crisis.[82] By the end of the 1970s, he was speaking publicly on the importance of expanding alternative methods. Governments across western Europe were considering the possibilities of organic agriculture and figuring out how best to manage it alongside the dominant industrial model.

But for those suspicious of state co-optation, the treatment of organic agriculture by mainstream institutions fell short of the ideals established by the early crusaders. The Orientation Law spoke of organic agriculture strictly in terms of chemical inputs. Nothing was said about the environment, or about the farm as a closed system. Organic agriculture for these practitioners was about more than simply eschewing chemical products. It was about respecting the land, a holistic approach to health, and maintaining autonomy from a dirigiste state. When the leaders of GABO had first set out to articulate organic methods in the late 1950s, they had reached well beyond the simple exhortation that farmers abjure chemical inputs. They had argued that the farmer's primary duty was to maintain the natural fertility of the soil. Heavy tillage was forbidden. Composts derived from manure and other natural fertilizers were required. In short, the farmer was first and foremost a guardian of the soil. From that vocation followed the production of quality agricultural goods that improved consumer health and sustained the environment. The state had reduced this philosophy to one single element, the absence of chemical inputs, an oversimplification that was an affront to those practitioners who believed in a deeper connection between farm and farmer.

Conclusion
Slipping through the Cracks

> We hear this affirmation everywhere: "Farms must be profitable."
> Money must produce more money. We fail to recognize that this
> production of more money is realized at the expense of capital;
> the essential capital that is life, Man, body, and soul.
>
> —JEAN BOUCHER, *Une veritable agriculture biologique* (1992, 32)

In 1969, Roger Roblot, an electrician working at a plastics factory in Eure-et-
Loir attempted to purchase farmlands and was preempted on behalf of an
established farmer. In a letter of protest addressed to the minister of agriculture, Roblot explained that he had been forced to leave the family farm for
the factory because there had not been enough land to support all of the
siblings who wished to farm. When he saw an advertisement in the paper for a
piece of land in his home county of Corvées-les-Yys, he jumped at the
chance to return to agriculture and quickly made arrangements with the
seller to effect the purchase.[1] The SAFER then exercised its right of preemption on the grounds that (1) Roblot was not already employed as a farmer,
and (2) the piece of land in question could be used to reinforce a neighboring
operation.[2] Roblot joined the ranks of those whose dreams had been dashed.

There was no question that the SAFER was acting according to its mandate and supporting area farmers to improve the size and distribution of their
holdings. In this regard, this case was like many others. What makes this
story interesting, however, is the manner in which Roblot defended his interests. He began with a desperate personal attack on the SAFER beneficiary, an almost universal tactic that was more often than not fueled by panic
and a complete lack of knowledge (and this case was no different, with
Roblot falsely accusing the beneficiary of the SAFER redistribution of
being neither a farmer nor in possession of lands contiguous to those he
received). But then he pushed further, questioning the foundations of the
market and of the Fifth Republic itself.

In Roblot's first letter, he questioned the limits of his rights as a consumer. In a frantic series of increasingly urgent questions put to the minister of agriculture, Roblot asked: "What is the SAFER for? What is its

goal? What are the limits of its power? Who has the right to buy lands? Why do the notaries use the press to advertise that lands are for sale when only the SAFER has the right to buy them?"[3] Roblot had freely purchased lands on the market, with a consenting seller, and had signed all necessary papers with the notary. Yet they were taken away from him. Roblot therefore came to the conclusion that the market was simply not functioning as it should. In his final letter, referring to the political climate following the events of 1968, Roblot went so far as to question the very democracy and rule of law on which the Fifth Republic was founded: "In an age when we talk a lot about progress, about democracy, about dialogue and legality, I ask myself if all of this is actually embodied in the case that I have presented."[4] Unable to appeal his case, for the SAFER was indeed acting according to the letter of the law, and faced with an intractable bureaucracy at every turn, Roblot finally gave up. After seven months of exchanging letters with various administrative officials, Roblot conceded that he would be unable to return to farming and that he would have to continue commuting eleven kilometers to a factory job he had never wanted in the first place. While many of these letters to the SAFER and to the Ministry of Agriculture communicated a certain level of desperation and frustration, the persistence with which Roblot pursued his case, and the utter helplessness he expressed in doing so, demonstrates the degree to which life options for individual citizens were foreclosed by a state hungry with global ambitions.

It often fell to the SAFER to deal with the complaints of those such as Roblot, who were simply not able to meet the requirements established by modernizing agricultural policies. Ultimately, the SAFER was a means for the state to displace some of its responsibility for the welfare of its citizens to the vicissitudes of local politics. As part of the deliberations process behind the Orientation Laws, it was openly acknowledged that one-half of all French farms were too small and would therefore either need to evolve or disappear.[5] It was also the case, however, that many of the individuals behind the Orientation Laws and the SAFER, and in particular Eugène Forget and Michel Debatisse, had hoped that these new measures would not only further modernization efforts, but that they would likewise soften the blow for those who were unable to carry on as farmers—through funding for retraining or retirement. But given the general refusal of both the Ministry of Agriculture and the office of the president to intervene in SAFER decisions, it was clear that state administrators, exhausted by the legal troubles that *remembrement* had produced, had come to see the SAFER as a means of deflecting responsibility for the agricultural revolution that they had mandated. As local institutions, the SAFER were often the first point of contact for farmers trying to engage with an incomprehensible state apparatus that was seemingly calling for their eradication. As such, they could likewise shoulder the blame.

While the administrators of the SAFER fought hard to protect those farmers they could, the organization ultimately functioned as a brutally competitive selective aid program. Those farmers deemed worthy of investment were provided with support and the rest were left to their own defenses. For the poorer owners, and for the elderly, this often meant being passed over for farmers who promised to fulfill state plans for modernization. The bottom line was that economic growth required a healthy and competitive agricultural sector. Consequently, the SAFER was designed to restructure holdings in the *aggregate*—and not to come to the rescue of individual farmers, a difficult truth that was often misunderstood by those who sought out its assistance. If individual claimants could not convince the SAFER that their own particular interests intersected with those of the state, they were simply out of luck. Men and women like Roblot, who would have preferred to farm modest "unviable" holdings than work in a factory, were denied access to farmland on the grounds that a more deserving individual would better serve the collective needs of the modernizing nation.

BY THE 1980S, French agriculture had triumphed on the world stage. The green gas of the French economy was performing as Jean Monnet and Pierre Pflimlin had hoped, earning credit on global markets and buttressing service-oriented growth. Between 1960 and 1982, earnings from agricultural exports skyrocketed from five million to eighty million francs—an increase of 1,600 percent.[6] Cereals accounted for the bulk of French exports, followed by wine and spirits, and then meat and animal products. In other words, the principle export product of the farm sector was industrially produced grain and not the gourmet items, such as wine or cheese, that one typically associates with French agriculture. The common market had paid off. By 2000, the EU accounted for almost three-quarters of all French agricultural exports. And even after agricultural spending declined, having reached its peak in the early 1980s, support from the CAP continued to represent a substantial portion of French agricultural incomes—a full 25 to 30 percent at the end of the century.[7]

As the French moved into position as the world's second largest exporter of agricultural goods, support for small-scale agricultural products was gaining a wider audience. In 1982, the regional daily *Presse-Océan* published a piece about how consuming farm products had become fashionable, while *Ouest France* a few months later told readers about the rise in popularity of buying direct from the farm.[8] Similarly, *Le Quotidien de Paris* briefed readers on the growing empire of La Vie Claire, which included 420 stores specializing in health foods and alternative medicine, as well as a small publishing house.[9] Needless to say, no mention was made of the company's anti-Semitic past.

As the boom years drew to a close, thanks to the oil crisis and rising inflation, the virtues of economic growth came to be questioned by a well-educated urban populace that had come to value the natural environment in new ways. In an article in the popular French weekly *Le Point*, industrial agriculture was publicly taken to task for its pollution of French waterways. The byline read: "Throughout France, the level of nitrates in our water has risen in a deadly manner. The number-one suspect: fertilizers used to 'dope' agriculture."[10] The article acknowledged that it was generally taboo to discuss the polluting effects of industrial farming, but the problem had grown so acute that something needed to be done and it was up to the press to raise awareness. The water in several French departments was in fact undrinkable according to the standards of the World Health Organization. The article then stated that the presence of chemicals in French drinking water could lead to gastrointestinal problems, and possibly even cancer.

Between the dangers of industrially produced food and the nostalgic allure of the countryside, the terrain was ripe for the rise of terroir. A concept that dated back to the eighteenth century, but which had been dormant since the interwar period, terroir bridged the gap between urban consumers and their rural past. Defined as "traditional local agricultural products and foodstuffs, whose qualities cross time and space and are anchored in a specific place and history," terroir products provided consumers with an alternative to the industrial standardization and amorphous placelessness of the postwar food chain.[11] In 1984, the Ministry of Culture decided to create a twenty-two-volume collection, one for each region in the hexagon, documenting the culinary heritage of France, from *poulets de Bresse* to *escargots à la Bourguignonne*. Simultaneously, the Ministry of Agriculture was increasing its efforts in the direction of value-added niche markets and encouraging the expansion of the AOC system. Created in the 1930s as a means of guaranteeing provenance in the wine industry, the number of foods protected by AOC status rose dramatically through the 1980s and 1990s. Previously, the vast majority of these terroir products had been consumed locally in their regions of origin. It was not until the final decades of the twentieth century that they entered national, and even international, distribution networks in large numbers. For instance, while only 15 percent of all French wine carried an AOC designation in 1970, during the following decade that share rose to 44 percent.[12] No longer the stuff of specialty stores, producers began selling their designated wines in big-box supermarkets.

In an early *Presse-Océan* article about this rising phenomenon, readers were schooled in the ABCs of terroir.[13] In light of efforts on the part of the AOC section for cheese to increase the presence of its products on the national market, readers were told that designated products carried a "seal of authenticity that guarantees the quality of the cheese," and that producers practiced traditional methods to comply with the exacting certification process. Consumers could be sure that AOC cheeses were higher in quality than the generic chèvre and Brie that were universally available across the country. Beyond the guarantee of quality, AOC products likewise guaranteed a deeper connection to the landscape, as they carried "the indissoluble and inalienable characteristics of the region, of the terroir, of the vintage, and of the producers." AOC products were rooted in the land, as were the farmers who produced them. Lastly, these superior goods were produced in concert with the environment. Unlike industrial agriculture that sought to tame the environment in order to exploit it, AOC production (so the story went) worked in tandem with the land. By eating and drinking these products, consumers could recapture their relationship with rural France one region at a time.

The consumption of these goods also allowed for the assertion of French identity in the midst of an increasingly European, and even global, system of food production and distribution. In this regard, regionalism worked both as an economic response to competition from the EEC and abroad (products with a terroir designation became highly desirable to international consumers) and as a cultural and political counterweight. While regionally specific French products cornered a niche market for high-quality goods, the rootedness of French sovereignty and the specificity of its cultural identity resisted the transnational political structure and the cultural imaginary of a homogenous united Europe.

The gap between agricultural practices and popular assumptions about what these practices entailed revealed a collective and voluntary case of misrecognition. Blind to the combine threshers and the concrete livestock operations, French men and women instead preferred to imagine a bucolic

FIGURE 16 Refusing the romantic idyll. *Source*: P. Jérome, "La loi des agroalimentaires," *Politique-Hebdo*, January 30, 1975; Kerleroux (Illustrator).

landscape in which farms were worked by human hands rather than machines, and livestock was pastured rather than confined. The regional inventories of culinary heritage were both a symptom, in that they embodied this collective nostalgia, and a cause, as they perpetuated these ideals. Announced in 1984, just before the first major reforms to the CAP and the first outbreak of mad cow disease, these inventories represented the apex of a nostalgia for the countryside that had begun to emerge in the early 1970s.[14]

The farmers who had broken their backs to industrialize and provide consumers with cheap food often resented this romantic imagining of the countryside and of the agricultural production that took place therein. In the radical *Politique-Hebdo*, for instance, an article on declining farm revenues was accompanied by a cartoon that portrayed a modern-looking farmer hard at work on a tractor, who asked, "What? You want me t' sing somethin' by Jean Ferrat?" (see figure 16).[15] The farmer was addressing a nonfarming public whose imagination of life on the farm relied on popular and idyllic representations, such as Ferrat's "La Montagne" and "Ma France," rather than on actual experience. This farmer was trying to tell urban romantics that farming was not all about being at one with nature, but that it was a livelihood like any other. Being called on to protect the landscape so that fair-weather ruralists might descend to consume it from time to time was hardly the victory that French farmers had envisioned for themselves when they had asked that the land be protected as something else entirely—as a tool of production.[16]

Attrition

In the summer of 2006, the *New York Times* published an article on how recent global trade talks had collapsed over issues concerning agriculture. When asked about why the deliberations had failed, one of the negotiators quipped, "If it's a toss-up between French farmers and the rest of the world, apparently it's French farmers who will win."[17] From the very first GATT (General Agreement on Tariffs and Trade) negotiations of the 1940s, when agriculture was deliberately left off the table because it was too controversial, through the recent Doha round of the World Trade Organization, which collapsed in large part due to inflexibility on farm subsidies, agricultural policy has persistently emerged as a breaking point in the sphere of international political economy. More recently, in the summer of 2015, as I finished the first draft of this manuscript, French farmers were once again in the streets, blocking roadways filled with Parisians heading out for summer vacation, dumping manure in the road, and marching to local prefectures. In spite of their dwindling numbers, French farmers have become a powerful interest group within the halls of French power. As such, they have also become a target for the kind of cynicism expressed in the above citation. Criticized for a seemingly disproportionate sense of entitlement, French farmers have become a thorn in the side of the French state, the European Union, and the members of the World Trade Organization.

What these critics fail to appreciate is that the French agricultural unions are the product of a cutthroat war of attrition that forced farmers to become ruthless negotiators in their own right.[18] The industrialization of French farming was one of the more stunningly thorough and brutally aggressive cases of agricultural transformation of the modern era. Often referred to as a revolution, the agricultural industrialization process in France effected an all-encompassing transformation of the countryside.[19] At the close of the Second World War, the average farm looked much as it had in the nineteenth century. Farmers used draft animals rather than tractors. They practiced polycultivation and distributed their goods through local networks. In the span of one generation, however, all of that had changed. Between 1955 and 1975, the active agricultural population was cut in half, and the number of farms decreased by roughly 2.5 percent per year, every year.[20] By the 1980s, the French farming population had been reduced to just 7 percent of the workforce.[21]

Statistics like these are often repeated in the literature on the agricultural revolution that took place in postwar France. But what is often missing is an examination of how these numbers translated into human experience. In twenty years, one million farms were lost. While it is presumably the case that many of these farms were transferred willingly and to the profit of their previous owners, it is also the case that many French men and women, whose labor had become unnecessary thanks to the advances of modernization, lost their farms in spite of great pains to hang on to them. The stories that emerged through *remembrement* and the SAFER attest to the ferocity with which farmers defended themselves as individual citizens when faced with a powerful state mandate that they did not always support.

In examining more closely how French farmers responded to a new system of production that made the vast majority of them superfluous, I have tried to emphasize that beyond the impressive statistics regarding increases in productivity and economic growth, there was a very real human cost to be paid for such accomplishments. While the collective nation may have achieved grandeur in the end, it did so at the expense of countless individual citizens. Roblot lost his place on the farm not once, but twice. Many of the farmers addressed by François-Henri de Virieu had lost their life savings and financial security by taking on too much debt. Farmers in isolated mountainous areas lost the rural communities that had once sustained them. Many lost the farm entirely.

In response to their obsolescence, different farmers reacted in different ways. To be sure, some simply sold off the farm and took up a new line of work. Others retired. But a great many tried to fight back, through protests, the creation of breakaway unions, the illegal occupation of lands, and the development of alternative local markets. That so many chose to resist the changing tide of agricultural industrialization is evidence of just how much was at stake in this process of transformation. That French farmers continue to fight to defend their interests, both at the negotiating table and in the streets, should come as no surprise given that they were forced to cut their political teeth through the war of attrition that was state-mandated agricultural modernization.

The French experience of agricultural modernization was both exemplary and anomalous. The French story was exemplary in that the industrialization of food production is an endeavor that was undertaken in the twentieth century by a wide variety of governments, from communist China and Russia to capitalist Canada and the United States, and everyone else in between. And here I would argue that the French experience was a classic example of what James Scott has called the ideology of high modernism, an ideology that was rooted in a belief in linear progress, technocratic expertise, and rational planning.

In other words, the sheer determination to pull off an economic and social revolution is not what set the French apart. What *did* make the French experience anomalous, however, was the disproportionate amount of power that the French state held over European integration, a position of political privilege that was exploited in order to rise to the top of the global food chain. It was this larger geopolitical context that afforded the French a decisive advantage over other states attempting to realize similar objectives. And it was this context that allowed the state to squeeze its farmers to such an exceptional degree.

The Organic Option

What does it mean that many of the early crusaders believed in eugenics, supported fascist politics, and were openly anti-Semitic? After all, the organic movement shifted squarely to the Left in the 1970s and abandoned its right-wing neo-fascist roots. But it is not that simple. Most contemporary proponents of organic production do not align themselves with fascist anti-Semitism, but they do value purity. And through the idiom of purification, organic supporters, both left and right, have been instrumental in cementing the connection between small producers, the rural landscape, and national identity. This connection has in turn been vulnerable to appropriation by contemporary French right-wing politics. And this appeal to purity, and to the authenticity of *la France profonde* (literally deep France, but metaphorically the heartland), has been instrumental in the early twenty-first century rise of the xenophobic National Front Party.

Moreover, what does it mean that these pioneers believed in the magical processes of transmutation? The cleaned-up version of the organic movement claims that organic foods are nutritionally superior and free from cancer-causing chemical residues. How do we evaluate that claim when we place it side by side with Jean Boucher's claim, based on the science of Kervran, that organic products fertilized with lithothamnion benefited from a process of nuclear transformation?

Twenty-first-century organic agriculture looks very different when viewed from its origins. Its claims to superior nutrition are haunted by a history of anthroposophy, vitalism, and pseudoscience. This early history, if made known, threatens to undermine the credibility of the movement. Perhaps this is why it is so rarely ever told. After reading the histories of industrial and organic farming side by side, it becomes difficult to determine who might be the more trustworthy party—the state that wanted to maximize productivity at all costs, or an oddball group of eccentrics who believed in magic? This early history makes it difficult to determine whether organic claims to that elusive "quality" were not just as suspect as those put forth by the agro-industrial complex.

Despite these suspect origins, or perhaps because they remained hidden from public view, the organic sector in France grew considerably in the first decades of the postwar period. By the 1980s, France accounted for a full 60 percent of all organic agricultural production in Europe. In 1995, however, that portion had fallen to just 10 percent.[22] Italy, Germany, Denmark, and Britain had all pulled ahead and today continue to outstrip the French in organic production. So what happened? How did France start off in such a strong position only to fall behind in the end?

The early split between the Raoul Lemaire and André Louis factions was certainly a contributing factor. In the 1980s, when it came time to negotiate with the state to advocate for the interests of organic farmers and to win them funding for technical and marketing assistance, a lack of unity in the sector diminished the strength of their lobbying power. Moreover, this lack of unity made it that much harder for organic farmers to challenge the monopoly of the FNSEA and the CNJA, and gain access to the halls of the Ministry of Agriculture. Under the neo-corporatist model, there was every incentive for the two major farm unions to refuse to cooperate with new organizations and to hang onto their power.

Perhaps most important, however, the process of institutionalization itself proved to be a real handicap for French organic farmers. By the 1990s, France was spending on organic agriculture just one-fifth of what the

Netherlands was spending, half of what Austria was spending, and considerably less than what was being spent in Germany and Belgium.[23] The EEC had earmarked special funding to support initiatives in sustainable and environmentally friendly farming. These countries tended to use that money to support the development of organic agriculture. France, however, tended to use the money to support the extensive pasturing of livestock in remote mountainous regions.[24]

The support of these isolated farmers was in keeping with broader plans for both the development of the AOC system and the proper balancing of the French landscape. Given that the AOC label and the reputation for quality were particularly important to the dairy industry, this investment in the extensive production of animal products might have been tied to a state decision to focus on the more malleable niche category of "quality," rather than on the more tightly defined organic. Moreover, as anxieties over the social desertification of the countryside mounted, maintaining equilibrium between urban and rural France was all the more important. Urban French would no longer be able to escape into the countryside if this balance was disrupted and there were no longer enough farmers to maintain the rural landscape. Providing subsidies to farmers to remain in these regions would fulfill the goal of *aménagement du territoire* that all of France continue to be inhabited. Between the joint efforts of the state and French agribusiness to develop quality goods in order to build niche markets and the myth that these products were all natural and artisanal, there was very little room for organic to maneuver, either within the halls of the Ministry of Agriculture or the hearts of French consumers.

The French agricultural sector was able to build on its initial success with industrial cereals by adding to its list of profitable exports both wine and dairy, products that were marketed as gourmet high-quality items. Agro-industrial processors mastered the art of selling foreign consumers on escargots, foie gras, Brie, and Camembert at such international trade events as the Fancy Food Show in New York City. And with the emphasis placed firmly on quality and terroir, the added value of organic was less important when it came to attracting discerning consumers.

While organic farmers and well-informed consumers pretended to understand the difference between the two, the increasing presence on the shelves of AOC labels and promises of quality led consumers to believe that whether a product was organic or not was irrelevant. In other countries, lacking this variety of traceability, organic served as a more important marker of trust. But in France, the labels indicating the origins, or the superior quality, of the goods on the shelves reestablished the consumer trust in the food chain that had been eroded by several decades of agricultural industrialization.

The Twenty-First-Century Ideal

The story of postwar French agriculture is really two stories that must be told in parallel: the story of a brutal state-mandated industrialization and the story of those who resisted it with alternative methods and markets. These alternatives began as local initiatives, developed by ideologues who existed on the fringe of mainstream agronomy. By the 1970s, these two stories began to converge as the French state pursued environmentalist policies designed to clean up industrial farming and to protect French lands from human development. A decade later, organic farming exited the fringe and entered the mainstream as a complement to industrial agriculture. The landscape could be both exploited *and* protected; agriculture could be both industrial *and* environmentally sound. In the 1980s, the state worked to merge these two stories together. The incorporation of alternative practices into the mainstream fold would cultivate the illusion that French agriculture remained an exception to the industrial rule, an illusion that would serve French agricultural exports well on global markets. And so the state co-opted the fringe by way of labeling laws, funding for organic agriculture, and the expansion of organic distribution networks into the aisles of big-box supermarkets such as Monoprix and Auchan.

But convergence was not easy. These two stories were constantly in tension with one another. Just as land in the Cévennes was set aside for conservation, land in Brittany was poldered to create more farms. The SAFER fought hard to control speculation on the real estate market in agricultural lands, but simultaneously facilitated state plans for the expansion of the market in second homes. Production and consumption came to inhabit the countryside in an uneasy coexistence. Farmers continued to produce cheap food in abundant quantities, while part-time urban residents and visitors consumed the land through recreational areas, new regional parks, and second homes.

At the root of these efforts to return symbolically to the land was a profound and absolute sense of loss. And yet, it was coupled with a blind faith that what was lost could somehow be recaptured. Farmers became a medium for this homecoming. For those who had lost their connection to the land, it was imperative that they believe that farmers had remained impervious to economic, social, and cultural change, and had maintained a meaningful connection to the land. And so, urban consumers of French food products ignored the concrete barns of Brittany, the increased reliance on chemical fertilizers, and the enormous combine harvesters that dotted the country-side. And the farmers, who stood to profit from this voluntary ignorance and whose reputation as quality small-scale traditional producers was highly bankable rarely saw fit to disabuse them of their fantasies.

Agriculture carried both market and symbolic values. As both an indispensable tool of production, *le foncier*, and a symbolically laden abstraction, *la terre*, the French landscape has long straddled the divide between farming as capitalist enterprise and farming as cultural cachet. Unlike the tractors and combines that came with mechanization or the pesticides and fertilizers that became common practice, farmland was not just an agricultural input. Farmland, as part of the French rural landscape, was (and still is) bound up with national heritage and identity, the ideological underpinnings of Republicanism, and the late twentieth-century emergence of a collective nostalgia for life on the farm. This complexity is embodied in the term itself—*la terre*. The multiple meanings that the term encompasses are laid bare as soon as one attempts to translate it into English. In choosing one of the available options—"land," "soil," "earth," "ground"—the meanings of the others are lost, for while the English language makes a distinction between the proprietary land, the productive soil, the romantic earth, and the positional ground, the French *la terre* captures them all, and is richer and more evocative than the simple sum of its parts.

The model farmer had become a combination of the industrial and alternative ideals. He was expected to be part *agriculteur* (farmer/entrepreneur) and part *paysan* (peasant/salt of the earth). While the popular imagination, unencumbered by the logistics of national food security or the economic potential of international markets in foodstuffs, had embraced the farmer as described by Jean Ferrat, the state required the ideal farmer to know how to operate a combine and to cultivate forty hectares or more. Moreover, this farmer was still decidedly a "he," supported a loving wife and one or two children who were committed to taking over the farm once their father retired. But the loving wife no longer necessarily worked alongside her husband. Instead, she probably supplemented his income with off-farm employment, as part of the broader attempt to keep families on the farm while curbing surplus production. She might even supplement the family revenue by converting an old barn into a rural *gîte* (a bed and breakfast or small inn), hosting urban families in search of pastoral tranquility on the weekends and during summer holidays.[25] The ideal farmer was moreover still an important part of the economy, producing wheat and sugar for the common market, bringing in the green gas that continued to buttress the French balance of payments. In short, despite the romantic fantasy that emerged in the 1970s, which imagined the French farmer as a steward to the nation's natural patrimony, much of the industrial ideal survived, for the ideal farmer was still a modern and efficient producer—what had changed was simply that he was expected to keep this fact to himself.

Notes

Unless otherwise noted, all translations of quotations are my own.

Introduction

1. Cleary, *Politicians and Producers*, 11.

2. France, La Direction de la documentation, *Le remembrement rural*, 6–7, and "La France a perdu le quart de ses exploitations agricoles en 10 ans," *Le Monde*, September 13, 2011.

3. Barral, *Les Agrariens Français*, 217; Alphandéry, Bitoun, and Dupont, *Les champs du départ*, 32.

4. Moulin, *Peasantry and Society*, 181.

5. Bairoch, Barral, and Tracy, Round Table Discussion (Barral speaking), 54.

6. Hervieu and Purseigle, "Troubled Pastures," 662.

7. Bairoch, "Dix-huit décennies de développement agricole," 15.

8. For more, see Tracy, *Government and Agriculture*.

9. Both biodynamic and organic farming are difficult to define given that different practitioners have stressed different elements. But broadly speaking, organic farming was most often defined by a lack of chemical inputs, whereas biodynamic farming was grounded in spiritual and mystical practices.

10. For more on the history of quality in all of its changing guises, see Stanziani, *Histoire de la qualité alimentaire*, and *La qualité des produits en France*.

11. Fel, "Les révolutions vertes," 11.

12. Wheelan, *Naked Economics*, 104.

13. Ibid., 105.

14. Some of the more widely read titles included Mendras, *La fin des paysans*, and Gervais, Servolin, and Weil, *Une France sans paysans*.

Chapter One

1. I have translated *commune*, the French administrative unit, as "county" throughout the text.

2. Serge Mallet, "Des paysans contre le passé," *France Observateur*, November 6, 1959, 12.

3. Dormois, *The French Economy*, 17, 54.

4. For more on the link between economic development and aspirations of political grandeur, see Hecht, *The Radiance of France*.

5. CAC (Centre des archives contemporaines), Fontainebleau, 800401 Ministère de l'agriculture, Direction de production et échanges, Service des relations internationales, Art. 7: "General Conditions of Agricultural Production in the Different

Countries," December 15, 1952. Anything that appears in English, except dates, in archival citations appeared in English in the original. This is not uncommon for either Marshall Plan or EU documents.

6. Migrant labor was another means by which industrial and tertiary positions could be filled. France certainly relied on this labor in its bid to modernize, but ultimately the transformation of the economy hinged on creating a new balance between town and country.

7. For an excellent study of how modernization operated within the context of rural electrification, see Frost, "Alternating Currents."

8. Treating the state as an actor can be problematic, if its inner workings are not made transparent. It is difficult, however, to provide detail when operating outside of the context of strict political or diplomatic history. When trying to make broader claims about the sociocultural stakes of land reform, I therefore treat the state as an economical, albeit insufficient, shorthand for a host of institutions and individuals, whose roles within this decision-making structure are discussed in greater detail when they intersect directly with the narrative.

9. Debatisse, *La révolution silencieuse*.

10. Claims about "farming in France" or "the agricultural sector" are gross generalizations. But to follow in the footsteps of Marc Bloch, I maintain that the use of such language is "an admissible convention, perhaps, so long as we recognize it for what it is." Short of producing a multivolume work, any attempt to examine agricultural industrialization in postwar France necessarily relies on the practice of elision. While differences are briefly introduced in this paragraph and subsequently underscored when deemed necessary to the integrity of the argument, Bloch's admissible convention allows for a fluid and coherent narrative. See Bloch, *French Rural History*, xxv.

11. *Paysans*, no. 55 (August/September 1965): 80.

12. Wright, *Rural Revolution*, 178.

13. Historian Deborah Fitzgerald provides an incisive analysis of how the principles of industry were applied to agriculture in the American case. See Fitzgerald, *Every Farm a Factory*.

14. The enormous changes that seemingly happened almost overnight after the Second World War therefore had their roots in the interwar period. Questioning the degree to which 1945 served as a breaking point has become an increasingly popular framework for historians of France—and with good reason. There were indeed meaningful continuities that bridged the 1920s, 1930s, and 1940s. But the economic and political obstacles of these decades made for uneven advances. See, e.g., Nord, *France's New Deal*; Bonneuil and Thomas, "Purifying Landscapes"; and, for an older example, Kuisel and Florentin, "Vichy et les origines de la planification économique."

15. Alphandéry, Bitoun, and Dupont, *Les champs du départ*, 178.

16. Kuisel and Florentin, "Vichy et les origines de la planification économique," 100.

17. The literature on the CGP and Monnet is vast. See, e.g., Duchêne, *Jean Monnet*, and Rousso, *De Monnet à Massé*.

18. As quoted in Alphandéry and Sencébé, "L'émergence de la sociologie rurale en France," 25.

19. Dumont, *Le problème agricole français*. For the argument that farms were turned into factories, in the U.S. context, see Fitzgerald, *Every Farm a Factory*.

20. For more on *planification*, see Cazes and Mioche, *Modernisation ou décadence*; Hall, *Governing the Economy*; Kuisel, *Capitalism and the State in Modern France*; and Levy, *Tocqueville's Revenge*.

21. The historical significance of these missions has been well documented. See, e.g., Barjot, *Catching Up with America*.

22. AN (Archives nationales), Paris, AJ81 42 Activités du commissariat général du plan, Productivity missions reports, André Douzon, *Le fermier américain et sa famille*, 1951, 17 (Italics in original).

23. AN, Paris, F10 5270 Ministère de l'agriculture, Production végétale, folder marked "Maïs," n.d.

24. Ibid., letter from the Corn States Hybrid Service to the Ministry of Agriculture, March 4, 1949.

25. Mendras, *The Vanishing Peasant*, 98–127.

26. For more on U.S. agricultural policy as foreign policy, see Cullather, *The Hungry World*, and Perkins, *Geopolitics and the Green Revolution*.

27. AN, Paris, F60 904 Secrétaire général du gouvernement et services du premier-ministre, Séances du comité économique, 1947–1948, "Communication de M. le Ministre de l'Agriculture sur les problèmes posés par la mise en oeuvre de l'aide américaine, la coopération économique européenne et le plan d'équipement et de modernisation," June 18, 1948.

28. AN, Paris, F6oter 440 Secrétariat général du comité interministériel pour les questions de coopération économique européenne, 1944–1958, Organisation et fonctionnement des services américains en France, Mission spéciale de l'ECA en France, 1948–1958, European Recovery Program, *France: Country Study* (Economic Cooperation Administration, February 1949), 21.

29. Ibid., 46.

30. M. B. Lefort, "Exigences du consommateur allemand en matière de produits agricoles," *Economie Rurale* 21 (July 1954): 11–16.

31. AN, Paris, F6oter 440 Secrétariat général du comité interministériel pour les questions de coopération économique européenne, 1944–1958, Propagande relative au Plan Marshall 1950–1960, speech delivered by Pflimlin at Le Havre, January 6, 1949.

32. France, La Direction de la documentation, *Le remembrement rural*, 6–7, and CAC, Fontainebleau, 880333 Répertoire numérique des archives de Jean Roche, Art. 175: World Land Tenure Conference, conference proceedings, 1951, Frederic O. Sargent and Philine R. Vanderpol, "Land Tenure in France," in *Conference on World Land Tenure Problems, Part IV: Handbook of References*.

33. Sargent, "Fragmentation of French Land," 218.

34. For instance, one heir could take over the family farm in exchange for a *soulte* (compensation payment) paid to his siblings, an amount that was usually so great it either indebted the young farmer for life or proved prohibitive. Certain regions in France, moreover, were less likely to follow the law of equitable inheritance than

others. This did not, however, necessarily mean that these regions were without sub
stantial parceling.

35. Sargent, "Fragmentation of French Land," 218–29.

36. AN, Paris, AJ80 10 Commissariat général du plan, Rural Report 1946, "Premier
rapport de la commission de modernisation de l'équipement rural," September 1946,
32, and Cheverry and Clergeot, *Paysages ruraux*, 17.

37. CAC, Fontainebleau, 860087 Etudes du ministère de l'agriculture, Art. 1:
1962–1963, and Art. 2: 1964. For spatial minimums, see CAC, Fontainebleau, 880333
Répertoire numérique des archives de Jean Roche, Art. 174: World Land Tenure Conference, planning documents, 1951, Jean Roche, "Important Aspects of Consolidation in France," in *Land Tenure: Proceedings of the International Conference on Land
Tenure and Related Problems in World Agriculture Held at Madison, Wisconsin, 1951*, and
France, La Direction de la documentation, *Le remembrement rural*, 13.

38. For reasons of economy and flow, I have chosen to use the French term *remembrement* throughout rather than the more cumbersome English phrasing.

39. Cheverry and Clergeot, *Paysages ruraux*, endnote 51.

40. CAC, Fontainebleau, 880333 Répertoire numérique des archives de Jean Roche,
Art. 175: World Land Tenure Conference, 1951, Frederic O. Sargent and Philine R.
Vanderpol, "Land Tenure in France," in *Conference on World Land Tenure Problems,
Part IV: Handbook of References*, and Cheverry and Clergeot, *Paysages ruraux*, 12.

41. France, La Direction de la documentation, *Le remembrement rural*, 19.

42. Cheverry and Clergeot, *Paysages ruraux*, 12.

43. France, Direction de la documentation, *Le remembrement rural*, 20.

44. Cheverry and Clergeot, *Paysages ruraux*, 14–15.

45. Peneff, *Remembrement de Cadours*, i–ii.

46. The archives contain several hundred linear meters of filed complaints, court
proceedings, and judicial rulings. Unfortunately, these holdings are restricted for one
hundred years. For accounts in the press of how *remembrement* divided communities,
see R.A., "Wormhoudt ne veut plus du remembrement," *La France Agricole*, August 30,
1974. Among the many complaints leveled against the procedure, farmers charged
that the mayor was planning to set aside ninety hectares of otherwise viable farmland for the creation of a golf course. See also "Sur 18,000 parcelles de la Combe de
Savoie: Une expérience malheureuse," *La France Agricole*, June 21, 1974, and Michel
Mortagne, "Dossier noir du remembrement en pays vosgien," *La France Agricole*,
November 9, 1973.

47. Peneff, *Remembrement de Cadours*, 92.

48. CAC, Fontainebleau, 880333 Répertoire numérique des archives de Jean Roche,
Art. 40: Correspondance diverse, 1950–55. No. 6075 Assemblée nationale deuxième
législature, session de 1953, Annexe au procès-verbal de la séance du 27 mars 1953,
Proposition de loi tendant à rétablir le caractère volontaire des opérations de remembrement, institué par la loi du 27 novembre 1918, 1–2.

49. Ibid., Art. 41: Correspondance diverse, 1961–65, letter from Marg Charasse,
September 27, 1961.

50. Hoffmann, *Growth in a Traditional Society*.

51. AD (Archives départementales) Maine-et-Loire, Angers, 1350W Remembrement, Antoigné, letter from Eugène Guillemet to Justice of the Peace of south Saumur, President of the County Commission for *remembrement*, April 3, 1951.

52. For good examples of how this process was carried out, see Peneff, *Remembrement de Cadours*, 82–86, and Montpied, *Terres mouvantes*. For an especially impassioned attack on *remembrement*, see Beaufils, *Origines, implantation*. In a final example, referring specifically to the Haute-Loire, a government report stated that *remembrement* was difficult to carry out in the area because of fierce rivalries among neighbors. See Chassagne and Grandjean, *Les blocages fonciers*.

53. Peneff, *Remembrement de Cadours*, 171–73.

54. Montpied, *Terres mouvantes*, 163.

55. Cinémathèque du Ministère de l'agriculture, *Mécanisation et remembrement*.

56. Cronon, *Nature's Metropolis*, 120.

57. Fitzgerald, *Every Farm a Factory*, 5.

58. For more on Fourastié and productivity, see Boulat, *Jean Fourastié*.

59. Fourastié, *La productivité*.

60. Bouteille, *40 ans de politique foncière*, 10.

61. For two recent studies, see Cupers, *The Social Project*, and Pritchard, *Confluence*.

62. Gavignaud, *Les campagnes en France*, 74.

63. Béteille, *La France du vide*, and Gravier, *Paris et le désert français*. For desertification as it pertained directly to agriculture, see Alphandéry, Bitoun, and Dupont, *Les champs du départ*.

64. Pierre Roche, "Migrations rurales et sociétés d'établissement agricole," *Paysans*, no. 18 (June/July 1959): 37–50.

65. "Pourquoi ce malaise paysan?," *France Observateur*, February 18, 1960.

66. Allaire, "Modèle de développement," 347.

67. See, e.g., "L'agriculture française en evolution," *Combat*, July 14, 1959; "Pourquoi la crise dans les campagnes," *L'Express*, January 14, 1960; "Pourquoi ce malaise paysan?," *France-observateur*, February 18, 1960; and, for an academic treatment, Gachon, "L'évolution de l'agriculture française depuis 1940."

68. René Dumont, "Le malaise agricole," *Le Monde*, November 2, 1953.

69. André Ballet, "Les députés socialistes attaquent vivement la politique agricole du gouvernement," *Le Monde*, October 17, 1953.

70. Barral, *Les agrariens français*, 297, and Cleary, *Peasants, Politicians and Producers*, 16.

71. Keeler, *Neocorporatism in France*, 9.

72. Wright, *Rural Revolution*, 103–6, 114.

73. Keeler, *Neocorporatism in France*, 51.

74. To be sure, these are generalizations regarding the respective memberships of the two major agricultural unions. The sheer volume of FNSEA membership was such that its makeup certainly included competing opinions on which policies to pursue—and many would have supported structural reforms. That said, the general tenor of these two unions, as represented by their public statements and their

official support for various initiatives, was such that these generalizations remain productive.

75. Gervais, Jollivet, and Tavernier, *La fin de la France paysanne*, 469.

76. Wright, *Rural Revolution*, 150, and Alphandéry, Bitoun, and Dupont, *Les champs du départ*, 165–67.

77. Wright, *Rural Revolution*, 243n8.

78. Alphandéry, Bitoun, and Dupont, *Les champs du départ*, 168.

79. Keeler, *Neocorporatism in France*, 61.

80. For more on the Chambers of Agriculture, see Atrux-Tallau, "Histoire sociale d'un corps intermédiaire."

81. Hennis, *Globalization and European Integration*, 113.

82. Moulin, *Peasantry and Society in France*, 173; "Le discours de M. Debré sur l'agriculture n'a pas apaisé les inquiétudes du monde paysan," *Combat*, January 26, 1960.

83. The history of European integration has been well documented. See, e.g., Deighton and Milward, *Widening, Deepening*, and Knudsen, *Farmers on Welfare*. For a comprehensive study of the French case, see Sutton, *France and the Construction of Europe*.

84. Sutton, *France and the Construction of Europe*, 59.

85. CAC, Fontainebleau, 800401 Ministère de l'agriculture, Art. 7: Conférence européenne sur l'organisation des marchés agricoles, 1952–54.

86. Sutton, *France and the Construction of Europe*, 127.

87. Muth, *French Agriculture*, 107, 112, and M. Cuperly, "La politique agricole commune: 'Test' de l'Europe," *Paysans*, no. 23 (April/May 1960): 31–39.

88. Muth, *French Agriculture*, 107, 112.

89. See, e.g., "L'agriculture doit s'adapter pour profiter du Marché commun," *Les Echos*, January 26, 1965, and Michel Gabrysiak, "L'Europe a bouleversé la mentalité des paysans français," *L'Aurore*, July 15, 1965.

90. Jean Mennevret, "Vers une Europe économique," *Paysans*, no. 4 (February/March 1957): 39; see also, Michel Cuperly, "Face au marché commun l'agriculture française est-elle en peril?," *Paysans*, no. 12 (June/July 1958): 14–29.

91. "Agriculture, contre l'exode," *L'Express*, February 25, 1960.

92. AN, Paris, AJ80 Commissariat général du plan, Annexe 3: Poullain and Coquery, "Productivité de la main d'oeuvre en agriculture," circa 1946–47.

Chapter Two

1. Claude Louis, "3 exploitations en 'culture biologique,'" *Agri-7*, July 19, 1968.

2. Fonds Raoul Lemaire, Archives municipales d'Angers, 42J 241 Relations avec Pierre Poujade, 1959–1964, letter from Pierre Page to Pierre Poujade, May 11, 1956.

3. Ibid.

4. Address given on June 25, 1940, as recorded in Pétain, *La France nouvelle*, 25.

5. Cornu and Mayaud, *Au nom de la terre*, 18.

6. Conford, *The Origins of the Organic Movement*, 51–53, and Vogt, "Origins of Organic Farming," 24.

7. Jas, "Public Health and Pesticide Regulation in France," 372; see also Jas, *Au carrefour de la chimie et de l'agriculture.*

8. Treitel, *Eating Nature in Modern Germany.*

9. Paull, "Attending the First Organic Agriculture Course," 67.

10. Conford, *The Origins of the Organic Movement*, 65.

11. For more on Steiner, see Lachman, *Rudolf Steiner*, and Steiner, *The Agriculture Course.*

12. Conford, *The Origins of the Organic Movement*, 72.

13. Vogt, "Origins of Organic Farming," 22.

14. For more on Dorgères, and agrarianism, see Paxton, *French Peasant Fascism.*

15. For an extended discussion of how doctors intervened in the debate regarding bread and nutrition, see Kaplan, *Pain maudit*, 156–61. For the CNERNA study, see ibid., 1020–34.

16. Fonds Raoul Lemaire, Archives municipales d'Angers, 42J 208 Retours sur son parcours professionnel, April 1953, 75.

17. For more on how seed varieties were regulated, see Bonneuil et Hochereau, "Gouverner le 'progrès génétique.'"

18. Fonds Raoul Lemaire, Archives municipales d'Angers, 42J 191 Relations avec les autorités: Correspondance, 1938–1971, letter from Eugène Forget, president of the agricultural working group for the Economic Council, December 30, 1953.

19. Ibid., 42J 208 Retours sur son parcours professionnel, April 1953, 1.

20. Ibid., 42J 241 Relations avec Pierre Poujade, 1959–1964, letter to Poujade, April 27, 1963.

21. Ibid., 42J 181 Syndicats agricoles, 1952–1969, letter to Turaud, August 11, 1951.

22. Claude Monzies, "L'agriculture biologique et l'agriculture biodynamique en France: Réflexions d'un biodynamiste," *Nature et Progrès*, no. 73 (January–March 1982): 12.

23. Fonds Raoul Lemaire, Archives municipales d'Angers, 42J 181 Syndicats agricoles, 1952–1969, letter from Lemaire to Turaud, August 11, 1951, and ibid., 42J 186 Groupement d'agriculture biologique de l'Ouest, 1959–1969, letter from I. Bouvet, farmer at La Jaille Yvon (Maine-et-Loire), November 18, 1959.

24. Archives André Louis, Centre international de recherches sur l'écologie (CIRE)–AgroParisTech, Grignon, André Birre, "L'affaissement de la vie rurale," *L'Epoque agricole*, January 14, 1949. In the same collection, see also "Plans et réalités," *L'Epoque agricole*, January 7, 1949.

25. Ibid.

26. Boucher, *Pour une véritable agriculture biologique*, 12.

27. Archives André Louis, Centre international de recherches sur l'écologie (CIRE)–AgroParisTech, Grignon, André Birre, "Dans le sens de la vie," *L'Époque agricole* December 17, 1948.

28. André Birre, introduction to the journal, *Sol et Vitalité*, no. 1 (March 1950): 1.

29. "Vie de l'association: André et Paule," *Nature et Progrès*, no. 69 (January–March 1981): 35–36.

30. Silguy, *Bio*, 181.

31. Archives André Louis, Centre international de recherches sur l'écologie (CIRE)–AgroParisTech, Grignon, letter from Pierre Gentry, January 5, 1943.

32. Ibid., letter from Frossard, September 7, 1956.

33. Ibid., Louis to Ehrenfried Pfeiffer, December 31, n.d. See also Louis's rich correspondence with Richard Hediger, a regular contributor to *Triades*, an anthroposophist journal.

34. Viel, *L'Agriculture biologique*, 79.

35. As quoted in César, "Les métamorphoses des idéologues de l'agriculture biologique," 339.

36. Ibid., 340.

37. Morineau, "L'Agriculture biologique et commerce spécialisé."

38. Piriou, *L'institutionnalisation de l'agriculture biologique*, 113.

39. J. W. Bas, "Le rétablissement du normal dans le cycle sol, plante, animal, homme," *Sol et Vitalité*, no. 1 (March 1950): 23.

40. Henri-Charles Geffroy, "Sauvons les enfants!," *La Vie Claire*, no. 9 (April 1947): 1.

41. Raoul Lemaire, "La lettre de M. Raoul Lemaire," *La Vie Claire*, no. 24 (September 1948): 6.

42. J. W. Bas, "Le rétablissement du normal," 25.

43. Viel, *L'Agriculture biologique*, 62–65.

44. Fonds Raoul Lemaire, Archives municipales d'Angers, 42J 183 Association française de recherche pour une alimentation normale, 1955–1972, letter signed by J. W. Bas and sent out to AFRAN members, April 30, 1955.

45. *Sol-Alimentation-Santé*, various, 1956–59.

46. Fonds Raoul Lemaire, Archives municipales d'Angers, 42J 183 Association française de recherche pour une alimentation normale, 1955–1972, text of speech given by Lemaire at AFRAN meeting, June 5, 1955.

47. Kaplan, *Good Bread Is Back*, 28.

48. Lefebvre, "Role et responsabilité des médecins et des consommateurs dans la nouvelle structure de l'AFRAN," *Sol-Alimentation-Santé*, nos. 7/8 (September/October 1959): 6.

49. Fonds Raoul Lemaire, Archives municipales d'Angers, 42J 184 Label AFRAN, projet de création, 1958–1959, letter to SODAC (Société de diffusion des aliments controlés), November 26, 1958.

50. Archives André Louis, Centre international de recherches sur l'écologie (CIRE)–AgroParisTech, Grignon, letter from Xavier Florin, April 6, 1956.

51. Silguy, *Bio*, 132.

52. Viel, *L'Agriculture biologique*, 65.

53. Fonds Raoul Lemaire, Archives municipales d'Angers, 42J 186 Groupement d'agriculture biologique de l'Ouest, "Présentation de Groupement d'agriculture biologique de l'Ouest," n.d.

54. Ibid., liste des adhérents, July 25, 1959.

55. Cadiou et al., *L'Agriculture biologique*, 30, and Conford, *The Origins of the Organic Movement*, 82.

56. Fonds Raoul Lemaire, Archives municipales d'Angers, 42J 191 Relations avec les autorités: Correspondance, 1938–1971, letters to various deputies and ministers.

57. Cadiou et al., *L'Agriculture biologique en France*, 7.

58. Fonds Raoul Lemaire, Archives municipales d'Angers, 42J 186 Groupement d'agriculture biologique de l'Ouest, "Présentation de Groupement d'agriculture biologique de l'Ouest," n.d.

59. Ibid.

60. Fonds Raoul Lemaire, Archives municipales d'Angers, 42J 186 Groupement d'agriculture biologique de l'Ouest, letter from René Juillet, June 29, 1957.

61. Ibid., letter from René Juillet, October 18, 1959.

62. Fonds Raoul Lemaire, Archives municipales d'Angers 42J 280 Coupures de presse: Politique, 1936–1970, Raoul Lemaire, "En toutes choses il faut considérer la fin et avec le Marché Commun . . . La Faim," *La Gazette Agricole*, September 14, 1957.

63. Fonds Raoul Lemaire, Archives municipales d'Angers, 42J 181 Syndicats agricoles, 1952–1969, letter from Lemaire to Turaud, August 24, 1951.

Chapter Three

1. CAC (Centre des archives contemporaines), Fontainebleau, 880333 Répertoire numérique des archives de Jean Roche, Art. 41: Correspondance diverse, 1961–65, letter from Mr. Renauld to President de Gaulle, March 17, 1962.

2. Ibid.

3. Ibid.

4. Ibid., letter from Mr. Reynders to Jean Roche, April 20, 1962.

5. CAC, Fontainebleau, 880333 Répertoire numérique des archives de Jean Roche, Art. 41: Correspondance diverse, 1961–65, letter from farmers of Montois to the prefect of Meurthe-et-Moselle, May 10, 1962.

6. As quoted in Coutin, "La politique agricole de la Ve République," 785.

7. "Au courrier des lecteurs: À propos des lenteurs du remembrement," *La France Agricole*, September 17, 1964.

8. Pierre Coutin, "La politique agricole de la Ve République," 789.

9. "Evolution du remembrement," *Paysans*, no. 49 (August 1964): 34.

10. CAC, Fontainebleau, 800010 Ministère de l'agriculture, Direction de l'inspection générale, Art. 27: Dossiers de M. Forestier, 1952–1976, "Introduction aux problèmes fonciers," March 28, 1960.

11. René Massot, "Nouvelle déclaration officielle sur le regroupement foncier: Les mésures à prendre," *La France Agricole*, March 10, 1960.

12. René Massot, "Importantes déclarations sur le regroupement foncier," *La France Agricole*, March 3, 1960.

13. Mendras, *The Vanishing Peasant*, 51.

14. CNJA, *Investir*; see also L. Douroux, "Exploitation agricole et problèmes fonciers," *Paysans*, no. 24 (June/July 1960): 36–48.

15. "Quoi de nouveau cette semaine?," *La France Agricole*, March 19, 1964.

16. L'Agence européenne de productivité de l'OECE, *La petite exploitation agricole familiale*, 3.

17. René Massot, "Le regroupement foncier et le Marché commun," *La France Agricole*, April 21, 1960.

18. CAC, Fontainebleau, 800010 Ministère de l'agriculture, Direction de l'inspection générale, Art. 27: Dossiers de M. Forestier, 1952–1976, Forestier, "Introduction aux problèmes fonciers," March 28, 1960.

19. *L'Express*, Les Affaires Françaises, January 28, 1960.

20. Ibid., February 25, 1960.

21. Michel Legris, "Les dirigeants agricoles régionaux déplorrent le rôle d'éléments étrangers à la profession," *Le Monde*, February 13, 1960.

22. Jean Cau, "L'explosion paysanne," *L'Express*, February 18, 1960.

23. As reported in "Debré: 'Le malaise paysan es le reflet d'une crise profonde,'" *Combat*, March 5–6, 1960.

24. For an excellent study of how these protests played out in Brittany, see Berger, *Peasants against Politics*.

25. Pol Echevin, "Paysans: Au Secours!," *L'Express*, March 22, 1971.

26. Maxime de Coniac, President of the National Federation of Agricultural Property (Fédération nationale de la propriété agricole), "La propriété privée agricole?," *L'Opinion Agricole*, September 1, 1970, 4; Buchou, *Partager la terre*, 30.

27. Debatisse, *La révolution silencieuse*, 183.

28. Wright, *Rural Revolution*, 104–6.

29. For a general overview of how the SAFER worked, see SCAFR, *Société d'aménagement*.

30. CAC, Fontainebleau, 880333 Répertoire numérique des archives de Jean Roche, Art. 88: Elaboration de textes législatifs et réglementaires, 1959–1961, report attached to letter from the Ministry of Agriculture to Roche, October 19, 1960.

31. Buchou, *Partager la terre*, 101.

32. Ministère de l'agriculture, *Le prix des terres agricoles*.

33. These associations included the Chambres d'agriculture, the departmental branches of the FNSEA and CNJA, Syndicats de migrations et d'établissement ruraux, Caisses régionales de Crédit agricole, Caisses de mutualité agricole, and Syndicats de propriétaires fonciers. In addition, representatives from the national SCAFR and ANMER were also included in the General Assembly.

34. After the initial contributions made by the members of the General Assembly, funding for SAFER was derived from both state subsidies and a tax imposed on all SAFER land sales.

35. CAC, Fontainebleau, 880333 Répertoire numérique des archives de Jean Roche, Art. 89: Organisation nationale des SAFER, 1962–1973, "SAFER de Gascogne–Haut Languedoc, janvier 1967."

36. Fédération nationale des sociétés d'aménagement foncier et d'établissement rural, *Société d'aménagement foncier et d'établissement rural*, 14.

37. The state program for retirement was known as the Indemnité viagère de départ. The minimum age requirements changed over time, but generally speaking, farmers nearing retirement age were provided with an indemnity by the state if they sold their lands to a young farmer. This program was an important 1962 addition to the land reform legislation as it freed up thousands of hectares of farmland that could then be used to buttress the operations of younger, more enterprising, farmers.

38. CAC, Fontainebleau, 880333 Répertoire numérique des archives de Jean Roche, Art. 89: Organisation nationale des SAFER, 1962–1973, "SAFER de Gascogne–Haut Languedoc, janvier 1967."

39. "1848–1961," *Le Figaro*, June 27, 1961; Serge Mallet, "Les paysans contre 'l'agriculture de papa,'" *France-Observateur*, June 29, 1961; Mendras and Tavernier, "Les manifestations de juin 1961."

40. *L'Express*, Les Affaires Françaises, July 6, 1961. Lambert would go on to become one of the most important figures of the radical agricultural Left, establishing in the 1970s a new movement that would later become the Confédération Paysanne. For more on Lambert, see Chavagne, *Bernard Lambert*, and Lambert, *Les Paysans*.

41. "Hier matin au Palais Bourbon," *Le Figaro*, July 21–22, 1962.

42. Fédération nationale des sociétés d'aménagement foncier et d'établissement rural, *Société d'aménagement foncier et d'établissement rural*, 66.

43. In practice, however, this was rarely done, as the courts tended to interpret the SAFER mandate as conservatively as possible and so exercised a lot of leeway in determining what constituted a fair price in the local market.

44. CAC, Fontainebleau, 800389 Ministère de l'agriculture, Correspondance concernant les particuliers en relation ou en conflit avec les SAFER, Art. 53: Languedoc-Roussillon, 1971–1973, letter from Jacques Madalle to the deputy of Hérault, February 29, 1972.

45. Ibid., letter from the Ministry of Agriculture to the deputy of Hérault, June 2, 1972.

46. CAC, Fontainebleau, 800389 Ministère de l'agriculture, Correspondance concernant les particuliers en relation ou en conflit avec les SAFER, Art. 19: Aveyron-Lot-Tarn (SAFALT), 1970–1975, letter from Laval to the Ministry of Agriculture, August 30, 1972.

47. Ibid., Art. 42: Franche-Comté, 1970–76, letter from CDJA (Centre départemental des jeunes agriculteurs) to André Tisserand, the deputy of Belfort, October 13, 1971.

48. Ibid., letter from the Secretary of Commerce to the Ministry of Agriculture, February 9, 1972.

49. CAC, Fontainebleau, 800389 Ministère de l'agriculture, Correspondance concernant les particuliers en relation ou en conflit avec les SAFER, Art. 27: Bretagne (SBAFER), 1965–1968, newspaper clipping of *Ouest-France*, May 25, 1967.

50. Ibid.

51. CAC, Fontainebleau, 800389 Ministère de l'agriculture, Correspondance concernant les particuliers en relation ou en conflit avec les SAFER, Art. 27: Bretagne (SBAFER), 1965–1968, letter from the Ministry of Agriculture to the SBAFER, September 25, 1967.

52. Another favored means of circumventing the SAFER was to wait until the administration took its vacation in August and then to effect a quick and quiet sale. For an example of this tactic, see CAC, Fontainebleau, 800389 Ministère de l'agriculture, Correspondance concernant les particuliers en relation ou en conflit avec les SAFER, Art. 18: Aveyron-Lot-Tarn (SAFALT), 1962–1970, letter from Crespy to the SAFALT, October 1, 1966.

53. Pierre Flandin, "Une atteinte aux droits civiques: Le droit de préemption des sociétés foncières," *France Agricole*, October 5, 1961.

54. CAC, Fontainebleau, 800389 Ministère de l'agriculture, Correspondance concernant les particuliers en relation ou en conflit avec les SAFER, Art. 41: Franche-Comté, 1962–1970, letter from René Meyer, director of the Technical College of Menton, to the Ministry of Agriculture, April 18, 1967.

55. Fonds Raoul Lemaire, Archives municipales d'Angers, 42J 13/1 Ferme expérimentale de la Glacière à Beaumont-Pied-de-Boeuf (Mayenne), Champ de chemin privé, expropriation: Enquête publique, ordonnance d'expropriation, correspondance, 1936, 1966–1970.

56. Ibid., letter to Maître Richou Père (notary), March 7, 1969.

57. CAC, Fontainebleau, 800389 Ministère de l'agriculture, Correspondance concernant les particuliers en relation ou en conflit avec les SAFER, Art. 52: Languedoc-Roussillon, 1962–1970, letter from Mr. Rives to the Ministry of Agriculture, February 13, 1968.

58. CAC, Fontainebleau, 880333 Répertoire numérique des archives de Jean Roche, Art. 89: Organisation nationale des SAFER, 1962–1973, "SAFER de Gascogne–Haut Languedoc, janvier 1967."

59. CAC, Fontainebleau, 800389 Ministère de l'agriculture, Correspondance concernant les particuliers en relation ou en conflit avec les SAFER, Art. 52: Languedoc-Roussillon, 1962–1970, letter from Granier, director of the SAFER Languedoc-Roussillon, to the Ministry of Agriculture, July 31, 1964.

60. Ibid., Art. 26: Bourgogne, 1973–1976, collection of letters exchanged between Duvernoy, the SAFER, and the Ministry of Agriculture, 1973–1976.

61. CAC, Fontainebleau, 770416 Ministère de l'agriculture, Art. 11. Libre circulation des salariés à l'intérieur de la CEE, 1960–70, "Note concernant les dispositions du traité de marché commun relatif à la libre circulation des personnes," November 15, 1957.

62. F. F. Legueu, "Le prix de la terre," *Le Bulletin de Paris*, June 6, 1962.

63. CAC, Fontainebleau, 800010 Ministère de l'agriculture, Direction de l'inspection générale, Art. 27: Dossiers de M. Forestier, 1952–1976, Chambres d'agriculture, "La Valeur de la terre en France," supplément no. 254, October 15, 1962.

64. Letter from Marcel Deneux and Michel Debatisse to Georges Pompidou, September 1, 1962, as reproduced in Noël and Willaert, *Pompidou*, 55.

65. Noël and Willaert, *Pompidou*, 57.

66. The full text of the Treaty of Rome is available at http://eur-lex.europa.eu/en /treaties/dat/12002E/htm/C_2002325EN.003301.html.

67. "Accaparement des terres par les exploitants étrangers," *Fraternité Paysanne*, February 25, 1961; "Le sol européen," *La France Agricole*, August 16, 1968.

68. For concern about North Africans leading to an increase in land prices, see "Evolution du prix de la terre," *Fraternité Paysanne*, March 13, 1959, and CAC, Fontainebleau, 800010 Ministère de l'agriculture, Direction de l'inspection générale, Art. 27: Dossiers de M. Forestier, 1952–1976, "La Valeur de la terre en France," n.d. For a general overview of the repatriation of French Algerian farmers, see Brun, *Les français d'Algérie*.

69. Pierre Roche, "Migrations rurales et sociétés d'établissement agricole," *Paysans*, no. 18 (June/July 1959): 37–50.

70. Ibid., 38.

71. CAC, Fontainebleau, 880333 Répertoire numérique des archives de Jean Roche, Art. 88: Elaboration de textes législatifs et réglementaires, 1959–1961, Rapport présenté au comité supérieur consultatif d'aménagement foncier sur le projet de décret relatif à l'application des articles 15, 16 et 17 de la loi 60-808 du 5 août 1960 relatifs aux SAFER, January 13, 1961, 3.

72. For evidence of continued anxiety on the part of SAFER administrators with respect to the influx of member-state farmers and how they might drive up prices, see CAC, Fontainebleau, 880333 Répertoire numérique des archives de Jean Roche, Art. 89: Organisation nationale des SAFER, 1962–1973, "FNSAFER Assemblée générale du 23 septembre 1971: Rapport du Conseil d'administration."

73. CAC, Fontainebleau, 800467 Ministère de l'agriculture, Cabinet de presse, Art. 1: Edgard Pisani, 1961–1962, press conference, September 15, 1961.

74. "Le sol européen," *La France Agricole*, August 16, 1968.

75. CAC, Fontainebleau, 800389 Ministère de l'agriculture, Correspondance concernant les particuliers en relation ou en conflit avec les SAFER, Art. 25: Bourgogne, 1964–1973, letter from Marcel Ohl to the Ministry of Agriculture, May 9, 1967.

76. CAC, Fontainebleau, 800389 Ministère de l'agriculture, Correspondance concernant les particuliers en relation ou en conflit avec les SAFER, Art. 34: Centre, 1965–1970, letter from Jean-Paul Jaloux to the SAFER, May 11, 1962.

77. Ibid., letters from the CDJA and FDSEA (Fédération départementale des syndicats d'exploitants agricoles) of Indre-et-Loire to the SAFER, May 12, 1962.

78. Ibid., letter from the SAFER to the Ministry of Agriculture, July 18, 1962.

79. CAC, Fontainebleau, 770412 Ministère de l'agriculture, Dossiers de M. de Vaissière, Art. 124: Réunions divers, 1965–1966, APCA, *Journée nationale des Chambres d'agriculture*, March 11, 1970, "La situation de l'agriculture en 1967," 4.

80. P. Collet, "La réforme des 'structures' à l'heure de la révolution," *L'Opinion Agricole*, supplement to the Chambers of Agriculture periodical, September 1, 1968, 2.

81. CAC, Fontainebleau, 770412 Ministère de l'agriculture, Dossiers de M. de Vaissière, Art. 118: CNJA, Journées d'études, congrès, 1966–1973, Congrès de 1968, Hilaire Flandre, "Propositions pour une nouvelle politique agricole."

82. Ibid.

83. Pierre Cressard, "La manifestation des agriculteurs a fait quatre-vingts blessés, dont neuf sont sérieusement atteints," *Le Monde*, June 8, 1967.

84. Ibid.

85. François-Henri de Virieu, "Terroirs sans frontières," *Le Monde*, July 4, 1967. See also "Le point de vue du président," *L'Opinion Agricole*, October 1, 1967, and "France: Peasants Rising," *The Economist*, October 7, 1967.

86. CAC, Fontainebleau, 800467 Ministère de l'agriculture, Cabinet de presse, Art. 3: Edgard Pisani, 1964, debate between Pisani and representatives from professional farm organizations, March 13, 1964.

87. "Un devoir de modernization," *La Nation*, October 21, 1966.

Chapter Four

Epigraph source. Archives André Louis, Centre International de Recherches sur l'Ecolgie (CIRE)–AgroParisTech, Grignon. Text of speech delivered by Tavera to the Soil Association in England, October 12, 1965.

1. For more on the Crédit Agricole, see Gaudibert, *Le dernier empire*, and Guéslin, *Le crédit agricole*.

2. Rabhi, *Du Sahara aux Cévennes*, 193.

3. Ibid., 195.

4. Fonds Raoul Lemaire, Archives municipales d'Angers, 42J 267 Coupures de presse: Agriculture biologique, 1953–1971, Guy Gasnault, "A l'Ouest du nouveau avec . . . la culture biologique: Une technique nouvelle: la Culture Biologique," *Courrier de l'Ouest*, July 5, 1960. See also "L'agriculture biologique," *Agriculture Services* (Charente), November 26, 1966.

5. Fonds Raoul Lemaire, Archives municipales d'Angers, 42J 267 Coupures de presse: Agriculture biologique, 1953–1971, Guy Gasnault, "Notre enquête sur la culture biologique," *Courrier français de Bordeaux*, March 4, 1967.

6. Fonds Raoul Lemaire, Archives municipales d'Angers, 42J 187 Association française d'agriculture biologique, 1962–1964, Boucher, "Notes de voyage: Pour une agriculture fonctionnelle," 46.

7. J. W. Bas, "Lettre aux médécins," *Sol-Alimentation-Santé*, no. 8 (September/October 1959): 1.

8. Fonds Raoul Lemaire, Archives municipales d'Angers, 42J 183 Association française de recherche pour une normale, 1955–1972.

9. Fonds Raoul Lemaire, Archives municipales d'Angers, 42J 91/2 Activité de la SARL SVB Lemaire, 1960–1977, Boucher at L'Ecole nationale supérieure de mécaniqe de Nantes, April 13, 1961.

10. Archives André Louis, Centre international de recherches sur l'écologie (CIRE)–AgroParisTech, Grignon, Geffroy, "Défense du Consommateur," *La Vie Claire*, February 1967.

11. Fonds Raoul Lemaire, Archives municipales d'Angers, 42J 183 Association française de recherche pour une alimentation normale, 1955–1972, *Alimentation Normale*, no. 5 (October 1962): 7.

12. Jean Engelhard, "Poulets de 'Papa' ou poulets industriels," *Le Figaro*, July 8, 1966.

13. Ibid.

14. Fonds Raoul Lemaire, Archives municipales d'Angers, 42J 183 Association française de recherche pour une alimentation normale, 1955–1972, minutes from meeting held between the secretary-general of the Fédération des industries alimentaires (FIA), Mr. Dietlin, and AFRAN representative Mr. Martin, Paris, May 14, 1959.

15. Nancy was chosen as the research site simply because that is where AFRAN members interested in studying consumer behavior were located. Fonds Raoul Lemaire, Archives municipales d'Angers, 42J 183 Association française de recherche pour une alimentation normale, 1955–1972, summary of the Nancy study, May 20, 1959.

16. Fonds Raoul Lemaire, Archives municipales d'Angers, 42J 185 Label AFRAN, enquête auprès du public, 1959.

17. Fonds Raoul Lemaire, Archives municipales d'Angers, 42J 183 Association française de recherche pour une alimentation normale, 1955–1972, "Acheter c'est voter," *Documentation AFRAN*, February 2, 1963.

18. In the end, the translation from idea to practice would fail. As the organic movement developed over the course of the 1960s and moved in new directions, AFRAN began to quietly unravel before shutting down for good in the 1970s.

19. Fonds Raoul Lemaire, Archives municipales d'Angers, 42J 191 Relations avec les autorités, 1938–1971.

20. Fonds Raoul Lemaire, Archives municipales d'Angers, 42J 195 Relations avec le directeur du journal *Le Progrès Agricole*, 1951–1970, letter to M. G. Raquet, October 20, 1962.

21. Boucher, *Une véritable agriculture biologique*, 17.

22. Fonds Raoul Lemaire, Archives municipales d'Angers, 42J 91/2 Activité de la SARL SVB Lemaire, 1960–1977, letter to Boucher, July 26, 1963.

23. Fonds Raoul Lemaire, Archives municipales d'Angers, 42J 283 Journal *La Semaine du Lait*: Exemplaires, 1960–1966, "La Mer, le Maerl, Lemaire," *La Semaine du Lait*, January 28, 1961. See also *Le Courrier de l'Ouest*, January 13, 1961, and Fonds Raoul Lemaire, Archives municipales d'Angers, 42J 95 Contentieux sur le maërl produit, 1959–1961.

24. Viel, *L'Agriculture biologique*, 65.

25. Piriou, "L'institutionnalisation de l'agriculture biologique," 116.

26. Viel, *L'Agriculture biologique*, 68.

27. Fonds Raoul Lemaire, Archives municipales d'Angers, 42J 232 Précis pratique de la culture biologique de Jean Boucher, 1965, *La culture biologique et ses applications*.

28. Kervran, *Biological Transmutation*, 15.

29. Fonds Raoul Lemaire, Archives municipales d'Angers, 42J 232 Précis pratique de la culture biologique de Jean Boucher, publication, 1965, *La culture biologique et ses applications*, 5.

30. Conford, *The Origins of the Organic Movement*, 65.

31. Rabhi, *Du Sahara aux Cévennes*, 243.

32. Fonds Raoul Lemaire, Archives municipales d'Angers, 42J 232 Précis pratique de la culture biologique de Jean Boucher, 1965, *La culture biologique et ses applications*, 6.

33. Saint Henis, *Guide pratique de culture biologique*, 7.

34. Ibid., 26.

35. Ibid., 23.

36. Fonds Raoul Lemaire, Archives municipales d'Angers, 42J 187 Association française d'agriculture biologique, 1962–1964, summary of AFAB general assembly meeting of September 29, 1963, and in the same collection, *AFAB*, no. 17/18 (November 20, 1963).

37. "Compte-Rendu de la réunion à Saint-Aubin," *AFAB*, no. 12/13 (October 20, 1962): 5–6.

38. Ibid.

39. Archives André Louis, Centre international de recherches sur l'écologie (CIRE)–AgroParisTech, Grignon, "Correspondance avec les particuliers."

40. Ibid., "Articles de Rich Hediger (*Triades*)," letter to Hediger, June 2, 1961.

41. Ibid., "Correspondance avec l'étranger."

42. Louis and Goachet, "Relation d'un voyage agrobiologique en Grande-Bretagne," *AFAB*, no. 17/18 (November 20, 1963): 6–17.

43. Viel, *L'Agriculture biologique*, 103.

44. Archives André Louis, Centre international de recherches sur l'écologie (CIRE)–AgroParisTech, Grignon, "Articles de Rich Hediger (Triades) et Correspondance," letter to Hediger, June 22, 1964.

45. Ibid., "Correspondance avec les particuliers," letter to Étienne Giraud, agronomist in Perigueux, January 24, 1968.

46. Fonds Raoul Lemaire, Archives municipales d'Angers, 43J 100 SVB Lemaire, Relations avec l'Association Française de l'Agriculture Biologique, 1963–1965, "L'AFAB: Ses origines, ses buts," *AFAB*, no. 20 (1964).

47. Archives André Louis, Centre international de recherches sur l'écologie (CIRE)–AgroParisTech, Grignon, "Conférences CETA [Centre d'études techniques agricoles]," leaflet (presumably to hand out to CETA attendees) titled "Agriculteurs et horticulteurs de toutes spécialités: Savez-vous qu'il existe deux méthodes d'Agriculture?"

48. *Nature et Progrès*, no. 1 (January–March 1974): 1–3.

49. Ibid.

50. Ibid.

51. Ibid.

52. Piriou, "L'institutionnalisation de l'agriculture biologique," 116.

53. Ibid., 2.

54. Rimsky-Korsakoff, *Au delà du bio*, 170.

55. Charvolin, *L'invention de l'environnement en France*, 33.

56. CAC, Fontainebleau, 770412 Ministère de l'agriculture, Dossiers de M. de Vaissière, Art. 124: Réunions divers, 1965–1966, Report on the meeting of the European Committee for the Conservation of Nature and Natural Resources at Strasbourg, 1966.

57. Bess, *The Light-Green Society*.

58. J. W. Bas, "Commission supérieure de la qualité," *Documentation AFRAN* 4, no. 1 (January–March 1966): 11–12.

Chapter Five

Epigraph Source. CAC, Fontainebleau, 800389 Ministère de l'Agriculture, Correspondance concernant les particuliers en relation ou en conflit avec les SAFER, Art. 21: Basse-Normandie, 1965–1974, letter from the Ministry for the Protection of Nature and the Environment to the Ministry of Agriculture, October 1, 1973.

1. A polder is an area of land that has been reclaimed from the sea and enclosed by dikes.

2. CAC (Centre des archives contemporaines), Fontainebleau, 800389 Ministère de l'agriculture, Correspondance concernant les particuliers en relation ou en

conflit avec les SAFER, Art. 21: Basse-Normandie, 1965–1974, collection of letters exchanged between all interested parties between 1971 and 1974.

3. Ibid., SAFER report, April 1971.

4. Ibid., letter from the Ministry of the Protection of Nature and the Environment to the Ministry of Agriculture, October 1, 1973.

5. CAC, Fontainebleau, 890078 Ministère de l'agriculture, Direction de la modernisation des exploitations, Art. 14: L'établissement à la terre, 1975, "Les grandes characteristiques de l'agriculture française de 1959 à 1974."

6. "La France au second rang mondial pour l'exportation des produits agricoles," *Information Agricole*, December 1974.

7. The full text of the Mansholt Plan is available at http://www.ena.lu.

8. François-Henri de Virieu, "Vers des surplus permanents dans l'agriculture?," *Le Monde*, January 27, 1961.

9. CAC, Fontainebleau, 890078 Ministère de l'agriculture, Direction de la modernisation des exploitations, Art. 14: L'établissement à la terre, 1975, "Les grandes characteristiques de l'agriculture française de 1959 à 1974."

10. Fearne, "The History and Development of the CAP," 44.

11. *Paysans*, no. 55 (August/September 1965): 80.

12. François-Henri de Virieu, "Le Plan Mansholt provoque de sérieuses oppositions," *Le Monde*, December 13, 1968.

13. France, *Le Rapport Vedel*.

14. French agricultural production rose 50 percent from 1963 to 1970, and the average farm size increased from 20.4 to 27.6 hectares. But increases in productivity led to lower agricultural prices on the market. Coupled with rising costs for industrial agricultural inputs (e.g., land, fertilizers, machinery, and fuel), this situation led farm revenues to stagnate. See Fearne, "The History and Development of the CAP," 35.

15. Pol Echevin, "Paysans, Au Secours!," *L'Express*, March 22, 1971.

16. Allaire, "Modèle de développement," 349.

17. Ibid.; "Farm Snorts," *Economist*, October 18, 1969; and J.-J. Lauvergne and J.-C. Flamant, "Faut-il brûler le rapport Vedel?," *Le Monde*, December 18, 1969.

18. Raoul Serieys, "Quel dialogue?," *Le Monde*, November 29, 1969.

19. These statistics are for 1970. CAC, Fontainebleau, 800010 de l'Agriculture, Direction de l'Inspection Générale, Art. 1–3: Dossiers de M. Wallon, 1957–1977, "Inégalités de revenue et politique agricole," April 3, 1975.

20. Fearne, "The History and Development of the CAP," 42.

21. CAC, Fontainebleau, 880333 Répertoire numérique des archives de Jean Roche, Art. 89: Organisation nationale des SAFER, 1962–1973, "FNSAFER Assemblée générale du 9 octobre 1969: Rapport du conseil d'administration."

22. Buchou, *Partager la terre*, 64.

23. CAC, Fontainebleau, 880333 Répertoire numérique des archives de Jean Roche, Art. 89: Organisation nationale des SAFER, 1962–1973, "FNSAFER Assemblée générale du 26 septembre 1972: Rapport du conseil d'administration," and "Les SAFER s'enferrent . . . ," *La France Agricole*, October 29, 1976.

24. Pierre-Marie Doutrelant, "Les sociétés d'aménagement foncier sont prêtes à rendre à la nature une partie des hectares cultivés qu'elles achètent," *Le Monde*, October 10, 1969.

25. "Le hobereau et son kolkhoze," *Le Monde*, October 14, 1974.

26. See, for example, Prendiville, *Environmental Politics in France*, 6.

27. Szarka, *Environmental Policy in France*, 32, 50.

28. Charvolin, *L'invention de l'environnement en France*, 59.

29. Fel, "Les révolutions vertes," 9.

30. Cheverry and Clergeot, *Paysages ruraux*, 26.

31. Peneff, *Remembrement de Cadours*, 177.

32. Ibid.

33. CAC, Fontainebleau, 800005 Ministère de l'agriculture, Collection des circulaires, 1967–1978, Art. 21: 1970, memo from Duhamel to the departmental prefects, March 3, 1970.

34. Ibid., Art. 23: Memo regarding water pollution, April 29, 1971, and Art. 35: Memo regarding pork production and pollution, April 15, 1971. For a contemporary analysis of the new approach of the Ministry of Agriculture, see Simone Branglidor, "La protection de la nature est au service de l'homme," *La France Agricole*, March 6, 1970.

35. France, Remembrement et voirie agricole (Section technique centrale), *Remembrement rural et conservation de la nature. [2]*, report of the Chambers of Agriculture.

36. For more on this, see P. H. Bernard, "Le remembrement des exploitations rurales," *La France Agricole*, March 26, 1976.

37. CAC, Fontainebleau, 800389 Ministère de l'agriculture, Correspondance concernant les particuliers en relation ou en conflit avec les SAFER, Art. 36: Centre, 1974–1976, newspaper clipping, *Le Monde*, May 14, 1976.

38. Ibid.

39. "Conservation au naturel," *La France Agricole*, February 6, 1970; see also "Pollution: La lutte de l'homme pour sauver son environnement," *La France Agricole*, November 12, 1971, and "L'agriculture et l'écologie," *La France Agricole*, December 28, 1973.

40. Cheverry and Clergeot, *Paysages ruraux*, 34.

41. Jean Vuaille, "L'agriculture et l'environnement," *L'Opinion Agricole*, April 1, 1975. See also Chamboredon, "La 'naturalisation' de la campagne"; René Dalan, "Paysans-estivants: La guerre froide est déclarée," *Le Monde*, September 12, 1981; and J. M. Le Clair, "La cohabitation difficile de deux mondes," *Ouest France*, November 24, 1980.

42. For more on second-home buyers and the neo-rural movement, see Farmer, "The Other House," and Rouvière, *Retourner à la terre*.

43. Fédération nationale des sociétés d'aménagement foncier et d'établissement rural, *Société d'aménagement foncier et d'établissement rural*, 42.

44. CAC, Fontainebleau, 880333 Répertoire numérique des archives de Jean Roche, Art. 89: Organisation nationale des SAFER, 1962–1973, "FNSAFER Assemblée générale du 9 octobre 1969: Rapport du conseil d'administration," and "FNSAFER Assemblée générale du 23 septembre 1971: Rapport du conseil d'administration."

45. SAFER of Burgundy, Dijon, onsite archives, Assemblée générale ordinaire, June 21, 1971, 2.

46. CAC, Fontainebleau, 800389 Ministère de l'agriculture, Correspondance concernant les particuliers en relation ou en conflit avec les SAFER, Art. 19: Aveyron-Lot-Tarn (SAFALT), 1970–1975, letter from Maurice Clemente to the SAFALT, November 10, 1972.

47. For further examples, see CAC, Fontainebleau, 800389 Ministère de l'agriculture, Correspondance concernant les particuliers en relation ou en conflit avec les SAFER, Art. 36: Centre, 1974–1976, letter from François Pillard to the Ministry of Agriculture, July 24, 1976 (protesting that his plans to acquire new lands to plant a forest to redress the lack of trees in the area were preempted by the SAFER), and in the same collection, letter from Mr. Leguet to the Ministry of Agriculture, August 31, 1976 (protesting that he had been preempted even though he had planned to maintain the banks and hedgerows on the property).

48. Viel, *L'Agriculture biologique*, 81–83; Rimsky-Korsakoff, *Au delà du bio*, 102.

49. Ibid., 54–55.

50. Fel, "Les révolutions vertes," 13.

51. Béteille, *La France du vide*, 228.

52. Léger and Hervieu, "Les immigrés," 230.

53. Ibid., 71.

54. Ibid., 57.

55. François-Henri de Virieu, "Vers l'agriculture du métier," *Le Monde*, June 24, 1969.

56. Pierre Marchant, "Mort et résurrection de l'agriculture française: L'agonie des petites terres," *France Catholique*, June 25, 1971.

57. Piriou, *L'institutionnalisation de l'agriculture biologique*, 111.

58. Jean Cochard, "Un principe du maintient de l'équilibre biologique: La culture en bon père de famille," *La France Agricole*, October 8, 1971.

59. For more on pesticide regulation, or lack thereof, see Jas, "Public Health and Pesticide Regulation in France."

60. For other examples of this stance, see Georges Kletch, "Comment sauvegarder les équilibres biologiques dans les aménagements ruraux et les pratiques agricoles?," *La France Agricole*, April 3, 1970, and Pierre Lancrenon, "Questions à propos de 'l'agriculture biologique,'" *La France Agricole*, March 3, 1972.

61. "En Aquitaine: De la viande pour l'exportation sur des prairies sans azote ni potasse chimiques . . . ," *La France Agricole*, February 16, 1973.

62. In the interview, de Monbrison cited André Voisin as an influence. Voisin was an agronomist and a dairy farmer in Normandy. He was a member of the Académie d'Agriculture de France and wrote extensively on biodynamic grass-based farming. His most influential work was *La productivité de l'herbe* (1957), which inspired an entire generation of young farmers. Translated into several languages, his work became an essential text for anyone interested in alternative farming practices—even Fidel Castro was a fan and invited Voisin to Cuba in 1964. While Voisin's work remains influential and is regularly cited by proponents of grass-based farming throughout the world, there is very little secondary literature that addresses his historical significance.

As an early and enormously influential figure in the history of organic farming, André Voisin is someone well deserving of further academic research.

63. "Quoi de nouveau cette semaine?," *La France Agricole*, June 13, 1975.

64. Interview with Poly, *AgriSept*, no. 665 (January 6, 1978).

65. Piriou, *L'institutionnalisation de l'agriculture biologique*, 127.

66. Ibid., 129.

67. Silguy, *Bio*, 184.

68. Ibid., 115.

69. Viel, *L'Agriculture biologique*, 68.

70. Ibid., 73.

71. *Nature et Progrès*, no. 52 (October–December 1976), inside cover.

72. Jean-Luc Messe, "L'agriculture biologique: Solution aux problèmes économiques des paysans," *Nature et Progrès*, no. 1 (January–March 1974).

73. Archives André Louis, Centre International de Recherches sur l'Ecologie (CIRE)–AgroParisTech, Grignon, Nature et Progrès pamphlet for three-day conference at the City Hall in Tours, November 20–22, 1970.

74. Viel, *L'Agriculture biologique*, 78. Estimates on the number of organic farmers through the 1970s, before the state institutionalized the practice and started keeping track, are rough at best. For instance, in Piriou, *L'institutionnalisation de l'agriculture biologique* (107), it was estimated that there were four thousand.

75. Silguy, *Bio*, 18.

76. Archives André Louis, Centre International de Recherches sur l'Ecologie (CIRE)–AgroParisTech, Grignon, "Congrès 9–11 novembre 1968—Bordeaux," letter to Louis (return address illegible), circa 1968.

77. Piriou, *L'institutionnalisation de l'agriculture biologique*, 119.

78. To name just a few: FESA-Lemaire, FNAB, Fédération nationale d'agriculture biologique des régions de France (part of Nature and Progress), Institut de nutrition de la région centre, Union française pour la recherche sur l'environnement et la santé, Fédération des associations pour une écologie de la santé (FAPES), and the Union nationale de diététique (UNADIET).

79. "Début de reconnaissance de l'ag biologique," *Nouvelle République du Centre-Ouest*, March 24, 1981.

80. Sylvander, "Conventions de qualité," 83.

81. INRA, *Recherches sur la qualité du poulet label rouge*, 34.

82. Piriou, *L'institutionnalisation de l'agriculture biologique*, 138.

Conclusion

1. CAC (Centre des archives contemporaines), Fontainebleau, 800389 Ministère de l'agriculture, Correspondance concernant les particuliers en relation ou en conflit avec les SAFER, Art. 34: Centre, 1965–1970, letter from Roblot to the Ministry of Agriculture, May 13, 1969.

2. Ibid., letter from the SAFER of Centre to the Ministry of Agriculture, June 6, 1969.

3. Ibid., letter from Roblot to the Ministry of Agriculture, May 13, 1969.

4. Ibid., letter from Roblot to the Ministry of Agriculture, October 21, 1969.

5. CAC, Fontainebleau, 800010 Ministère de l'agriculture, Direction de l'inspection générale, Art. 27: Dossiers de M. Forestier, 1952–1976, "Introduction aux problèmes fonciers," March 28, 1960.

6. "La place de l'agro-alimentaire au sein de la balance commerciale," *L'Yonne Républicaine*, January 14, 1982.

7. Dormois, *The French Economy*, 110.

8. "Consommation produits de la ferme très en vogue," *Presse-Océan*, June 29, 1982, and Jean Le Douar, "Du producteur aux consommateurs: La vente en direct: 'un affaire de confiance!,'" *Ouest France*, August 3, 1982.

9. Bernard Delthil, "Bientôt des fast-food 'bio,'" *Le Quotidien de Paris*, June 23, 1982.

10. Roland Mihail, "Engrais: Comme un poison dans l'eau," *Le Point*, February 17, 1981.

11. Bérard and Marchenay, *Produits de terroir*, 54. For more on the history of terroir, see Demossier, "Culinary Heritage," and Parker, *Tasting French Terroir*.

12. Loubère, *Wine Revolution*, 125.

13. "Avec les appellations d'origine, voyagez au pays du fromage," *Presse-Océan*, December 30, 1982.

14. For more on the rise of nostalgia for rural life in the 1970s, see Sarah Farmer, "Memoirs of French Peasant Life."

15. P. Jérome, "La loi des agro-alimentaires," *Politique-Hebdo*, January 30, 1975.

16. For another example of the rejection of the romantic idyll, see Jean Vuaille, "L'agriculture et l'environnement," *L'Opinion Agricole*, April 1, 1975. Vuaille, an agronomist and president of the Association of Environmental Journalists, wrote: "If the farmer . . . through the ages and up to the present day, maintained the natural heritage, it was for these two simple reasons: first, a respectful fear of natural forces that outweighed the strength of his own meager arms, and second, the necessity of having to satisfy his vital needs, food, clothing, and heat. I don't believe that farmers carry a romantic love for nature. Virgil, Rousseau, they were not farmers."

17. Steven R. Weisman, "Failure of Global Trade Talks Is Traced to the Power of Farmers," *New York Times*, July 27, 2006.

18. While such situations might be humorous, the success of organized resistance in agricultural France, when compared, for instance, to the current situation in India, where tens of thousands of farmers have committed suicide in the last decade because they were unable to cope with the introduction of industrial agriculture, ought to be better appreciated. For more on the situation in India, see Somini Sengupta, "On India's Farms, a Plague of Suicide," *New York Times*, September 19, 2006.

19. See, for example, Baumier, *Les paysans de l'an 2000: Un siècle de révolution "silencieuse" dans les campagnes françaises*; Debatisse, *La révolution silencieuse*; Dibie, *Le village métamorphosé*; Rambaud, "Révoltes et révolution paysannes dans la France contemporaine"; Wright, *Rural Revolution in France*.

20. Cleary, *Peasants, Politicians and Producers*, 11.

21. Moulin, *Peasantry and Society in France*, 181.

22. Rimsky-Korsakoff, *Au delà du bio*, 170.

23. Piriou, *L'institutionnalisation de l'agriculture biologique*, 285.

24. Ibid., 246.

25. By 1980, 21 percent of farm heads had another stream of income, while two-thirds of all farming households had at least one outside source of income. See Moulin, *Peasantry and Society in France*, 186. As mentioned above, rural tourism was a common source of secondary income. By 1978, there were twenty thousand *gîtes* in four thousand counties. See Biancarelli, Parini, and Serradji, *Aménager les campagnes*, 77.

Bibliography

Archival Sources

AD (Archives départementales) Maine-et-Loire, Angers, 1350W Remembrement, Antoigné.

AN (Archives nationales), Paris, AJ80 10 Commissariat général du plan.

AN, Paris, AJ81 42 Activités du commissariat général du plan, Productivity missions reports.

AN, Paris, F10 5201 Ministère de l'agriculture, Service d'études et de documentation, Statistiques.

AN, Paris, F10 5270 Ministère de l'agriculture, Production végétale.

AN, Paris, F60 904 Secrétaire général du gouvernement et services du premier-ministre, Séances du comité économique.

AN, Paris, F60ter Secrétariat général du comité interministériel pour les questions de coopération économique européenne.

Archives André Louis, Centre international de recherches sur l'écologie (CIRE)–AgroParisTech, Grignon.

CAC (Centre des archives contemporaines), Fontainebleau, 770412 Ministère de l'agriculture, Dossiers de Monsieur de Vaissière, Inspecteur général.

CAC, Fontainebleau, 770416 Ministère de l'agriculture, Travail et emploi.

CAC, Fontainebleau, 800005 Ministère de l'agriculture, Collection des circulaires.

CAC, Fontainebleau, 800010 Ministère de l'agriculture, Direction de l'inspection générale.

CAC, Fontainebleau, 800389 Ministère de l'agriculture, Correspondance concernant les particuliers en relation ou en conflit avec les SAFER.

CAC, Fontainebleau, 800401 Ministère de l'agriculture, Direction de production et échanges, Service des relations internationales.

CAC, Fontainebleau, 800467 Ministère de l'agriculture, Cabinet de presse.

CAC, Fontainebleau, 860087 Études du ministère de l'agriculture.

CAC, Fontainebleau, 880333 Répertoire numérique des archives de Jean Roche, ingénieur du génie rural et des eaux et forêts.

CAC, Fontainebleau, 890078 Ministère de l'agriculture, Direction de la modernisation des exploitations.

Cinémathèque du Ministère de l'agriculture, Paris. *L'Étape du remembrement.* Directed by Armand Chartier. Ministère de l'agriculture, 1964.

Cinémathèque du Ministère de l'agriculture. *Mécanisation et remembrement.* Directed by Dimitri Kirsanoff. Ministère de l'agriculture, 1955.

Fonds Raoul Lemaire, Archives municipales d'Angers, 42J.

Fonds Groupe Lemaire, Archives municipales d'Angers, 43J.

SAFER (Société d'aménagement foncier et d'établissement rural) of Burgundy, Dijon, onsite archives, Assemblée générale ordinaire.

SAFER of Burgundy, Dijon, onsite archives, Procès verbaux du conseil administratif.

Journals and Newspapers

Association Française pour l'Agriculture Biologique, 1962–68.

Dossiers de presse historique at Sciences-Po, Paris, France.

La France Agricole, 1945–80.

Fraternité paysanne, 1959–1965.

Nature et Progrès, 1964–82.

L'Opinion Agricole, 1969–1975.

Paysans, 1957–76.

Sol-Alimentation-Santé, 1956–59.

Sol et Vitalité, 1950.

La Vie Claire, 1946–1980.

Published Sources

L'Agence européenne de productivité de l'OECE. *La petite exploitation agricole familiale, problème européen: Méthodes pour la création d'unités viables.* Paris: OECE, 1959.

Allaire, Gilles. "Le modèle de développement agricole des années 60 confronté aux logiques marchandes." In *La grande transformation de l'agriculture,* edited by Gilles Allaire and Robert Boyer, 345–76. Paris: INRA, 1995.

Alphandéry, Pierre, Pierre Bitoun, and Yves Dupont. *Les champs du départ: Une France rurale sans paysans?* Paris: Editions La Découverte, 1988.

Alphandéry, Pierre, and Yannick Sencébé. "L'émergence de la sociologie rurale en France (1945–1967)." *Études Rurales,* no. 183 (2009): 23–40.

Amann, Peter H. *The Corncribs of Buzet: Modernizing Agriculture in the French Southwest.* Princeton, NJ: Princeton University Press, 1990.

Association des ruralistes français. *Le foncier agricole dans l'ouest: Travaux et documents.* Caen: Centre de publications de l'Université de Caen, 1987.

Atias, Christian, and Didier Linotte. *Le remembrement rural.* Paris: Libraries techniques, 1980.

Atkin, Michael. *Snouts in the Trough: European Farmers, the Common Agricultural Policy, and the Public Purse.* Cambridge, U.K.: Woodhead, 1993.

Atrux-Tallau, Mélanie. "Histoire sociale d'un corps intermédiaire: l'Assemblée permanente des chambres d'agriculture (1924–1974)." PhD diss., Université Lumière Lyon 2, 2010.

Bairoch, Paul. "Dix-huit décennies de développement agricole français dans une perspective internationale." *Économie Rurale,* no. 184–86 (1988): 13–23.

Bairoch, Paul, Pierre Barral, and Michael Tracy. Round Table Discussion. *Économie Rurale,* nos. 184–86 (1988): 51–62.

Barjot, Dominique, ed. *Catching Up with America: Productivity Missions and the Diffusion of American Economic and Technological Influence after the Second World*

War. Proceedings of the Caen Preconference, September 18–20, 1997, Workshop C 45 of the Twelfth International Economic History Congress of Madrid. Paris: Presses de l'Université de Paris-Sorbonne, 2002.

Barral, Pierre. *Les agrariens français de Meline à Pisani*. Paris: Presses de la Foundation Nationale des Sciences Politiques, 1968.

Bas, Jacques-William, "Le rétablissement du normal dans le cycle sol, plante, animal homme." *Sol et Vitalité*, no. 1 (March 1950): 23.

Baumier, Jean. *Les paysans de l'an 2000: Un siècle de révolution "silencieuse" dans les campagnes françaises*. Paris: Plon, 1979.

Beaufils, Maurice. *Origines, implantation, consequences du remembrement agraire*. Poitou: Editions P.S.R., 1991.

Bérard, Laurence, and Philipe Marchenay. "A Market Culture: *Produits de Terroir* or the Selling of Heritage." In *Recollections of France: Memories, Identities and Heritage in Contemporary France*, edited by Sarah Blowen, Marion Demossier, and Jeanine Picard, 154–67. New York: Berghahn Books, 2000.

Berger, Susan. *Peasants against Politics: Rural Organization in Brittany, 1911–1967*. Cambridge, MA: Harvard University Press, 1972.

Bess, Michael. *The Light-Green Society: Ecology and Technological Modernity in France, 1960–2000*. Chicago: University of Chicago Press, 2003.

Béteille, Roger. *La France du vide*. Paris: Librarie Technique, 1981.

Biancarelli, Jacques, Philippe Parini, and Christian Serradji. *Aménager les campagnes*. Paris: Editions du Moniteur, 1978.

Bloch, Marc. *French Rural History: An Essay on Its Basic Characteristics*. Translated by Janet Sondheimer. Berkeley: University of California Press, 1970.

Bodon, Virginie. *La modernité au village: Tignes, Savines, Ubaye . . . la submersion de communes rurales au nom de l'intérêt général, 1920–1970*. Grenoble: Presses Universitaires de Grenoble, 2003.

Bonneuil, Christophe, and François Hochereau. "Gouverner le 'progrès génétique': Biopolitique et métrologie de la construction d'un standard variétal dans la France agricole d'après-guerre." *Annales. Histoire, Sciences Sociales* 63, no. 6 (November/December 2008): 1305–40.

Bonneuil, Christophe, and Frederic Thomas. "Purifying Landscapes: The Vichy Regime and the Genetic Modernization of France." *Historical Studies in the Natural Sciences* 40, no. 4 (November 2010): 532–68.

Boswell, Laird. "Rethinking the Nation at the Periphery." *French Politics, Culture and Society* 27, no. 2 (Summer 2009): 111–26.

Boucher, Jean. *Pour une véritable agriculture biologique*. Nantes: self-published, 1992.

Boulat, Régis. *Jean Fourastié, un expert en productivité: La modernisation de la France (années trente-années cinquante)*. Besançon: Presses Universitaires de Franche-Comté, 2008.

Boussard, Isabel. *Les agriculteurs et la république*. Paris: Economica, 1990.

Bouteille, Arnaud. *40 ans de politique foncière en France*. Paris: Economica, 1986.

Brun, Françoise. *Les français d'Algérie dans l'agriculture du Midi méditerranéen: Etude géographique*. Gap: Editions Ophrys, 1976.

Bryant, Christopher R. "Metropolitan Development and Agriculture: The SAFER de l'Ile de France." *Land Economics* 51, no. 2 (May 1975): 158–63.

Buchou, Hubert. *Partager la terre: L'histoire des SAFER*. Biarritz: Atlantica, 1999.

Cadiou, Pierre, Françoise Mathieu-Gaudrot, André Lefebvre, Yves Le Pape, and Stéphane Oriol. *L'Agriculture biologique en France: Écologie ou mythologie*. Grenoble: Presses Universitaires de Grenoble, 1975.

Caron, François, and Maurice Vaïsse, eds. *L'aménagement du territoire, 1958–1974: Actes du colloque tenu à Dijon les 21 et 22 novembre 1996*. Paris: L'Harmattan, 1999.

Carson, Rachel. *Silent Spring*. Boston: Houghton Mifflin, 1962.

Cazes, Bernard, and Philippe Mioche, eds. *Modernisation ou décadence, contribution à l'histoire du plan Monnet et de la planification en France*. Aix-en-Provence: Publications de l'Université de Provence, 1990.

Centre national des jeunes agriculteurs (CNJA). *Dossiers de travail 1966–1967, Investir, c'est préparer l'avenir, le financement des exploitations agricoles*. Paris: SEPJA, 1966.

Cepède, Michel, and Gérard Weill. *L'agriculture*. Paris: Presses universitaires de France, 1965.

César, Christine. "Les métamorphoses des idéologues de l'agriculture biologique: La voix de *La Vie Claire* (1946–1981)." In *Au nom de la terre: Agrarisme et agrariens en France et en Europe du XIXe siècle à nos jours*, edited by Pierre Cornu et Jean-Luc Mayaud, 335–47. Paris: Boutique de l'histoire, 2008.

Chamboredon, Jean-Claude. "La 'naturalisation' de la campagne: Une autre manière de cultiver les 'simples'?" In *Protection de la nature: Histoire et idéologie. De la nature à l'environnement*, edited by Anne Cadoret, 138–51. Paris: Editions L'Harmattan, 1985.

Charvolin, Florian. *L'invention de l'environnement en France: Chroniques anthropologiques d'une institutionnalisation*. Paris: Editions la découverte, 2003.

Chassagne, Marie Elisabeth, and A. Grandjean. *Les blocages fonciers en montagne*. Paris: Ministère de l'agriculture, 1982.

Chavagne, Yves. *Bernard Lambert, 30 ans de combat paysan*. Baye: Editions La Digitale, 1988.

Cheverry, Pierre, and Pierre Clergeot. *Paysages ruraux: Un perpétuel devenir: 1800–2000, histoire de l'aménagement foncier*. Paris: Editions Publi-Topex, 2005.

Cleary, M. C. Peasants. *Politicians and Producers: The Organisation of Agriculture in France since 1918*. Cambridge, U.K.: Cambridge University Press, 1989.

Conford, Philip. *The Origins of the Organic Movement*. Edinburgh: Floris Books, 2001.

Cornu, Pierre. "Déprise agraire et reboisement. Le cas des Cévennes (1860–1970)." *Histoire et sociétés rurales*, no. 20 (2003): 173–201.

Cornu, Pierre, and Jean-Luc Mayaud. *Au nom de la terre: Agrarisme et agrariens, en France et en Europe, du 19e siècle à nos jours*. Paris: Boutique de l'histoire, 2007.

Coulomb, Pierre, Hélène Delorme, Bertrand Hervieu, Marcel Jollivet, and Philippe Lacombe. *Les agriculteurs et la politique*. Paris: Presses de la Fondation Nationale des Sciences Politiques, 1990.

Coutin, Pierre. "La politique agricole de la Vᵉ République." *Revue Économique* 10, no. 5, l'Economie de la Vᵉ République (September 1959): 784–92.

Cronon, William. *Nature's Metropolis: Chicago and the Great West.* New York: W. W. Norton, 1991.

Cullather, Nick. *The Hungry World: America's Cold War Battle against Poverty in Asia.* Cambridge, MA: Harvard University Press, 2013.

Cuperly, Michel. "La politique agricole commune: 'Test' de l'Europe." *Paysans*, no. 23 (April/May 1960): 31–39.

———. "Face au marché commun l'agriculture française est-elle en peril?" *Paysans*, no. 12 (June/July 1958): 14–29.

Cupers, Kenny. *The Social Project: Housing Postwar France.* Minneapolis: University of Minnesota Press, 2014.

Debatisse, Michel. *La révolution silencieuse; le combat des paysans.* Paris: Calmann-Lévy, 1963.

Deighton, Anne, and Alan S. Milward. *Widening, Deepening and Acceleration: The European Economic Community, 1957–1963.* Baden-Baden: Nomos, 1999.

Demossier, Marion. "Culinary Heritage and *Produits du Terroir* in France." In *Recollections of France: Memories, Identities and Heritage in Contemporary France,* edited by Sarah Blowen, Marion Demossier, and Jeanine Picard, 141–53. Oxford: Berghahn Books, 2000.

Dibie, Pascal. *Le village métamorphosé: Révolution dans la France profonde.* Paris: Plon, 2006.

Domergue, René. *L'intégration des pieds-noirs dans les villages du Midi.* Paris: L'Harmattan, 2005.

Dormois, Jean-Paul. *The French Economy in the Twentieth Century.* Cambridge, U.K.: Cambridge University Press, 2004.

Duchêne, François. *Jean Monnet: The First Statesman of Interdependence.* New York: W. W. Norton, 1980.

Dumont, René. *Le problème agricole français.* Paris: Editions Nouvelles, 1957.

Farmer, Sarah. "Memoirs of French Peasant Life: Progress and Nostalgia in Postwar France." *French History* 25, no. 3 (2011): 362–79.

———. "The Other House: The Secondary Residence in Postwar France." *French Politics, Culture and Society* 33, no. 1 (Spring 2016): 104–21.

Fearne, Andrew. "The History and Development of the CAP 1945–1985." In *The Common Agricultural Policy and the World Economy: Essays in Honour of John Ashton,* edited by Christopher Ritson and David Harvey, 22–63. Wallingford: C.A.B. International, 1991.

Fédération nationale des sociétés d'aménagement foncier et d'établissement rural. *Société d'aménagement foncier et d'établissement Rural: Organisation, fonctionnement.* Paris: SCAFR, 1970.

Fel, André. "Les révolutions vertes de la campagne Française (1955–1985)." *Vingtième Siècle*, no. 8 (October–December 1985): 3–17.

Fitzgerald, Deborah. *Every Farm a Factory: The Industrial Ideal in American Agriculture.* New Haven: Yale University Press, 2003.

Fourastié, Jean. *La Productivité.* Paris: Presses universitaires de France, 1952.

France, La Commission sur l'avenir à long terme de l'agriculture française. *Le Rapport Vedel*. Paris: SECLAF, 1969.

France, La direction de la documentation. *La documentation française illustrée n° 68: Le remembrement rural*. Paris: Secrétariat général du gouvernement, December 1958.

France, Ministère de l'agriculture, Service central des enquêtes et études statistiques. *Le prix des terres agricoles depuis 1950 (Terres labourables et prairies naturelles)*. Paris: Ministère de l'agriculture, April 1984.

France, Remembrement et voirie agricole (Section technique centrale). *Remembrement rural et conservation de la nature. [2], Les Effets du remembrement rural sur l'évolution des structures des exploitations agricoles*. Paris: Ministère de l'agriculture, 1970.

Frost, Robert L. *Alternating Currents: Nationalized Power in France, 1946–1970*. Ithaca, NY: Cornell University Press, 1991.

———. "The Flood of 'Progress': Technocrats and Peasants at Tignes (Savoy), 1946–1952." *French Historical Studies* 14, no. 1 (Spring 1995): 117–40.

Gachon, Lucien. "L'évolution de l'agriculture française depuis 1940." *Revue Économique* 6, no. 1 (1955): 35–55.

Gatty, Ronald. "The Consolidation of Farming Lands in France." *Journal of Farm Economics* 38, no. 4 (November 1956): 911–22.

Gaudibert, Jean-Claude. *Le dernier empire français: Le Crédit agricole*. Paris: Seghers, 1977.

Gavignaud, Geneviève. *Les campagnes en France au XXe siècle: 1914–1989*. Gap: Editions Ophrys, 1990.

Geffroy, Henri-Charles. "Sauvons les enfants!" *La Vie Claire*, no. 9 (April 1947): 1.

Gervais, Michel, Marcel Jollivet, and Yves Tavernier. *La fin de la France paysanne de 1914 à nos jours*. Vol. 4 of *Histoire de la France rurale*, edited by Georges Duby and Armand Wallon. Paris: Seuil, 1976.

Gervais, Michel, Claude Servolin, and Jean Weil. *Une France sans paysans*. Paris: Seuil, 1965.

Gravier, Jean-François. *Paris et le désert français*. Paris: Le Portulan, 1947.

Gueslin, André. *Le crédit agricole*. Paris: Editions la découverte, 1985.

Hall, Peter. *Governing the Economy: The Politics of State Intervention in Britain and France*. Oxford: Oxford University Press, 1986.

Hecht, Gabrielle. *The Radiance of France: Nuclear Power and National Identity after World War II*. Cambridge, MA: MIT Press, 1998.

Hennis, Marjoleine. *Globalization and European Integration: The Changing Role of Farmers in the Common Agricultural Policy*. Lanham: Rowman & Littlefield, 2005.

Hervieu, Bertrand, and François Purseigle. "Troubled Pastures, Troubled Pictures: French Agriculture and Contemporary Rural Sociology." *Rural Sociology* 73, no. 4 (December 2008): 660–83.

Hoffman, Philip. *Growth in a Traditional Society: The French Countryside, 1450–1815*. Princeton, NJ: Princeton University Press, 2000.

Howard, Albert. *An Agricultural Testament*. Oxford: Oxford University Press, 1940.

Institut national de la recherche agronomique (INRA). *Recherches sur la qualité du poulet label rouge*. Rungis: Laboratoire de recherches économiques, 1984.

Jas, Nathalie. *Au carrefour de la chimie et de l'agriculture: Les sciences agronomiques en France et en Allemagne, 1850–1914*. Paris: Editions des Archives contemporaines, 2001.

———. "Public Health and Pesticide Regulation in France Before and After *Silent Spring*," *History and Technology* 23, no. 4 (2007): 369–88.

Jollivet, Marcel, and Henri Medras. *Les collectivités rurales françaises; étude comparative de changement sociale*. Paris: A. Colin, 1971.

Kaplan, Steven Laurence. *Good Bread Is Back: A Contemporary History of French Bread, the Way It Is Made, and the People Who Make It*. Durham, NC: Duke University Press, 2006.

———. *Le pain maudit: Retour sur la France des années oubliées, 1945–1958*. Paris: Fayard, 2008.

Keeler, John T. S. *The Politics of Neocorporatism in France: Farmers, the State, and Agricultural Policy-Making in the Fifth Republic*. New York: Oxford University Press, 1987.

Kervran, C. Louis. *Biological Transmutation*. Translated by George Ohsawa. Chico: George Ohsawa Macrobiotic Foundation, 1971.

Knudsen, Ann-Christina. *Farmers on Welfare: The Making of Europe's Common Agricultural Policy*. Ithaca, NY: Cornell University Press, 2009.

Kuisel, Richard. *Capitalism and the State in Modern France: Renovation and Economic Management in the Twentieth Century*. New York: Cambridge University Press, 1981.

Kuisel, Richard, and Marie-Claude Florentin. "Vichy et les origines de la planification économique, 1940–1946." *Le mouvement social* 98 (January–March 1977): 77–101.

Lachman, Gary. *Rudolf Steiner: An Introduction to His Life and Work*. New York: Penguin, 2007.

Lacour, Claude, Aliette Delamarre, and Muriel Thoin. *40 ans d'aménagement du territoire*. Paris: La Documentation française, 2003.

Laferté, Gilles. *La Bourgogne et ses vins: Image d'origine controlée*. Paris: Belin, 2006.

Lambert, Bernard. *Les paysans dans la lutte des classes*. Paris: Seuil, 1970.

Lefebvre. "Role et responsabilité des médecins et des consommateurs dans la nouvelle structure de l'AFRAN." *Sol-Alimentation-Santé*, nos. 7/8 (September/October 1959): 6.

Lefort, M. B. "Exigences du consommateur allemand en matière de produits agricoles." *Economie Rurale* 21 (July 1954): 11–16.

Léger, Danièle, and Bertrand Hervieu. "Les immigrés de l'utopie." *Autrement* 14 (June 1978): 46–71.

Lemaire, Raoul. "La lettre de M. Raoul Lemaire." *La Vie Claire*, no. 24 (September 1948): 6.

Levy, Jonah D. *Tocqueville's Revenge: State, Society, and Economy in Contemporary France*. Cambridge, MA: Harvard University Press, 1999.

Loubère, Leo. *The Wine Revolution in France: The Twentieth Century.* Princeton, NJ: Princeton University Press, 1990.

The Mansholt Plan. http://www.ena.lu.

Matthieu, Nicole. "La notion de rural et les rapports ville-campagne en France: Des années cinquante aux années quatre-vingts." *Économie Rurale* 187 (May/June 1990): 35–41.

Mendras, Henri. *La fin des paysans; changement et innovations dans les sociétés rurales françaises.* Paris: SEDEIS, 1967.

———. *The Vanishing Peasant: Innovation and Change in French Agriculture.* Translated by Jean Lerner. Cambridge, MA: MIT Press, 1970.

Mendras, Henri, and Yves Tavernier. "Les manifestations de juin 1961." *Revue française de science politique* 12, no. 3 (1962): 647–71.

———. *Les paysans et la politique dans le France contemporaine.* Paris: SEDEIS, 1969.

Mennevret, Jean. "Vers une Europe économique." *Paysans,* no. 4 (February/March 1957).

Montpied, Ernest. *Terres mouvantes; un maire rural au coeur du remembrement.* Paris: M. F. R. Edition-Librarie, 1965.

Monzies, Claude. "L'agriculture biologique et l'agriculture biodynamique en France: Réflexions d'un biodynamiste." *Nature et Progrès,* no. 73 (January–March 1982): 12.

Morineau, Michel. "L'Agriculture biologique et commerce spécialisé." In *L'agriculture biologique et son devenir.* Annales du colloque APRIA-CNAB du 30 novembre et du 1er décembre 1989, 119–28. Paris: Association pour la Promotion Industrie Agriculture, 1989.

Moulin, Annie. *Peasantry and Society in France since 1789.* Translated by M. C. and M. F. Cleary. Cambridge, U.K.: Cambridge University Press, 1991.

Muth, Hans Peter. *French Agriculture and the Political Integration of Western Europe.* Leyden: A. W. Sijthoff, 1970.

Noël, Gilbert, and Emilie Willaert. *Georges Pompidou, une certaine idée de la modernité agricole et rurale.* Brussels: P. I. E. Peter Lang, 2007.

Nord, Philip. *France's New Deal: From the Thirties to the Postwar Era.* Princeton, NJ: Princeton University Press, 2010.

Parker, Thomas. *Tasting French Terroir: The History of an Idea.* Berkeley: University of California Press, 2015.

Patel, Kiran Klaus. "Europeanisation à contre-coeur. Germany and Agricultural Integration, 1945 to 1975." In *Fertile Ground for Europe? The History of European Integration and the Common Agricultural Policy since 1945,* edited by Kiran Klaus Patel, 139–60. Baden-Baden: Nomos 2009.

Paull, John. "Attending the First Organic Agriculture Course: Rudolf Steiner's Agriculture Course at Koberwitz, 1924." *European Journal of Social Sciences* 21, no. 1 (April 2011): 64–70.

Paxton, Robert. *French Peasant Fascism: Henry Dorgère's Greenshirts and the Crises of French Agriculture, 1929–1939.* Oxford: Oxford University Press, 1997.

Peneff, Nicolas. *Histoire du foncier et du remembrement de Cadours.* Nantes: Presses Universitaires de Nantes, 1980.

Perec, Georges. *Les Choses*. Paris: Editions Julliard, 1965.

Perkins, John H. *Geopolitics and the Green Revolution: Wheat, Genes, and the Cold War*. New York: Oxford University Press, 1997.

Pétain, Philippe. *La France Nouvelle: Principes de la communauté, appels et messages, 17 juin 1940–17 juin 1941*. Paris: Les Editions Fasquelle, 1941.

Pfeiffer, Ehrenfried. *Fécondité de la terre*. Paris: Editions Triades, 1972.

Piriou, Solenne. "L'institutionnalisation de l'agriculture biologique (1980–2000)." PhD diss., Ecole nationale supérieure agronomique de Rennes, 2002.

Prendiville, Brendan. *Environmental Politics in France*. Boulder, CO: Westview Press, 1994.

Pritchard, Sara B. *Confluence: The Nature of Technology and the Remaking of the Rhône*. Cambridge, MA: Harvard University Press, 2011.

Rabhi, Pierre. *Du Sahara aux Cévennes: Itinéraire d'un homme au service de la Terre-Mère*. Paris: Albin Michel, 2002.

Rambaud, Placide. "Révoltes et révolution paysannes dans la France contemporaine." *Sociologia Ruralis* 4 (1964): 101–13.

Rimsky-Korsakoff, Jean-Pierre. *Au delà du bio: La consom'action*. Gap: Editions Yves Michel, 2003.

Rivière-Wekstein, Gil. *Bio: Fausses promesses et vrai marketing*. Paris: Le Publieur, 2011.

Roche, Pierre. "Migrations rurales et sociétés d'établissement agricole." *Paysans*, no. 18 (June/July 1959): 37–50.

Rousso, Henri, ed. *De Monnet à Massé. Enjeux politiques et objectifs économiques dans le cadre des quatre premiers Plans (1946–1965)*. Paris: Editions du CNRS, 1986.

Rouvière, Catherine. *Retourner à la terre: L'utopie néo-rurale en Ardèche depuis les années 1960*. Rennes: Presses Universitaires de Rennes, 2015.

Saint Henis, Antoine de. *Guide pratique de culture biologique: Méthode Lemaire-Boucher*. Angers: Edition Agriculture et vie, 1972.

Sargent, Frederic O. "Fragmentation of French Land: Its Nature, Extent, and Causes." *Land Economics* 28, no. 3 (August 1952): 218–29.

SCAFR. *Société d'aménagement foncier et d'établissement rural: Organisation, fonctionnement*. Paris: SCAFR, 1970.

Servolin, Claude. *L'agriculture moderne*. Paris: Seuil, 1989.

de Silguy, Catherine. *L'Agriculture biologique*. Paris: Presses Universitaires de France, 1991.

Stanziani, Alessandro. *Histoire de la qualité alimentaire: France XIXe–XXe siècles*. Paris: Seuil, 2005.

———, ed. *La qualité des produits en France XVIIIe–XXe siècles*. Paris: Belin, 2003.

Steiner, Rudolph. *The Agriculture Course: The Birth of the Biodynamic Method*. Translated by George Adams. London: Rudolph Steiner Press, 2004.

Sutton, Michael. *France and the Construction of Europe, 1944–2007: The Geopolitical Imperative*. New York: Berghahn Books, 2007.

Sylvander, Bertil. "Conventions de qualité, concurrence et coopération: Cas du 'Label Rouge' dans la filière volailles." In *La grande transformation de l'agriculture:*

Lectures conventionnalistes et régulationnistes, edited by Gilles Allaire and Robert Boyer, 73–96. Paris: INRA, 1995.

Szarka, Joseph. *The Shaping of Environmental Policy in France*. New York: Berghahn Books, 2002.

Tavernier, Yves. *Le syndicalisme paysan: F.N.S.E.A., C.N.J.A.* Paris: A. Colin, 1969.

Tavernier, Yves, Michel Gervais, and Claude Servolin, eds. *L'univers politique des paysans français*. Paris: A. Colin, 1972.

Tracy, Michael. *Government and Agriculture in Western Europe, 1880–1988*. 3rd ed. New York: NYU Press, 1989.

Treaty of Rome. http://eur-lex.europa.eu/en/treaties/dat/12002E/htm/C _2002325EN.003301.html.

Treitel, Corinna. *Eating Nature in Modern Germany: Food, Agriculture, and Environment, c. 1870–2000*. New York: Cambridge University Press, 2017.

Viel, Jeanne-Marie. *L'Agriculture biologique: Une réponse?* Paris: Editions Entente, 1979.

Vogt, G. "The Origins of Organic Farming." In *Organic Farming: An International History*, edited by William Lockeretz, 9–29. Oxfordshire: CAB International, 2007.

Voisin, André. *La productivité de l'herbe*. Paris: Flammarion, 1957.

Wheelan, Charles. *Naked Economics: Undressing the Dismal Science*. New York: W. W. Norton, 2010.

Wright, Gordon. *Rural Revolution in France: The Peasantry in the Twentieth Century*. Stanford, CA: Stanford University Press, 1964.

Index

Illustrations are indicated by page numbers in *italics*.

French Union of Organic Farming (Union française d'agriculture biologique, or UFAB), 163, 167

Gambetta, Léon, 2
Gas prices, 143
Geffroy, Henri-Charles, 67–69, 119, 129
General Agreement on Tariffs and Trade (GATT), 176
General Association of Wheat Producers, 70
General Directorate for Environmental Protection, 153
Germany, 23, 43, 55, 61, 66, 89, 109, 168, 179–80
Greece, 44
Guide pratique de culture biologique: Méthode Lemaire-Boucher (A practical guide to organic farming: The Lemaire-Boucher Method), 130–31

Health, 54–55, 71, 118–19, 122
Healthy Food (L'Aliment sain), 68
Heart disease, 122
Hediger, Rich, 133
Herbicides, 48–49. See also Pesticides
Hervieu, Bertrand, 159, 160
High Commission on Quality (Commission supérieure de la qualité), 140
Highways, 10
Howard, Albert, 53–54, 56–57, 66, 131
Human capital, 6
Hydroelectric dams, 10

Illness, livestock, 48–49, 54, 79–80. See also Health
Improvement projects, after World War II, 14–15
Indemnité viagère de départ, 194n37
Independence, 50–51. See also Autonomy
India, 53, 54, 205n18
Indore Method, 53–54
Industrialized agriculture. See Agriculture, industrialized

Infant mortality, 3
Inheritance, 24–25, 187n34
Insecticide, 130, 133. See also Pesticides
Institutionalization, 52, 157, 167, 179–80, 204n74
Ireland, 89
Italy, 89, 108–9, 133, 179

Jaloux, Jean-Paul, 109
Joint-stock associations, 89
Juillet, René, 81–82

Kaplan, Steve, 57–58
Kervran, Cotentin Louis, 128–29, 131

Label Rouge, 168
Labels, 180–181. See also AOC system
Lambert, Bernard, 95, 195n40
Land banks, 7–8, 13, 52, 92–93, 97
Land parceling, 24–37, 26, 27. See also Remembrement
Land prices, 32, 149
"Land problem," 87–88
Land use, 9–12, 11, 150–51. See also Remembrement
League of Nations, 19
Léger, Danièle, 159, 160
Legitimacy, 163–69
Lemaire, Jean-François, 118, 125, 125, 163–64
Lemaire, Pierre-Bernard, 118, 131, 163–64
Lemaire, Raoul, 3, 6, 8, 58–64, 75, 76, 83–84, 100–101; AFAB and, 132; AFRAN and, 70–72, 73, 74; in codification of method, 117–18; common market and, 83; death of, 146; GABO and, 77, 79; Geffroy and, 69; lithothamnion and, 126–28; Louis vs., 134–35, 138–39; papers of, 8; Poujade and, 51; Racineux and, 49; struggle of, 124–25; wheat and, 125, 125–26
Lemaire-Boucher Method, 117–18, 126, 128, 129–34, 137, 138, 163–64, 166